# Dying in Good Hands

# Dying in Good Hands

## PALLIATIVE MASSAGE AND THE POWER OF TOUCH

*Christine Sutherland, RMT*

**Brush**
Education Inc.

Brush Education Inc.
www.brusheducation.ca
contact@brusheducation.ca

Cover and interior design: Carol Dragich, Dragich Design

Front cover image: Peter Schramm; back cover artwork by Katherine Whitney

Photo credit: Figures 9.4, 9.4b, 9.5a, 9.8, 9.10a, 9.10d, 9.10e by James Munroe of SerpMedia

**Disclaimer**

The publisher, authors, contributors, and editors bring substantial expertise to this reference and have made their best efforts to ensure that it is useful, accurate, safe, and reliable.

Nonetheless, practitioners must always rely on their own experience, knowledge and judgment when consulting any of the information contained in this reference or employing it in patient care. When using any of this information, they should remain conscious of their responsibility for their own safety and the safety of others, and for the best interests of those in their care.

To the fullest extent of the law, neither the publishers, the authors, the contributors nor the editors assume any liability for injury or damage to persons or property from any use of information or ideas contained in this reference.

**Library and Archives Canada Cataloguing in Publication**

Title: Dying in good hands : palliative massage and the power of touch / Christine Sutherland, RMT

Names: Sutherland, Christine, 1951- author.

Description: Includes bibliographical references and index.

Identifiers: Canadiana (print) 20200323695 | Canadiana (ebook) 20200324187 | ISBN 9781550598506

(softcover) | ISBN 9781550598513 (PDF) | ISBN 9781550598520 (Kindle) | ISBN 9781550598537 (EPUB)

Subjects: LCSH: Massage therapy. | LCSH: Touch—Therapeutic use. | LCSH: Palliative treatment. |

LCSH: Terminal care.

Classification: LCC RM721 .S88 2021 | DDC 615.8/22—dc23

We acknowledge the support of the Government of Canada
Nous reconnaissons l'appui du gouvernement du Canada | Canadä

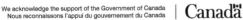

This book is dedicated to my mom, Margaret, my dad, Bill, my stepmom, Valerie, and my daughter, Crystal. They helped me spread the most love in the best way by teaching you how to help others die in good hands.

This book honors all those helping to provide a peaceful parting through palliative massage and the power of touch.

# Contents

# Palliative Massage and the Power of Touch

Therapeutic massage is gaining increased attention as a way to provide both physical and emotional benefits to people in palliative care. Chief physical benefits include the following:

- Preventing pressure sores
- Keeping food moving through the digestive system
- Helping to clear the lungs so breathing is easier
- Lessening physical pain

More than just tangible, hands-on benefits, massage also creates a host of intangible comforts related to connection and communication; these benefits are reciprocal, affecting both the massager and the massaged.

For massage professionals and those in training, and for volunteers at hospices and hospitals, this book will provide all the tools needed to massage for every stage of dying, from the diagnosis of a chronic terminal illness with months or years to live to a short-term departure with only days to prepare. I cover the important aspects of traditional massage theory and stroke sequences for the entire body, taking into consideration that palliative bodies are often swollen or emaciated.

Medical professionals will learn how to use massage techniques for patients and will get tips for teaching massage to others. By teaching massage to your patients' family and friends—individuals who may be providing much of your patients' daily care and comfort—you will not only augment the care you provide, but also give these loved ones a

way to direct their energy and anxiety in positive directions. Even children can participate.

This book is also meant for friends and family members of someone who is dying. As family, you may be in the best position to provide hands-on help. Professionals and volunteers sometimes have to abide by protocols and restrictions that keep them at bay, unable to do everything that palliative massage can offer to keep a dying patient comfortable. Even if you have never massaged before, this book teaches what you need to know to provide hands-on care that will make your loved one more comfortable until their last breath.

## Book Organization

The **Introduction** begins with a look at dying and the discomfort many people, both those dying and those around them, feel about this transition. It then looks at research into the physical and emotional benefits of massage on palliative patients and those caring for them. **Chapter 1** includes some of the practical preparations and equipment you might need to massage your patient. **Chapter 2** gives instruction on basic massage strokes. **Chapter 3** runs through a full-body massage routine. **Chapter 4** suggests specific massage treatments for some of the most common circulatory conditions in palliative people. **Chapter 5** is concerned with the respiratory system and how to keep people breathing comfortably as long as possible. **Chapter 6** discusses massage for the digestive system, which may include tubes, drains, and pouches. **Chapter 7** deals with the last moments of life and how to make that final breath more comfortable. **Chapter 8** gives massage ideas for the physical and emotional needs of caregivers, family, and friends. **Chapter 9** talks about options we have today for where to die, from hospital to hospice to home and beyond. **Chapter 10** explains massage techniques to address the challenges of bereavement. Finally, the **Conclusion** talks about expanding the power of touch beyond your family and loved ones to the broader community.

Tucked between these chapters are stories about some of the patients who have most influenced my work as a massage therapist, filmmaker, and educator. I have always loved the power of story, the "how to" of life—how to live and die most dynamically, and how to best spread the most love along the way. It's my hope that you will identify with these stories and not feel alone in the natural processes of death and dying.

## Online Classroom

I encourage you to visit the online classroom I've prepared for many of the chapters of this book. You will find a list of videos at the end of most chapters and can see the full list of videos available by visiting brusheducation.ca/dying-in-good-hands. The videos are arranged according to chapter and were specifically created to help readers understand the techniques and concepts in this book.

One of my mentors, Balfour Mount, the father of palliative care in North America, is a veteran surgical oncologist from Montreal. He describes his experience in palliative care as "an odyssey in which the dying and their families became my teachers."[1] Like Balfour Mount, I credit everything I know to the generosity of the patients, friends, family members, and caregivers with whom I have had the opportunity to work. I hope, in this book, to pass on that knowledge and help us all give life a better ending. I hope, too, to continue massaging until it's my turn to be on the receiving end of palliative massage and touch.

# Dying for Beginners

The dying part of life is scary. There is no training, no practice session for such a big event, and no one comes back to tell us how to do it better when it's our turn. This book is about touching the untouchables—those who, in dying, seem like they should not be disturbed; those whom we are reluctant to touch. But touch can massage away our loved ones' pain, making them less afraid of their death, and possibly making us less afraid of our own.

## Talking about Death

In 1969, Elizabeth Kübler-Ross published *On Death and Dying: What the Dying Have to Teach Doctors, Nurses, Clergy and Their Own Families.* Her groundbreaking book opened up the possibilities for a dialogue about death. She gave the public permission to explore not just dying, but the art and science of being well loved while doing so. Her work ignited a sea change in the world of palliative care. She helped us care more fully for those in pain—to care for them emotionally and physically as they died.

I was nineteen and part of the Chaplaincy Committee at Selkirk College when Kübler-Ross's book was published. We organized a conference on death and dying, inviting Dr. Kübler-Ross to Canada for the first time. Without Dr. Kübler-Ross's influence, my dreams of teaching palliative massage might still be daydreams. Her talks on the stages of dying, her outlook on the politics of medicine, and her stories were woven, all those years ago, into a powerful weekend that changed my life and my approach to therapeutic massage.

Upon meeting Dr. Kübler-Ross, I found that I didn't just admire her, I identified with her. Small in stature, like me, she was a crusader who went fearlessly into the difficult subject of death. I saw in myself the same crusading spirit; we shared a similar work ethic. And when she discussed her work in palliative care, she sparked in me the curiosity of how I could be of service in our endlessly interesting human drama of birth and death, and the spark turned into a fire. She showed me how to make a difference in this world.

It is my hope that, in my lifetime, I can spark a similar fire in others. I believe that anybody with a passion, a mission, or simply a yearning to ease human suffering can equip themselves with palliative massage and the power to change the world of those dying, one massage at a time.

### Witnessing the threshold moments

Before my father, my stepmother, and my mother died, I had fortunately had lots of professional experience in palliative massage. I also had my brother. We worked as a team as we went through the death of each of these people we loved. We worked together to help our family members die, one by one, hands-on, and surrounded with love.

This kind of hands-on approach to death is not always the norm. Some cultures have great rituals and special ceremonies for pivotal times such as birth and death. In North America, however, these transformational times have often been institutionally hidden from view and everyday conversation. Most people in our culture get very little guidance for the dramatic events of birth and death. But these are transformational experiences—threshold moments. To witness a threshold moment—the moment someone enters or leaves the world—is magical, giving us a glimpse of the connection between this world and the beyond. Yet these transitions, like all transitions, can be difficult, uncomfortable, and marked by struggle. With touch, we can ease these transitions. We can make them a peaceful entry or a gentle exit.

## The Power of Touch

When I was a teenager, I burnt my face with a sunlamp so badly I thought I was dying. My face was swollen beyond recognition. This was the first time I really understood, albeit instinctively, the power of loving touch.

My dad sat beside me on my bed and kept a steady vigil, staying up all night to bathe my face with cool water. He sang Scottish lullabies, coaching me through the agonizing hours. Whenever he touched me, the pain was bearable. If he thought I was sleeping and lifted his hands off, the pain started to climb again. The witch-hazel compresses he applied to my burning skin were positive contact, therapeutic pressure, and pain-relieving magic. He stroked my hair while the compresses baked on my face. I remember that stroking as the most dramatic pain reliever.

It is our instinctive human response to reach out and help someone in pain. This is our greatest asset in challenging emotional and physical times. The aches and pains of everyday life are a good training ground for touch and massaging away discomfort in a palliative care situation.

Taking away someone's pain is not rocket science. The easiest illustration of this relief is that comforting squeeze of the hand when someone gets emotional during a friendly cup of tea. We feel heard at that moment, not alone. That simple hand squeeze makes us feel much better, but in our "hands-off" culture, tactile courage is sometimes needed in order to reach out.

## Politics of Touch

Churches, schools, and public institutions alike have reined in touching due to revelations about inappropriate touch. The healing of institutional trauma around sexual abuse has given rise to protective laws, rules, and regulations that restrict touch, even in health professions where it is most needed.

Years ago when I was teaching at the Vancouver School of Theology, I had to change my hands-on massage program to accommodate changing church policies that restricted physical contact. Today, the tide is starting to return to a healthier balance, and respectful approaches to appropriate touch are part of the protocol for professionals and volunteers.

With patients I've been hired to massage, I don't need to ask whether I can touch, but I do communicate about how, when, and where, especially with someone new who might not know what to expect. I teach my students to check in continually with the person on the receiving end of their massage (e.g., "Would you like more pressure, or less?" "Should I move slower here?" "Do you want a break now?")

With caregivers and other people outside the professional relationship I have with a patient, I need a more direct approach to securing consent: "Can I massage your shoulders?" or "I bet your husband/wife/mother/father would love to see you relax with a shoulder rub. May I?"

### Palliative care during the COVID-19 pandemic

COVID-19 added extra layers to the protocols surrounding touch, but uncertain times mean we need human contact more than ever before. Remember that safe touching is still possible within your social or familial bubble.

In palliative care, COVID-19 heightened the sense of helplessness people feel as their loved ones die. It was a new reality that people in long-term or chronic care facilities were dying in isolation or with only one family member allowed to attend. Reach out where it is safe, and be hands-on not only to help the palliative symptoms of death and dying, but also to reduce the anxiety of those left behind. Now wearing the gloves and mask that are a new constant in palliative care, I might approach a caregiver with something like, "I'd love to shake your hand, but this is the best I can do to introduce myself [as I fake the shake from 2 meters away]. May I go around behind you and massage your shoulders while you take a break?" I can't shake hands or give a hug, but properly masked, I can massage someone's neck and shoulders.

## Palliative Massage in the Long and Short Run

People with chronic disabilities such as amyotrophic lateral sclerosis (ALS) and multiple sclerosis (MS) are perfect candidates for palliative massage. These people are sometimes given a life full of physical challenge from their birth to their death. With daily massage, we can give them a more painless life and, eventually, a gentler departure. And who knows? There might be a cure around the corner; our massages will help keep their bodies ready for that miracle.

Often these people feel like they are a burden to their families, especially when their disease is long lasting or predictably terminal. Regular massage can help change that. I have seen dying people who are shy about asking for help until they are introduced to palliative massage through family and friends. Massage gives them an alternative for dealing with worry and anxiety about their ending and how it will be. This is one reason massage is so popular, not just because of the physical high of the aftermath, but because of the feelings that happen when we are touched—feelings of belonging, of being well-loved, and of being alive. Massage helps recover those feelings of well-being.

Of course, not all deaths are slow and lingering. Recently, I helped Richard, a practicing Buddhist, through a "short run" disease. He was in his late sixties with a terminal lung cancer diagnosis. One week before he died, he came home to Nelson, British Columbia, and the shores of Kootenay Lake to be near his three kids, Wren, Nick, and Toby, after a three-month South American pilgrimage. He died 10 days later, leaving everyone stunned

that he was able to travel alone and make it home alive!

From the moment he arrived in British Columbia, his family rallied around and prepared for him to die. They took shifts for an around-the-clock caring cycle, filling the house with laughter, playing card games, and learning to massage him. It made his death real. He accepted his verdict. I asked Richard when he thought he would die, more for the family politics than my own curiosity on his outlook. He smiled and said that not only did he not know, he didn't care. He was ready—but before he died, he wanted to leave some palliative massage films so he would be remembered for teaching something meaningful, even in his final days.

Richard and his massage dream team.

Family massage. Wren and River rub Richard the right way to the last day.

He died two days after we had that conversation, in the hands of his grandson, River, who excelled at massaging his grandad's swollen feet; Jessie, a freshly graduated massage therapist; and Richard's two adult kids, Wren and Toby, newly educated in palliative massage. I was impressed with the thoroughness of their care, wheeling their dad outside for his last massage in the sunlight, pointing him toward the sandy beach and lake he loved and where they had all grown up. It was the perfect version of what I call the short run, from one of my best "sprinting" families.

## WHEELCHAIR MASSAGE

I am evangelical about the possibilities wheelchairs bring to the short and long runs of palliative care. Wheelchairs are a bridge for bringing palliative people to the land of the living and ensuring that they do not die in social isolation, stuck in their homes and bedrooms. You can massage people everywhere and anywhere, including sitting in their wheelchair at family gatherings, restaurants, or public parks. Wheel them out into their favorite places and then park them with a great view. The palliative wheelchair life might be short-lived, but it need not be ill-lived.

My summer massage students each experience 24 hours of life in a wheelchair. They also learn to give and experience receiving massages in the chair. I think this should be something everyone experiences before finishing high school.

Experiment with massage locations. Massages in the public eye are clothes-on massages, so it doesn't matter where they are. Exposing feet for a foot massage is acceptable anywhere, but watch out that you don't get a lineup of people hoping for the same treatment!

I suggest keeping the same routes for palliative wheelchair activities as the person had in the rest of their life. For example, if they went for a morning walk, then try to take them wheeling at the same times and along the same route as was their daily routine. If they walked their dog in the morning and at night, then do the same with the wheelchair and take their dog along. This is probably comforting to both the human and the animal, and these routines offer new locations for mini-massages. In the case of my mother, I would wheel her every morning to the local coffee shop that her young friend frequented and spend an hour interacting.

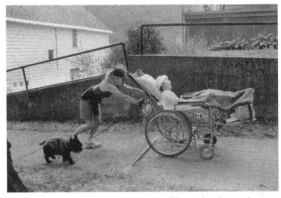

Me, my mom, and Bert, my terrier. Although I dressed my mom every day in her favorite dresses and jewelry, she could have easily been wheeling around in her pyjamas. Our evening wheelchair walks and wheelchair massages are my best memories of my mom's last days.

## Emotional Discomfort, Fear, and Consent

Dying is not easy for anyone. It can feel frightening and uncomfortable. It is natural to feel reluctant to disturb the person who is dying. Many parts of the dying experience are unnerving—even for professionals. The patient cannot cheerfully ask us to massage them; they are labored in their breathing and may be too weak to even speak or nod.

I still get scared. I still wonder if the patient wants me to continue massaging them after they have passed the point of being able to tell me. Even if I have talked to them about this early on, and they have requested that I massage them until the end, I still sometimes feel like I am an intruder.

I get scared, too, of family politics, of the family stresses, stories, and expectations that I may not necessarily know, but in which I may nonetheless be swept up. Even as a seasoned professional, I worry about doing the wrong thing with families. Am I putting them in a hands-on situation that is too much of an emotional stretch? In these situations, I turn both inward and outward, and ask for clarification whenever I can: "How do you feel about showing your brother the massage routines for your dad?"; "Do you think your mom wants us to continue massaging her?"; "How do you feel about massaging your mom now that she cannot smile and sigh with each stroke?"; "How do you feel about me continuing to massage your father now that he is comatose?"

It's always important to ask these questions. It gives a reality check and helps reduce or eliminate fears. Families are usually full of positive feedback about the effects of the massages, not only for their loved ones, but also for family and care team as a whole, and checking in with our own fears helps us turn our focus away from family politics and back towards the palliative person and the massaging.

## Comfort in the Face of Death

Though I've encountered many difficult family politics, and the fear and uncertainty that come with them, my fear is always quickly replaced with interest in the next experience. Using touch, we can help people who are inexperienced with death feel their fears and push through them. For me, it's intensely interesting to understand why some people break under these tough circumstances and how they can be made whole again through touch.

One of the best ways to prepare for this natural passage ourselves is to help people who are dying.

Offer them your touch, your amateur massages. Massage your grandmother's feet and hands. Teach your kids to massage them. Go looking for volunteer opportunities in a hospice.

Massage is critical for families who have loved ones in palliative care. Friends and families can integrate their emotions better, sleep better, and more fully enjoy the time they have left with their dying loved ones if they can connect through touch on a daily basis.

Death is not something to be feared, but—as my patient Cec once said—simply a transition from this place to a better place. Regardless of his spiritual beliefs, having the loving hands of his family massaging him made his passing not only comfortable, but gently poetic.

## Frequency Fosters Confidence

I always encourage people to try massaging a dying person. You might like it. You might feel instantly useful, relieved, fulfilled, or simply relaxed. We are all, however, beginners in the art of death and dying. Nonetheless, we are entrusted with the care of those around us in their dying, and sometimes, our inexperience may cause us to feel awkward about this responsibility, and especially about a hands-on approach.

Lorraine told me that she initially felt intimidated when her friend Mary, who had ALS, asked for massage. Still, she decided she had to try to make her friend more comfortable, even

Loraine and Mary, best friends since the age of four.

if she didn't know what she was doing. She used her intuition and did the best she could. Working through her discomfort helped Lorraine develop confidence in her ability to use positive touch to make a difference to Mary's life.

We need all the hands-on skills we can find to help those we love die in the best way possible. To get started, we simply need our first sense—our sense of touch—to be tuned up. With this innate power at our fingertips, we can minister to the sick and the dying, to our friends, and to our families. We can take the care of our loved ones into our own hands.

My goal is to create a world where my daughter will feel confident massaging me when I die and, in turn, where her family will feel the same for her, when the time comes. This requires a lifestyle of massage in growing families, seniors programs, youth programs, sports teams, couples' courtships, and on-site office wellness programs. Palliative massage training helps create an inner confidence and an outer dexterity. Repeated practice is the key to feeling comfortable; frequency fosters skill.

### Bring in the family and friends

Massage shouldn't be restricted to the hands of the professional. Every massage session is an opportunity to teach family and friends simple and safe massage techniques. Death has a way of disempowering those closest to the dying, and massage is a way to re-empower them. The physical act of massaging their loved one gives them a role, a function that makes a difference, not only for their dying loved one but for themselves.

All my professional life, I have advocated for "bringing in the family and friends" in a hands-on way, especially in a palliative care setting. Family and friends are one of the most important resources in palliative care. They are the people with a vested interest; they care deeply for the palliative person in question. I always work to build massage teams using family, friends, and volunteers. Massage techniques can easily be taught shoulder to shoulder through in-person demonstration, Zoom classes, DVDs, or YouTube videos.

## Research and the Power of Touch

Touch is our first experience of living. Our first experience of being massaged is the rhythmic squeezing in utero and then through the birth canal as we are delivered into life. As Ashley Montagu so clearly points out in *Touching: The Human Significance of the Skin*, "We are first touched and then hurled towards spatial freedom," and at the end of our life, after our years of spatial freedom, we instinctively "curl back into that fetal position."[2] In palliative care, touching becomes as comforting and as important as in infancy. Often, with the dying, it is our last means of communication.

Montagu's book was my bible, my most important resource, both when I was teaching and when Grace Chan and I were setting up the Sutherland-Chan School of Massage Therapy in Toronto, Ontario. Using many early research studies, Montagu was able to show how important and vital touching—tactile stimulation—is to human and nonhuman animal development, and even survival. Since the 1970s, when *Touching* was first published, there has been a lot of new research on touch. Unsurprisingly, much of the research has been done in neonatal units, oncological units, and palliative care environments.

As Montagu's book shows, the importance of touching in babies (both human babies and those of nonhuman animals) is well documented. By and large, the research shows that infants who are not touched do not thrive. Rene Spitz's early studies on human infants in the 1940s[3] and Harry Harlow's studies on infant monkeys in the 1950s and 1960s showed the catastrophic results when infants are not touched,[4] and a later, less dramatic study led by Tiffany Field, director of the Touch Research Institute (University of Miami, Miller School of Medicine), demonstrated that, in preterm babies, a "15-[minute] massage therapy protocol three times per day for 10 days resulted in 21%–47% greater weight gain than standard care alone."[5]

In adults, the majority of studies on the benefits of massage and healing touch have been with cancer patients. One of the largest studies to date began in 2000 at the Cancer Center at Memorial Sloan-Kettering Hospital in New York. For three years, researchers measured the impact of massage therapy for symptom control in 1290 cancer patients. They found that with massage, patients' symptom scores were reduced by an average of 50%. They concluded that massage therapy appeared "to be an uncommonly non-invasive and inexpensive means of symptom control." It was also found to be a therapeutic method that was comforting; achieved major reductions in pain, fatigue, nausea, anxiety, and depression; and was free of negative side effects.[6]

### Pain management

Massage for pain management is well documented in research conducted all over the world. It can relieve some forms of pain by relaxing painful, tight muscles, tendons, and joints, and by reducing stress and anxiety. Other research is focused on how massage may stimulate nerve fibers to block pain messages from reaching the brain.[7]

In a 2010 study conducted at the Flagstaff Medical Center in Flagstaff, Arizona, 53 hospital inpatients each received one or more half-hour massage sessions. Their pain levels were measured on a 0 to 10 scale before and after massage therapy. Before massage, the average pain level in these patients was 5.18. After massage, their average level was 2.33—a statistically significant change. Participants also showed significant improvements in "overall pain levels, emotional well-being, relaxation, and ability to sleep."[8]

### What happens when we are touched?

While touch itself may be simple and intuitive, the benefits of touch are physiologically complex. In a 2010 National Public Radio interview, two pioneers in the science of touch research discussed the biology of touch. Researcher Tiffany Field (University of Miami) and psychologist Matt Hertenstein (DePaul University) explained that human connections start with a friendly touch. When we are touched, pressure sensors under our skin send messages to a nerve bundle deep in the brain: the vagus nerve. The vagus nerve communicates with all the major organs in the body. If the vagus nerve tells the heart that the touch is friendly, the heart responds by slowing down. This lowers blood pressure, and we start producing oxytocin: the trust, devotion, and bonding hormone. These physiological findings explain why massage has been so effective in palliative care for reducing anxiety and depression. When we touch or are touched, the oxytocin that is released helps us form or strengthen bonds with the person touching us.[9]

The interesting part about touch is that it is a two-way street. As Field says in the interview, when we reach out and touch someone, we "may reap all the same benefits as those we're touching." Hertenstein echoes this, saying that "you can't touch without being touched."[10] When we give a massage, our own stress hormones lower and our oxytocin levels rise along with those of the person being massaged; we all benefit.

### Reciprocity

Teaching and learning, like touch, are reciprocal. When you are teaching, you are being taught, just as when you are massaging, you are being touched. And all of these processes are ways of communicating and transmitting information. We have conversations through the skin. If you remember this, it will make your massages a well-rounded experience.

I usually teach massage in teams of two. This method of teaching is simple and usually brings out the best in everyone. Team members can see how easy it is to pass along the massage procedures, how fast they can learn in the tutorial, how quickly they learn that massage is a reciprocal act. If you are a medical professional, teach family, friends, and volunteers through tandem massage. Remember that both the person giving the massage and the person receiving the massage benefit.

An interesting study I came across recently involves the relationship between caregivers and oncology patients. It was led by psychotherapist William Collinge, an author and researcher in the field of integrative health. The study evaluated the outcomes of a multimedia program teaching massage to family caregivers of cancer patients at home. Almost one hundred families from diverse ethnic backgrounds were chosen and roughly divided into two groups. Using the same time frequency and duration, one group read to patients and the second group massaged patients using techniques learned through a DVD and study manual. While patients in both groups showed significant symptom reduction, the massage group's numbers were considerably higher (12%–28% reduction in the reading group vs. 29%–44% in the massage group).

The study concluded that massage was a viable means of enhancing "self-efficacy and satisfaction in caregiving while decreasing patient pain, depression, and other symptoms." The study also found that the people giving the massages showed "significant gains in confidence, comfort and self-efficacy using touch and massage as forms of caregiving."[11]

This type of reciprocity also gives the dying person an opportunity to have a caregiving role. The dying person can leave a positive legacy by allowing families and friends to massage them. Caregivers often aren't sure what to do. An invitation to massage gives people a helpful job. This sense of involvement helps families grieve more easily (although grieving is never easy), and will leave them with tactile memories to comfort them. They will have the knowledge that they did everything they could to make the departure gentle and pain free.

## Online Classroom

Visit brusheducation.ca/dying-in-good-hands to watch these videos:

The power of touch

Richard's massage team

Benefits of massage

# 1

# Palliative Massage Preparations

One of the first preparations for palliative massage is to gather the support team: the people who will do the massaging. The palliative massage team is generally formed with a foundation of the most important people in the life of the dying person: family and friends. It may also include some of the newest people in the last part of this person's life—medical professionals, massage therapists, end of life doulas, and hospice volunteers.

Usually, the people we inform about our illness are the first ones to become important players on our team. When I was diagnosed with neutropenia and given five years to live (20 years ago), I told my ex-husband first, and then my parents and best friends. I knew my team would be these people, who would be there for me, hands-on at every stage, if this diagnosis was going to run its course.

Over the years, I have worked with an incredible variety of massage teams, and every one of them has been different. I've had couples in which the patient did not want their spouse on the massage team, as well as couples that curled around each other and breathed nose to nose until the last breath. I've had people who were isolated in life and now popular in dying with volunteers massaging them every day. The teams I have taught have ranged from very small (the smallest being two: one person and one animal) to teams of 20, all vying for their turns to massage.

One patient, Mary Coletti, had a wonderful family who showed up *en masse* to learn to massage her. Mary's team included her son, daughter, and husband, her best friend since kindergarten,

and many other volunteers. Everyone signed up to massage Mary on a weekly basis. Nik, who had just met Mary through one of the other volunteers, ended up being the team's superstar with three or four massage shifts every week. To this day, Mary's crew is the biggest palliative massage team I've worked with.

**Figure 1.1.** Mary's team reading from her logbook, which the volunteers used to communicate with one another. Mary and her team's story is told in the documentary *Massaging Mary: Hands On with ALS.*

Although the people on a massage team might not all be instinctively good at massage, they share your devotion and dedication to granting the dying person "a peaceful parting," as palliative massage volunteer Melissa Cataford termed it in an interview in the documentary *Massaging Mary: Hands On with ALS.*[12] I am always surprised at the efforts families make to become comfortable massaging their dying loved ones. With the right feedback about their touch, even those who struggle most with tactility can be taught to massage with a touch that is not only therapeutic but also comforting.

## Forming the Massage Support Team

If you are organizing massage sessions for someone at home or in a hospice or hospital, include both professionals and amateurs, including friends and family.

My ideal basic massage team formula is based on a seven-volunteer schedule for a once-a-day patient massage in which volunteers sign up for one shift a week. This, however, isn't always possible, and sometimes you'll have to make do with fewer volunteers, some of whom will take more than one shift a week. For instance, I currently volunteer to massage one palliative person three times a week. Another massage volunteer is massaging the same person another three times a week, so this person gets six massages a week, guaranteed. This massage schedule is supplemented by one of the person's friends, who usually comes once or twice a week.

**Figure 1.3.** Suzy was serenaded by her husband, Earl, as she was massaged in her last days.

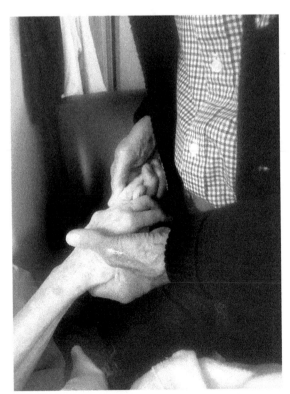

**Figure 1.2.** My patient Suzy's handyman, her brother.

**Figure 1.4.** The family massage team.

In collaboration with the palliative patient, try to come up with a list of *at least* five people to commit to a once a week massage time. Some people are the foot-massage-only types, others might be just hands, while others can take on the whole works! This variety of skill and comfort levels within a team is not a problem. All these forms of hands-on support are important and useful.

## TOUCHING THE UNTOUCHABLE

You *can* make contact with growths or unusual skin surfaces, and this touch can be tremendously beneficial. I remember my first breast cancer patient. She had a tumorous breast that felt like tree bark to the touch, and yet she could feel my fingers as though they were massaging on her natural skin. She taught me not to leave out the tumor; she wanted all of her body included in my massages during the last months of her life. I learned to massage her tumor as though it was a special part of her, a part that needed extra love and attention.

Now, I always ask my patients if I can include their tumor in my massage. If it is within reach, the patient may want to touch it and apply the oils or lotions himself or herself. I have also taught volunteers to do this when they are working with a person with a tumor that is accessible. I heard from one of them 25 years later about the importance of that experience in her palliative work today. Tumors are still part of the person and worthy of thoughtful touch.

Including tumors in massage can also help with skin maintenance. Like in pregnancy, tumors sometimes grow in fits and spurts, stretching the skin at different rates. Unlike pregnancy, these growths can develop into completely unexpected sizes and shapes. Just as we massage a pregnant abdomen to keep the skin's elasticity so it can stretch without damage or tearing, so too can we include cancerous growths in our massage in order to maintain the integrity of the skin that covers them.

My patient Gaston, for example, had a massive tumor on his abdomen that his family massaged with oil every day, and they credited this massaging with keeping the skin intact, even over such a large growth. Another patient, Bridget, had a tumor the size of a large orange on top of her head, which she

covered up with toques and funny hats. She was open to including her tumor in her face and scalp massage and appreciated the encouragement I gave her to make contact with this part of herself. She also had other tumor sites that stuck straight up and out from her body like spools of thread. We negotiated around these little creatures and tenderly treated them with the same oils that we were using on the rest of her body.

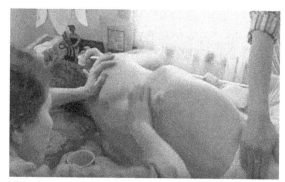

**Figure 1.5.** Miryam massaging Gaston's tumor.

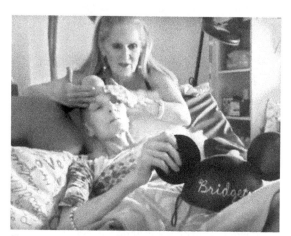

**Figure 1.6.** Bridget's adaptive face and scalp massage.

Neither Gaston nor Bridget presented with the pressure sores and tissue breakdown that frequently present with similar growths. Even the gentlest touch carried the necessary oils and skin stimulation to counteract any tissue tearing associated with fast or unusual skin growth. I recommend at least daily massage of these areas, but two or three times per day is better.

## Massage Preparations

You don't need much in the way of special equipment for massage. You probably already have most of what you need at home.

### Lubricant

Almost any viscous substance will do as a lubricant, as long as it is healthy: choose a high-quality oil that is edible and nourishing to the skin. Almond oil and cold pressed virgin olive oil are excellent, although they can stain your linens. Nonstaining oils such as walnut and coconut are excellent alternatives. Coconut oil has been my go-to lubricant for over 45 years. I used to find it only in health food stores, but today it's readily available at nearly every grocery store. With a little warmth (either from your hand or from placing the container inside a bowl of hot water), coconut oil melts beautifully and feels warm on the skin. Grapeseed oil is another good choice, and is high in antioxidants.

A dying person experiences the breakdown of body functioning; sometimes, this includes the breakdown of the skin. Skin degradation may result in hair loss, rashes, and dryness to the point of large, thick, flaking patches of skin. With such extreme dryness, I find the usual nursing lotions are not heavy enough to moisturize the skin for very long. In these cases, I use ordinary kitchen olive oil, rubbed in twice daily. It restores, nourishes, and maintains the skin in a good and flexible condition.

Some people believe you should not use softening lotions or oils while rubbing, as softening the skin at this point may make it more vulnerable to more breakdown and bedsores. However, my experience from many years of massaging spinal-cord injury wheelchair patients is that medicinal oils and plant-based healing mixtures can have positive benefit. Rubbing alcohol and witch hazel have traditionally been used to toughen skin and make it less susceptible to rupture.

You might want to try aromatherapy oils and lotions, but remember to first check with the patient about sensitivities to scent. Some people may like strong smells such as Tiger Balm, while others may find even the scent of olive oil to be too much (or think that it smells too much like a Greek salad lunch special). For palliative massage, the most popular oils with fragrance are lavender, cardamom, frankincense, myrrh, and rosewood. I also like orange, vanilla, and coconut. You may also use oils as a kind of ceremony. For instance, we anointed my dying friend Don Grayston with oils that had been blessed by religious colleagues. After his death, we used these same oils to bathe and dress him for his funeral.

> **A word of caution that aromatherapy is its own form of medicine. It is always good to read up about these powerful additives or check in with an aromatherapist before liberally adding them to your baths or massage oils. Keep in mind also that some dying people are very sensitive to fragrance and might not be able to tolerate any strong or formerly favorite fragrances.**

You don't always have to massage with an oil. Working with oil allows more ease of movement on the part of the massager and more tolerance to repeated work on an area on the part of the massagee. But working without oil allows you to massage over layers of clothing in public places. Wheelchair massage, for example, is normally done with patients fully clothed, so no lotions are needed.

### GLOVES AND MASKS

I have always taught my students to be comfortable in tight-fitting surgical gloves and masks for massage protocols in hospitals, chronic care facilities, and hospices. Now with COVID-19 precautions and protocols, gloves and masks have gone mainstream.

When working with a palliative person, you need to be especially vigilant about using gloves and masks properly, both for their protection and your own. If you'll be massaging someone at home, ask your patient's healthcare provider or consult your local public health agency for current glove and mask protocols.

If you'll be massaging in a hospital or care facility, you may be required to wear a mask the whole time you are in the building. If you will be

**Figure 1.7.** Due to COVID-19, gloves and masks may become standard precautions when visiting or attending to anyone in a long-term or chronic care facility.

wearing gloves, wash your hands thoroughly before touching the them. Don't touch or adjust the mask once your gloves are on. Change your gloves after the massage or after touching anything other than the patient.

### Warmth, heating, and hot-water bottles

Make the room comfortably warm. Electric blankets and heating pads will keep the bed warm, and microwaveable bean bags, hot-water bottles, and wool socks will warm your patient. I often massage right through long underwear, mittens, and layers of wool blankets! Some patients are not able to tolerate any air on their skin, so I massage them with extra covers so they are not exposed.

I like to warm the person's feet and neck while working on other parts of their body. If the person has an especially tight area, you might want to warm up the area before massage. When I am massaging my patient in a faceup (supine) position, I tuck the hot-water bottle under their neck before or after I finish massaging the head, neck, and shoulders. This both gives support to the neck and creates warmth.

Having four bottles handy is ideal. Distribute them where most comforting to the patient: one for each hand and foot; or behind the neck, on the abdomen, at the lower back, or for hip positioning. A hot-water bottle can be filled with different amounts of water to give different shapes. Depending on the patient's needs, it can also be filled with different temperatures of water—and yes, a hot-water bottle *can* be used for cooling! Applying "cold-water bottles" along with hot-water bottles can, in fact, help stimulate the patient's circulation, and this is, ultimately, the goal of hot-water bottle application.

### KNEIPP HYDROTHERAPY

I always rinse my hands with cold water at the end of a massage, an aspect of Kneipp therapy that I learned in Bad Wörishofen, Germany, which I visited in 1984 to see if they would let me bring their Kneipp hydrotherapy treatments to Canada.

In the nineteenth century, Sebastian Kneipp, a Catholic priest and naturopath, developed the practice of using cold water (and sometimes alternating warm and cold water) as a therapy for various ailments. He became famous for his "water cure" after curing his own tuberculosis with cold water from the Danube River. He went on to research cold water applications to promote health and to treat patients with various diseases.

The rationale for cold water treatments lies in how well cold temperatures help stimulate the body's circulation—and circulation, in turn, promotes healing. With the shock of cold on the skin, the blood vessels immediately constrict. This is called vasoconstriction. Then there is a secondary response—vasodilation—as the blood vessels open again and the body sends blood rushing to the cold area, creating warmth and a reddening color. It is as if the body, to fight the cold, decides to send in the (circulatory) troops to warm things up as quickly as possible.

It's easier to stimulate circulation with cold than with heat alone. At 98.6°F (37°C), the body is already warm, so you can't heat it up much more without burning or causing other damage to the tissues. However, if you first reduce the temperature in a particular area with cold, you have a greater temperature range with which to warm the tissues without causing damage.

I had been using cold water therapeutically years before I started massage school and long before I knew the circulatory principles behind Kneipp cold water applications. In my late teens and early twenties, I started daily dipping in the cold Slocan River and felt an improvement in my circulation. Today, I still do a daily dip to create a vascular flush, helping me keep a healthy lifestyle and happy hands.

These days, Kneipp's treatments are used by many medical professionals; massage therapists often find it to be a wonderful enhancement to their work. Hydrotherapy, the use of water to treat various conditions, is a big part of my massage practice. I use cold water and ice as a way to speed up the body's natural healing processes. I also use a small bucket of cold water and some witch hazel to wash each body part after I massage it. In an adaptation of Kneipp's techniques, I use ice massage as a pain remedy and to treat everything from surgical incisions to adhesions around wound sites. Ice massage stimulates the cells around the perimeter of wounds or ulcer sites to accelerate cell renewal.

A favorite use of hydrotherapy for palliative patients is the hot/cold water contrast footbath to encourage circulation, reduce swelling, and alleviate headaches.

*COLD WATER CONTRAST FOOTBATH*

1. Soak feet for five minutes in a bucket of warm water (approximately 97°F [36°C]).
2. Move feet for 10 seconds to a bucket of cold water (approximately 65°F [18°C]).
3. Remove feet from the cold water for 10 seconds.
4. Repeat steps 2 and 3 ten times, and then dry the feet.
5. Have the patient put on warm socks or, if they can, move around to warm the feet again.

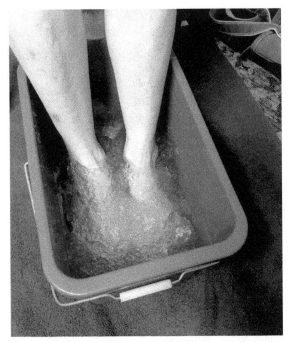

**Figure 1.8.** An ice water or snow footbath is good for both swollen feet and headaches. Contrast bathing can also be done with both hot and cold water. Take two buckets in your car and do this in the park, at the beach, at the family picnic, or wherever you take the patient out and about in their wheelchair.

### Lighting and music

Create a comfortable atmosphere with low lighting and the patient's (or your) favorite music. Playing your patient's favorite music during your palliative massages allows you to use that same music later on, in end stage, when the patient may not be able to communicate any longer. Getting the brain to associate relaxation with certain music is a handy tool to lessen the discomfort or anxiety of the final transition of life. Repeating the same music with each massage creates a Pavlovian-like response in your patient, and the massage music can be use when you need to soothe the patient, with or without your touch. For some people, this soothing music will be classical or New Age, while others want country ballads or rock and roll. Try also integrating musical favorites of the massage team so everyone will have a lasting musical memory of this special time.

From my experience, some patients who express no musical preference grow in the last weeks and days of their lives to love the favorites of their massage team. The music becomes associated with the pleasant sensation of massage. I can still hear my friend Don's favorite arrangement of the Brandenburg concertos—Wendy Carlos's electronic *Switched-On Bach*—more than a year after his death.

### Logbook

Keep a notebook or journal beside the patient's bed to record the dates or times of massages, massage highlights, visitors, and other comments. These notes are often not just useful for the caregivers, but also valuable reminder for families reading the logbook long after the person has passed. You can also take notes about how pressure sores are healing or where pressure points are reddening, the dying person's ability to respond to the massage, deepening respiration, or any issues or concerns that might impact the massage. The logbook serves as a reporting tool from one caregiver to the next, as well as suggestions about which caregivers should receive a shoulder rub during their shift crossovers. I always look forward to the hands-on welcome when I show up to do my massages from the person who has been massaging or reading or praying. I talk more about the importance of care for the caregivers in Chapter 9.

### Table

Portable massage tables are great if the person you are massaging can be moved. Sometimes I've set up a massage table in a garden to massage someone in a favorite location. A portable massage table can also facilitate a group massage. I've taken tables to a dying patient's home so family and friends can circle around. Usually, two people can fit at the foot of any massage table and two at the head of the table.

However, massage tables are not a prerequisite to doing a great home massage. In fact, palliative massage is rarely done on a massage table. Most people are massaged in their bed in the hospital or hospice, or at home. Often the bed that someone has slept on for their entire adult life or senior years is the same bed that I am massaging them on until they die. They can also be massaged in their wheelchairs or in the bath. Some wheelchairs can be turned into beds to allow the person to stretch out comfortably.

I have the stature of a 12-year-old, so I find it easy to move around on the top of a bed to do a massage. However, this is not true of everyone. You might find it easier to stand beside the bed. Some beds today are so high that only a pole vaulter can access them easily. But these high beds do make it easier for tall people who find it hard to squat or kneel on the bed while massaging.

If the bed seems too awkward for you, try a dining room or kitchen table or the living room rug. And remember, dying people need never be kept in the corner. If they can be moved and can tolerate the weather, get them out of isolation and into the fresh air. Massage them with all your creative energy on whatever available surface is appropriate! Massage tables can be created anywhere and everywhere. Two sawhorses and a door, for instance, can make an instant indoor or outdoor massage table.

If you will be massaging on a hard surface, however, put down something soft, such as a couple yoga mats, to create a comfortable surface for the patient to lie on for about an hour.

### Ice

I sometimes use ice to treat uncomfortable palliative conditions such as swollen extremities that are boiling hot and feeling ready to burst. Ice massage is exactly as it sounds. Hold an ice cube in a facecloth. Use the ice to massage and the loose end of the facecloth to mop up the melting ice as you go.

Icy hands are another simple cold application. Hold your hands in ice water for at least a minute, and then dry off and massage, dipping back into the cold as needed.

Although you may not need ice massage with every palliative situation (especially where there is no swelling or any heated body surfaces), it is still a useful tool to have in your repertoire. Ice massage works particularly well to soothe the tissue around wounds, discolorations, and pressure sores.

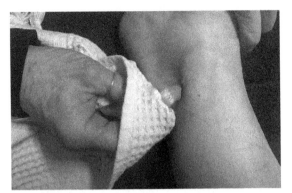

**Figure 1.9.** Massage with an ice popsicle can soothe swollen ankles.

### Support pillows and towels

You will want lots of towels and pillows to support the patient in different massage postures. Keep a stack of towels and five or six pillows at the ready. You can never have too many pillows for your patient. Different pillow sizes work well for uncomfortable days, tube drain support, or packing around tumor sites. There are now fancy body pillows that can help support a palliative patient comfortably, though these aren't necessary; you can get enough pillow support with regular pillows.

## Underwater Massage

I highly recommend massage in a warm water pool or tub for my palliative patients as a non-pharmacological approach to relax patients and manage pain. If patients go to a pool or hot spring, they see and experience the bigger world, familiar places, and people they know. The excursion gets them out of bed and into a warm, gentle, buoyant world where their bodies are not so heavy or so pain-ridden. Even when people are dying, they are not without the ability to experience good things. Much depends upon the patient themselves. Two of my patients, my mom and Freya, loved Ainsworth Hot Springs. For them the drive along the lake, seeing where they had lived and talking about who they had known, was a trip down memory lane before we even got to the hot springs!

Underwater massage is easily practiced on a daily basis in your palliative patient's bathtub. I

**Figure 1.10.** Here Freya gets a massage in the pool with some help from her son, Finn, and husband, Stan.

A. One hand under the lower back supporting the sacrum, with the other hand holding the neck.

B. Both hands at the waistline or hips, or one hand at the hip and the other at the sacrum. The patient can rest their head on your shoulder.

**Figure 1.11.** Two supporting positions for floating your patient in the pool.

**Figure 1.12.** Here I do some single-handed fingertip kneading on the rhomboids while supporting my patient across the upper chest. I'm sitting on the pool bench with my patient sitting on my knees.

kneel alongside many bathtubs with families that are going to be washing and bathing their loved one. The underwater massage is a wonderful addition to that daily dose of warm relaxation.

Epsom salt baths can also lead to improved pain management and sleep patterns. My mom loved Epsom salt baths and would lie in there for an hour, occasionally asking for more hot water in her bathtub while I massaged her. It was the only time she didn't ache all over.

### EPSOM SALT BATHS

I recommend an Epsom salt bath after massage or each night before bed. Salt baths are great for general relaxation, as well as for pressure sore discomfort or other tissue breakdown. Salt baths

and saunas, sweat lodges, and steam rooms have long been seen as a way to detoxify and promote good health. Although research into the benefits of sweating is ongoing, studies have shown that various natural toxins and salts are found in human sweat, indicating that the sweat is helping to remove wastes from the body. So even if research on salt baths is inconclusive, if a palliative patient's kidneys are shutting down and the liver is malfunctioning, a salt bath to stimulate sweating seems worth a try to me.

Epsom salts are readily available at pharmacies, garden centers, farming supply stores, and shopping outlets. It's generally worth buying 50-pound bags from the farming supply store, if you can. Use about four cups of salt for each bath. Add the salt to a few inches of tepid water, and then gradually heat the bath up by adding warmer water.

You might want to put a bathing suit on to help lift your patient into the bath, as I have found it best to step into the bath myself. I got into the bath with my mom and was able to lie there with her as she rested on my arm across the back of her neck. Whether the dying person is small or large, always get another person to help with delivery in and out of the bath. This safety measure will ensure your back stays happy.

Submerge your patient up to the top of their chest. Place a cold towel around the person's neck to equalize the temperature in their head and keep them comfortable. Soak for 20 minutes to one hour. Don't add any other bathing solutions, oils, or soap since these will alter the chemistry of the water. Never use peppermint oil or any other pure carminative oils since they may irritate or burn mucus membranes.

Encourage your patient to drink lots of water. Keep a large glass of cold water handy on the side of the tub to sip during the bath. After the long soak in salt water, rinse in warm water straight from the hand-held shower.

Dying people can balloon to twice their size in their legs or arms. This edema buildup can be helped by the Epsom salt baths combined with massage. If the person is afflicted with extreme swelling and lymphatic distress, slowly turn the water to cooler and cooler. Have the patient stand or sit in front of the faucet and let cool water run down the back of the legs and over the puffy feet.

Be sure your patient gets out of the bath slowly and carefully, sitting on the edge of the tub to stabilize before getting out. I installed a hand grip for my mom even though I was helping her out of the bath.

Caregivers should take plenty of Epsom salt baths, too!

---

**Caution: If the patient is over 50 or has diagnosed heart trouble, you should moderate the water temperature and avoid submerging their body above heart level. You should definitely use a cold towel around the patient's neck, keeping a bucket of cold water available beside the tub for wringing. If you have any concerns about whether a hot tub will affect the patient adversely, please consult with a doctor before using the Epsom salt bath.**

---

## Draping Protocols

Draping helps keep your patient relaxed and not worried about exposing their private parts, especially when friends and extended family are part of the massage team. But aside from questions of modesty, proper draping is important to help the patient conserve the heat generated by the massage. This heat helps the relaxation response, so you want to retain as much of it as possible. I always tuck the sheeting firmly up against the person so they can feel its pressure. Expose only the part of the body you are directly massaging, and tell the patient what you are doing as you work. You don't want to upset or confuse them by hiking their underwear into a G-string arrangement without any explanation!

Use big towels or a sheet to cover parts of the body that aren't being worked on. For example, while massaging the abdomen, use a towel to cover the chest. Tuck the ends of the towel under the armpits or over the shoulders.

When massaging the legs, use towels or a sheet to cover the person's torso and arms. Secure the draping by tucking edges into underwear (when working on the gluteal muscles or leg) and/or under an opposite leg or body part. Like other underwear, adult or hospital diapers have elastic edges into which you can tuck the draping, still pulling it up to uncover the entire gluteal area for thorough massaging. Use a "diaper" draping method (a sheet tucked in at the crotch, both legs exposed) when doing tandem massage.

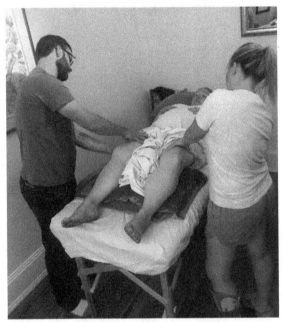

**Figure 1.13.** Tandem massage with a diaper-style drape.

Your patient can be draped with sheets or towels if you want to massage outdoors, or they might be undraped if you're massaging in private and that is their preference. I had a patient who did not want to be draped, no matter what I said about heat retention or therapeutics. Only when faced with the protocols of the massage school did he become more flexible and accept the draping that students needed to practice.

When I am doing garden or other outdoor massages, usually in wheelchairs, I will use a sheet or thicker covering to keep the patient warm or to keep the sun off. I have a chronically ill patient who must be covered with two layers of blankets

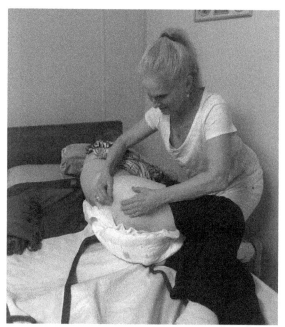

**Figure 1.14.** Side-lying diaper drape adaptation. Draping for a person lying on their side may take some practice. I try to expose the entire hip.

for heat retention as I massage her through the covers.

### Institutional linens

In hospitals or hospices, I usually use the linens they supply. The top sheet and blanket can be used for draping. Because I often use coconut oil, which doesn't stain, and because I am a professional in the amount of oil that I use, there isn't extra oil to stain the sheets. But if I am using a highly staining oil, like olive oil, then I use sheets that are dedicated to massage and can get stained—usually old sheets the family has provided. However, the draw sheet (a small bed sheet placed across the bed under the patient's torso to help move patients) is usually tough enough to handle both staining and nonstaining oils.

No matter what kind of covers you use for your patient, and no matter whether they are using their own underwear, diapered, or *au naturel*, the draping techniques you will use are the same as those used for able-bodied massages. Check in with your patient about heat loss or overheating as you go along, and drape accordingly.

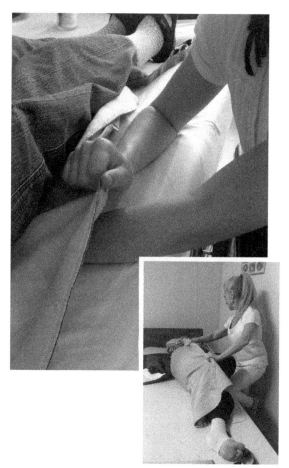

**Figure 1.15.** You can use the draw sheet to help you adjust the patient's position while massaging and can massage with the sheet between the patient and your hand.

## Massage Length

Most professional massages run about an hour in length, which is ideal for a full-body massage. However, palliative massages have no predictable timing. Some people are massaged for hours as the people that come to be with them are saying goodbye with their touch. Other visitors might only stay briefly, with just enough time to massage the hands or feet.

The therapeutic aspects of massaging someone who is dying depend on their condition and other symptoms such as sleep patterns and pain management. Some massages can be continuous, around the clock affairs, while others are focused on specific needs, such as late-night massages to establish better sleep. Be creative in your timing, and abandon the notion of hour-long massages

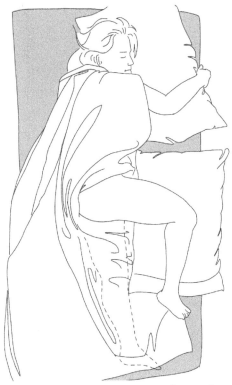

**Figure 1.16.** Draping for patient comfort, modesty, and warmth.

in the usual daytime hours. I spend more time in hospitals and hospices after 10 p.m. and often throughout the night because nights are often the hardest time for dying people to be comfortable.

When administering a tandem massage (a massage given by two or more people at once), be conscious of the fact that the massage will not take as long as it would with just one person. Be careful, too, not to overwork any areas.

Above all, however, I find that *frequency* is my watchword. Some people can tolerate only short periods of touch, and yet they want so many short massages that, at the end of the day, they get more massage than a traditional one-hour massage would provide! The more massages the better, I say, even if each massage is quite short.

## Patient Positioning

Patient positioning is an important focus of palliative massage training. As someone weakens,

moves less, and lies down a lot, the lungs are in a vulnerable state and predisposed to congestion. Passive drainage postures are critical for getting or keeping the lungs clear. We discuss drainage postures in detail on pages 125 to 126.

Most patients rest in the position that causes the least discomfort or pain. However, this quickly brings on the potential problem of pressure sores. As much as possible, encourage patients to change position regularly. You can help them lie in their most uncomfortable or least favorite position by massaging away their aches and pains. If your patient is uncomfortable with certain positions, be prepared to massage in short sequences, changing the patient's position frequently.

Traditional massage positions (lying flat, facedown or faceup) are usually only possible until the person has tubes, tumors, drains, pouches, or oxygen masks that get in the way. Most palliative people find it easiest to breathe faceup with an elevated upper body. As they get closer to the end, you may need to elevate the head higher and higher as they get weaker and more congested.

Some patients lie on their side from the beginning, and lying facedown is never an option for them. As time goes on, the patient might not be able to move or be moved, so you will need to adapt your massage methods, position, and timing in order to massage them through to the end.

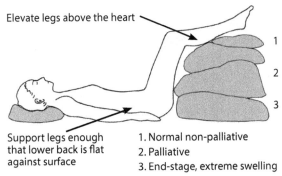

Elevate legs above the heart

Support legs enough that lower back is flat against surface

1. Normal non-palliative
2. Palliative
3. End-stage, extreme swelling

**Figure 1.17.** Supine position with patient's legs elevated above the heart for good passive drainage from the lower extremities.

## *Massage positions*

### SUPINE (FACEUP POSITIONING)

Place pillows under the knees and under the head to flex the head slightly up for better breathing. If the patient has leg swelling, you might use extra pillows to elevate the legs for drainage.

If the person is having trouble breathing, use more pillows behind the back and head to elevate their upper body even more. By the end stage, you might have to support the person with enough pillows to allow them to almost sit upright so they can breathe.

**Figure 1.19.** Supine wheelchair position: seated, leaning forward with shoulder support from your hand.

You will learn more about this type of massage in Chapter 2.

### PRONE (FACEDOWN POSITIONING)

I rarely massage people in a prone, facedown position when they are dying. However, I have had a number of dying patients who were comfortable in this position, which allowed me to massage their lower back and hips. Pillows and rolled towels can be strategically placed to make sure any drains and tubes are not squished. For obvious reasons, artificial bladders must be drained before the massage begins. Bowel bags can be placed to the side or between the legs.

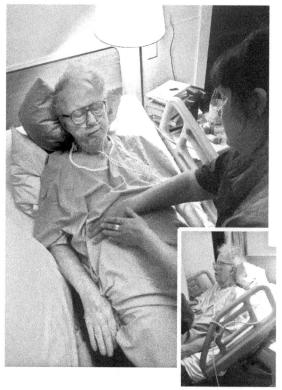

**Figure 1.18.** Supine position with the patient's head elevated with pillow support.

### SEATED AND LEANING FORWARD IN A CHAIR, BED, OR WHEELCHAIR

Patients can be massaged in bed, sitting up. Or some palliative patients might be in a wheelchair, so you can adapt your massages to this position by sliding your hands under the legs and gluteal muscles and between the chair back and patient's back.

People with respiratory impairment rarely stay in this position for long periods, but it can be useful, even if the patient can only tolerate it for a short time. The position gives you easy access to the full back and the hips. Your patient can let you know when they have had enough. Ask them—more

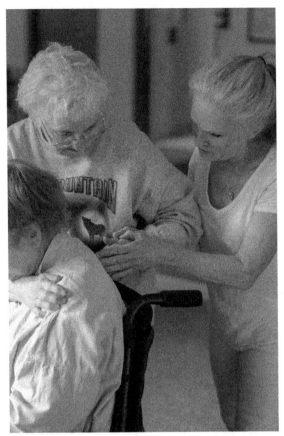

**Figure 1.20.** My massage volunteer learns to work on the patient's erector spinae muscles.

often than usual—if they are comfortable being facedown.

Women may need a rolled towel across the upper chest, supporting the sternum and taking pressure off the breasts. The towel needs to be long enough to curl around under the armpits. This support will also help the person extend and turn their neck without discomfort. If they want, they can rest their head on stacked hands or another rolled towel under the forehead.

Use two pillows under the person's ankles to semi flex the legs and take pressure off the low back. Those who have a bit of a sway back may need extra support for the lower back. I also position pillows to support the abdominal area, giving the back a more even and horizontal line. Place a hot-water bottle on the feet.

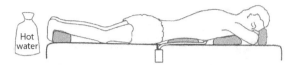

**Figure 1.21.** Pillows and rolled towels are the key to comfortable prone positioning, even when accommodating tubes, drains, and pouches.

Having the legs in a semi flexed position will relieve pressure on the low back. Anyone with a lower-back problem will be able to tell you this simple technique is highly effective for making lying down comfortable. With this support, you can press on the patient's back and not cause any discomfort for the vertebrae.

With the right pillow support for tubes, pouches, or drains, even a person with an abdominal tumor can lie comfortably facedown.

### SIDE-LYING POSITION

The side-lying position is a classic palliative treatment posture from early until end stage. The side-lying position is particularly useful in the beginning of convalescence if the patient has lower-back issues like sciatica or lumbago. This position avoids increasing strain on the lower back during the massage.

Place one pillow under the patient's head to keep it up, not angled downward. This will help their breathing so they don't get stuffed up. Angle the pillow toward the front of the chest. Many people will instinctively push the pillow back and over their shoulder; if this happens, bring the pillow back down around to the front and have the patient place one hand on top of the pillow and one hand underneath the pillow. Then place one or two pillows between the knees to support the person in the side-lying position.

Side-lying positions can be full-crooked or half-crooked. I use the full-crooked position most of the time, but I'll use half crooked if that is more comfortable for the patient.

- **Full-crooked side-lying patient position:**
  A full-crooked position means the palliative patient is on their side in a curled position,

both knees bent at a right angle, one on top of the other, with chin tucked slightly toward the chest. This position is ideal for allowing the massager to lean on the patient's back without rolling the patient onto their front. Place pillows between the knees to bring the top knee up so the leg is horizontal and not angled downward.

Figure 1.23. Half-crooked side-lying patient position.

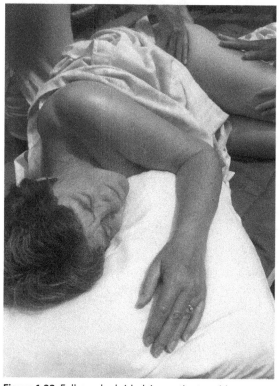

Figure 1.22. Full-crooked side-lying patient position.

- **Half-crooked side-lying patient position:** In a half-crooked position, the upper knee is bent up and the bottom leg is straight. Place a pillow under the top knee to keep the hip from twisting. Tucking the patient's head down so their chin is toward their chest puts the patient into a more curled and fetal position. This position is a good resting position for many patients, but for side-lying massage, the half-crooked posture is not as stable, and the patient may roll forward when you exert massage pressure on the back.

## Massage Postures for the Massager

Palliative massage can be a marathon of days and weeks of massaging. As part of the palliative massage team, you, as the massager, need to keep healthy and strong. It is so important to preserve your posture and protect your back. If your back goes down, the entire palliative support system may be down. In general, your position should be comfortable and sustainable, and should use the least amount of energy with maximum efficiency. The following tips should help you avoid strains or injuries:

- Wear comfortable shoes and clothing.
- If the patient is lying on a table, have them lie near the edge so they are close to your body. This will help you keep your back upright and prevent you from straining and leaning too far over.
- Keep your knees slightly bent with one leg in front of the other to be in a stable position and

able to execute a smooth rocking motion with as little effort as possible. This is called stride posture. The leg that is behind (i.e., farthest away from the bed or table) will be more stretched out; this is the push leg. The leg in front is more bent at the knee so you can vary your height according to the patient's bed height.

- Never stand with two legs together as you will not last long and your back will not thank you later.

**Figure 1.24.** The stride position is an effective way to get strength in your stroke using your body, not just your arms.

**Figure 1.25.** The shiatsu position provides good back support if you're working on the floor or the bed.

- When moving massage strokes down a large part of the patient's body, take a step or two alongside the table at the same time as the arm movement to prevent overreaching.
- If you're working on a patient in a hospital bed, remember you can adjust the bed; both the head and feet positions can be raised and lowered.
- Most hospital beds are on castors, so you can roll the bed into an optimum position of comfort for you.
- If the patient is able, you can have them switch head/foot positions so you can work on the other side of their body without strain.
- If you're working on the floor or on the bed beside the patient, take a shiatsu position, with one knee down and one knee up. The knee that is down should be closest to the person you are massaging. Use your legs, not your back, to get a forward rocking motion.

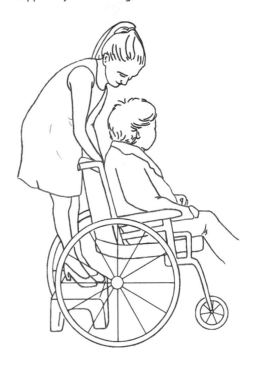

other so you can lean forward without straining your back. Use the chair to support your posture.

The bottom line is this: learn how to position yourself comfortably and safely. This is the key to stamina so you don't give in to awkward postures that can hurt your back.

## MASSAGE ETIQUETTE

- Always check with the patient about how they are feeling: Is there a particular place they would like worked on? Is your hand pressure too hard or too light?
- Ask about the location of any shunts, tumors, or current or old injuries.
- Ask the patient if they are comfortable in the position you have them in. Use pillows and extra rolled blankets for support.
- Ask the patient if they are warm enough. Use hot-water bottles, heaters, and blankets as needed.
- Be aware of subtle signs from the patient about a bowel movement or passing gas. You can say, "If you feel something moving around, let me know." This gives the patient a sense of ease to bring up the topic, or you could make an excuse to leave the room to get Tiger Balm or whatever. (Tiger Balm may also mask the smell and save the patient undue embarrassment.)

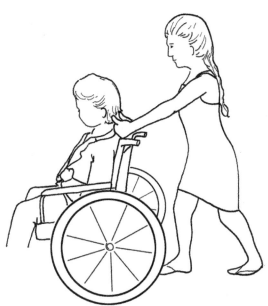

**Figure 1.26.** Wheelchairs present an obstacle, but you can safely massage around the wheels and backrest. Remember the stride position as a way to protect your back, even while straddling a wheel.

- If you're working on the floor, try sitting cross-legged or on your heels.
- When the patient is in a seated position, take a stride position with one foot ahead of the

## Contraindications for Palliative Massage

Many classic contraindications for professional therapeutic massage do not apply in the palliative, end-of-life-stage scenario, where the primary goal is to keep the patient comfortable until their last breath. For instance, those with heart conditions are often contraindicated for massage therapy. In my experience, however, palliative patients with a heart transplant, heart surgery, and heart failure are perfect candidates for the therapeutic effects of massage. Massage therapy offers the best passive way of encouraging the palliative patient's compromised circulation without the patient having to exert themselves, which could stress the heart muscle.

Patients with high blood pressure or hemophilia are also found in therapeutic training program contraindications. However, these patients can again be included in palliative massage, with the precautionary practice of avoiding varicosities, especially in the lower extremities.

The following sections presents some common contraindications for massage and how to approach them in the context of palliative care.

### Damaged blood vessels

As with all massage, palliative or not, avoid any direct contact with varicose veins or damaged blood vessels. Don't even massage beside them. Instead, apply hydrotherapies such as leg wraps, cold washes, and compresses to the affected areas. You can use these hydrotherapies while massaging nonaffected areas.

Diabetic cortisone users, patients taking blood thinners, and patients with hemophilia are usually told to avoid massage, but in palliative scenarios, gentle massage is appropriate.

### Open lesions or wounds

Massage is locally contraindicated over open lesions or wounds (common sense prevails here). However, massage is fine *near* these sites to promote tissue healing by increasing blood circulation and drainage from the site. Gentle massage strokes should be done towards the lesion; to avoid further tissue damage, never pull away from the site.

Gentle massage (such as a mild effleurage, described on pages 38 to 39) may be done over closed or raised lesions. Just remember that the tissue is traumatized by disease and requires very gentle massage treatment.

In general, most contraindications for lesions and wounds are as much about your own safety as they are about the patient's. Open lesions are prone to infection, so take care to practice impeccable hygiene prior to massaging a patient with an open lesion. Some lesions, such as those with a fungal infection, may also carry contagions that could affect you. When massaging around any area that carries the threat of infection, always wear medical gloves.

### Body fluids

Areas that contain body fluids, such as the rectum and the ischial tuberosity pressure sites (those bony bumps we sit on), are not contraindicated for massage. In fact, it is extremely important that the hip and gluteal areas be prevented from tissue breakdown. You should, however, use great care when massaging around these areas and always use gloves. The tissue in the lower gluteal muscles is close to the genital area and therefore highly susceptible to infection if the skin is broken. This area must be cleaned (if patient is in diapers or on the blue pad) before massage. After massaging this region, be sure to wash your hands or change your surgical gloves before moving on to massage any other body part.

### High body temperature

When I went to massage school in the early 1970s, I was taught not to do a full-body massage if a patient's body temperature exceeds 102°F. Today, however, a dying patient's extreme temperature would not stop me. In a palliative context, if the patient's body temperature is high, I use hydrotherapy to make them more comfortable. For example, I might use a fan to blow cool air on the patient throughout my massage. I might also keep a cold compress on their head or a "hot" water bottle filled with cold water at their neck, feet, or abdomen. A gentle, local massage provides comfort and contact, and a full-body massage can help speed up the body's regulating mechanism.

### Diarrhea

For patients with diarrhea, abdominal massage must be gentle. Deep massage is usually inappropriate when the colon is highly inflamed and easily irritated, but gentle digestive massage can help ease abdominal discomfort.

In AIDS patients, cryptosporidial diarrhea is common and can persist for weeks or months. Because this is a painful condition with an inflammatory element, you will need to adapt your pressure and use only light reflex stroking. Palliative patients who do not have AIDS can also be afflicted with ongoing diarrhea. Again, gentle digestive massage strokes can help settle the abdominal pain.

### Cancer

For many years, there was contraindication against using massage with cancer patients based on the belief that, because massage stimulates blood and lymph circulation, it might encourage cancerous growth. This belief has been repeatedly refuted. If it were true, says Deborah Curties, RMT, my former student and now co-owner of the Sutherland-Chan School of Massage Therapy, "many other normal activities…including hot showers, exercise, and sexual activity would also contribute to metastasis."[13] Her argument is supported by researcher William Collinge, who says there are necessary adaptations for oncological patients, but "the concern about metastasis is increasingly regarded as a myth in the massage profession."[14]

Although there is no evidence that massage stimulates cancerous growth, some people are still afraid massage will cause cancer cells to spread. Recent research suggests that the spread of cancer has nothing to do with increased blood or lymph flow. The Canadian Cancer Society says massage is safe for people with cancer. It also states that while there is no evidence that massage therapy can *treat* cancer itself, it can improve the quality of life of cancer patients by improving sleep and reducing nausea, pain, and stress.[15]

## Communication

Learning palliative massage requires feedback to tell you how you are doing. If your patient is still able to communicate, they can always tell you if you are on the right track. They can tell you if you are a little too far to the left or too far to the right, or if you are too firm or not firm enough. Remember to check in frequently and you can't go wrong.

I check in often to make sure my hunches about what a patient needs or wants are accurate, and I check in because I want the treatment to be patient driven as much as possible. I ask, "How's the pressure? Should I be lighter or heavier? Do you have any favorite spots that I should spend extra time on?" With feedback from your patient, you can guide yourself along a full-body massage routine with confidence.

A patient may be speaking one day and not the next. Weakness can come and go at random. If the patient is too weak to talk or form sentences, ask questions that make it easy for them to nod or shake their head in response. Try to ask yes-or-no questions, the kind of questions that simply require a nod or shake of the head. For instance: "Would you like more massage on your legs? Your feet? Your toes? Would you like me to keep going? Would you like it a little firmer? Would you like it a little gentler?" You can also try getting the patient to use blinks to communicate. I might say, "Just blink if you'd like me to do more massage on your feet. Blink if I can be firmer. Blink if you would like me to be lighter."

This chapter has given you practical tips to help you get ready to massage. The story of Gaston, next, will show you how to put these practical tips to positive use.

## Online Classroom

Visit brusheducation.ca/dying-in-good-hands to watch these videos:

Shower the people you love with love
Massaging Gaston's tumor
Acceptance
Mary's logbook
Ice massage
Using the draw sheets

# Gaston

"Massage gave us all a different way to live and a better way to die."

– Gaston Huchet

When I met Gaston he reawakened my dream. He had accomplished something that I had wanted to do since I was nineteen: he had built his own coffin. This was one of my first interests in things related to dying, in the world of the beyond, in preparations for the next unknown.

I always thought that my small stature would camouflage the cedar box. People would just think that it was a beautiful blanket box or coffee table!

But we had more than an interest in coffins in common, Gaston and I. We never stood beside each other, but I knew by his size in the bed that he was not a tall man. And we both shared a passion for education, for passing along what we knew to be true, and for sharing our expertise with those around us.

Gaston was French and looked French. He was always clean-shaven and had a tiny moustache. He had velvety skin, pale pink and smooth, and a full head of hair. Since his chemo, his hair had grown back to its original, youthful brown. He was 69 or, as his wife Monique said, "He will be 70 if he gets to 70."

Gaston and his wife, Monique, had come to the Kootenays from France 40 years before I met him. He was a highly respected member of a spiritual yoga community in rural British Columbia. He brought his family up with community values and high ideals. He was kind, loving, and unusually gifted with his hands.

We met over his illness. His days of bicycle racing were behind him and he was now racing a different course. His family was eager to learn about looking after Gaston from the onset of his illness, when he was still mobile, to the final days of bedridden paralysis.

I enjoyed hearing about all the different venues where his daughters had massaged him, from the garden to the lake and back to the bedroom. Gaston had been pushed around his neighborhood in a wheelchair and massaged at the park more than once.

From the beginning of my visits to Gaston's compact home, two blocks from our main street in Nelson, I was intrigued with his point of view. He wanted families to see that they could keep their loved ones at home. He wanted people to see that families like his could be families like theirs. Gaston and his family allowed me to bring classes of practical nurses, community workers, summer palliative students, hospice volunteers, and public health nurses to learn to massage him. We all piled into his attic-like bedroom and learned to massage him alongside his relatives.

"If I hadn't massaged my dad, I would have had so many regrets," declared Dominique as she glanced at her mother.

Monique nodded back in agreement. She laughed and said that she couldn't say no to

Gaston's wishes: "He wanted to have his story told, and give families the opportunity to die at home surrounded by loved ones."

At the first-year anniversary of Gaston's passing, his daughter Miryam expressed similar sentiments: "It wasn't about his dying, it was about his living. It was about how he taught us to not be afraid of death."

Miryam embodied Gaston's attitude in her daily care of her dad. She learned everything I could teach her about massage and proved to be a natural palliative caregiver. She is practical like her father, an elementary school teacher, a combination of artist and craftsperson with a flare for fun. She teased her dad and lightened up the atmosphere wherever she went. She talked to me about the woodwork her dad did with her one night trying to finish a puppet project for a deadline. Gaston had stayed up all night helping her.

But even before her father's illness, Miryam had already been acquainted with the world of palliative care: Miryam's husband is a music thanatologist—he plays the harp to people who are dying, as he played to my mother in the days before she died. He took my mom's pulse before he played, and he took her pulse after he played, and found he soothed her in her unconsciousness. As deep as my mother was, his music took her deeper. He was a similarly wonderful addition to Gaston's team.

Gaston's cancer was extreme. He had a massive tumor that had been removed from his side, but it grew back into the same site, anesthetizing his body by invading his spine. He became immobilized, with paralysis from the waist down. For the last six months of his life, the dining room downstairs became his bedroom.

However, for all the time Gaston spent in bed, he never had a pressure sore. This was because Dominique came every lunch hour from her job at the Credit Union to massage her dad. Miryam massaged him every morning when she bathed him and then again at night when she put him to bed. This daily treatment made all the difference in the world of palliative dangers. The preventative action of their daily massage therapy conditioned his skin and kept his circulation optimal.

Dominique noted, "His tumor had become monstrous, but we kept massaging it."

Miryam added, "We massaged it religiously every day. His skin became translucent, like rice paper, but it never broke open."

Gaston let me film the last two years of his life so I could document the work we did together teaching massage to his family. We took photos of the grandchildren attempting to reach his feet to massage them. The grandchildren were so small they could hardly stand, but they staggered over to his low bed, grabbed the edge, and balanced themselves, ready to work. They were determined to join in with the tasty coconut massages! They delicately scooped out the coconut oil and melted it onto his feet, their tiny fingers working it into his toes, the whole time overseen by their smiling grandpapa.

Gaston spoke the language of the heart. He had the serenity of someone who had lived well; it seemed to permeate the air around him. His enormous smile was as big in his waking hours as it was when he slept at the end of his massages.

Monique was a self-admitted "nontouchy type." She didn't like being massaged, which I didn't know the first time I automatically massaged her shoulders. I was dishing out my usual "care for the caregiver" shoulder rub and had no inkling that this was not her idea of a treat!*

She later admitted that she was a convert: she had been won over by the effect of massage on her husband and even her own shoulders. Now, Monique would be massageable in her final days; she would now be able to let her family touch her and comfort themselves in her passing.

Hearing Monique talk about being a convert made me think of my own conversion. My experience with Gaston and his family gave me the courage to scoop my mother from her senior's facility and bring her home to die. Gaston even had a profound influence on someone like me,

---

* This happened years ago. With my more-formalized protocols for consent today, I would have approached Monique differently to ensure her comfort with my hands-on approach.

who already *was* a convert to the experience of dying at home.

---

Gaston allowed me to film some of his massage treatments. When he said to me during filming, "Kreesteen, would you like to show the tumor?" I could not say no!

His daughters turned him over to a side-lying position and then showed how they applied oil to the entire tumor, which extended from Gaston's armpit to his waist. It must have weighed more than 20 pounds. It extended out of his side about a foot, making his arm angle outward.

They were not intimidated by Gaston's tumor size, nor were they afraid to touch it. They were the ones who taught me to be more hands-on with extremely large tumors.

They allowed Gaston to feel good about every part of himself as a whole and healthy person. This man was an athlete, someone who had extremely positive feelings about his body. He felt neither betrayed by the disease that was taking his life nor bitter about leaving early. His principles were reflected in the family around him. They were not in conflict with each other's different styles of caring for Gaston. They were harmoniously linked in love for him and for each other.

That's what it felt like every time I was in their presence. It was like being in the home of newlyweds: I always had the blush and bloom of their family love, of their love of touch—a honeymoon feeling!

After the last filming that Gaston and I did, he slowly smiled as I tucked him back into his blankets and said, "Kreesteen, thank you. That was a treat!"

I replied, "Gaston, you're the treat!"

And with that Gaston untangled his arms from under his blankets and said, "I'm going to give you a kiss."

He lifted his arms. I clicked the side of the bed down to lower the support railing and leaned into his embrace. With Gaston's kiss on one cheek and then the other, as was his habit, I felt blessed by an energy greater than either of us.

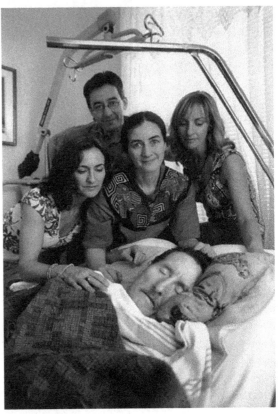

Gaston with family.

# 2

# Basic Massage Strokes

> "Anyone wishing to study medicine must master the art of massage."

> – Hippocrates, 460–377 BCE,
> Father of Modern Medicine

Massage is the manipulation of the tissues of the body for therapeutic purposes. The word itself is taken from an etymological root meaning "to knead" or "to handle." It is an ancient remedy; historical records show it being used in ancient China, India, and Greece. Today the most popular form of massage is known as Swedish massage, developed in the nineteenth century by Swedish gymnastics enthusiast Per-Henrik Ling and Dutch doctor Johann Georg Metzger. This chapter explains the basic massage strokes you can use and adapt for various parts of the body and for various palliative conditions.

## Learning Massage

The best way to learn massage is in person. It is an art passed on by mimicking and practicing alongside someone who knows more than you do. If this is not possible, a virtual classroom, using social media or online tutorials, is a good support. No matter how you learn—by book, person, or film—the most important part is to practice repeatedly and then pass it on to others.

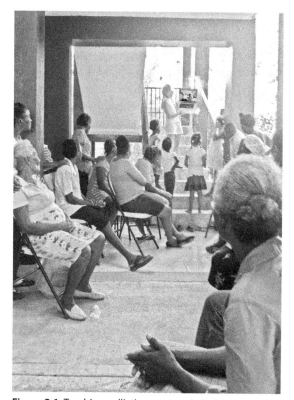

**Figure 2.1.** Teaching palliative massage in Haiti.

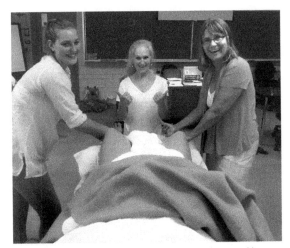

**Figure 2.2.** Family teaching tutorial with Sydnee and her granddaughter, Maya.

## Principles of Massage

There are four basic principles of massage that I always follow.

### 1. Uncork the bottle

When massaging, always work the part of a limb (an arm or leg) that is hooked up with the trunk of the body first before moving down its length. I call this uncorking the bottle. Think of it like this: if you want to get the contents out of a bottle, you need to uncork it first. So, for example, when giving someone an arm massage, massage the shoulder first, and then the upper arm, and then the lower arm. It's the same with the legs: massage the hips first, then the thigh, and then the calf.

### 2. Apply pressure toward the heart

I don't have many massage rules written in stone, but the direction of massage pressure is one. Although you start at the trunk and move out to the extremity, the pressure of each stroke must always go toward the heart. Don't push "downward" toward the extremities with any stroke, whether it be your starting general strokes or the nitty-gritty of therapeutic pressure—each stroke of pressure should go in an "upward" direction, always toward the heart.

This principle is based on the way blood travels around the body. The heart is the pump of the circulatory system. It gives the blood a big push from the center of the body out to our arms and legs, right to the tips of our fingers and toes. These extremities must then work against gravity to return blood to the heart, so our veins are designed with little one-way valves like gates to keep blood moving in the right direction. Directing your massage pressure up towards the heart helps promote the movement of blood back to the heart.

So, I repeat! Pressure upwards towards the heart!

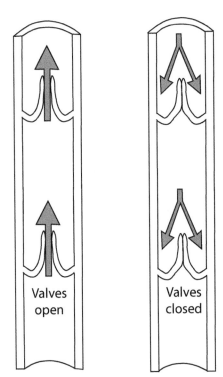

**Figure 2.3.** Veins have one-way valves that open as the heart beats, permitting blood to flow through and then close between heartbeats, stopping the blood from moving backward. These valves keep blood moving toward the heart.

There is only one exception to this rule: when massaging the trunk of the body. The heart is near the middle of the body and the circulatory system is more deeply buried, so the venous return is not directly affected by your direction of pressure.

### 3. Move from general strokes to local strokes and then back to general strokes

Massage strokes include some superficial, general, large strokes and other smaller, focused, and intense strokes. The superficial strokes tend to smooth out and soothe, while the local strokes really get in and work out tight spots, decreasing contractures and increasing mobility. A massage routine should always start with general strokes, move to specific strokes, and then move back out to general strokes.

Beginning with general strokes allows the patient's body to adjust and prepare for further therapeutic application. You want to get the patient's body used to your touch and you want to command the attention of the nervous system to the part being massaged before you work into it. If I start work on a sore spot too fast, the body will repel me—no thanks!—and then I can get locked out. Every situation is unique; every palliative person is different. Some need the same pressure when they are dying as in previous times. Other people need very little pressure.

Palliative people, like all people, may have aches and pains, tight muscles, and adhesions that have plagued them all their life. We can rehabilitate problems such as headaches or back pain while we treat people for end of life symptoms. Some of my palliative patients have gained therapeutic results from the daily massaging that should have been part of their lifestyle years before!

After giving a sore or tight spot focused attention, like the achy places that result from lying down for hours, I always end with general strokes that erase the memory of the deeper, stronger strokes. I learned this in the barnyard where I massaged all sorts of injured animals. I always left each animal I worked on with a stroke memory that was positive, if not necessarily therapeutic. If the animal remembered me as the person making them uncomfortable, even if there was later therapeutic gain, then it was going to be a lot harder to repeat the treatment. The animal would take one look at me coming into the barn and head for the other side of the stall. So, I learned early to "trick" the tissues and leave a lasting impression of positive contact. Leave the area of treatment with the same introductory strokes you started with. You want to leave the tissues happy to see you again.

### 4. Work both sides

My final principle is to balance your massage on both sides of the body. People tend to have a favored side to rest on and may not want to lie on the other side very long. Still to this day, I find it hard to ask a comfortable palliative patient to turn to their uncomfortable side. But even if you can only massage the disfavored side for a brief time, massaging both sides helps bring the person into balance.

However, sometimes it is impossible for palliative patients to turn even briefly. In those cases, you can massage their underlying side with success using a levering technique (see pages 45 to 49) to get to areas that are not otherwise easily accessible.

## Basic Anatomy

Professionally trained massage therapists have extensive knowledge of anatomy, which is critical for solid therapeutic massage. However, you can apply effective massages at home with just a basic knowledge of human anatomy. The illustrations that follow provide some of the basic anatomic knowledge and vocabulary you will find helpful as you work through the massages in this book. Understanding the human skeleton will help you understand the body's bony spots that are prone to bedsores.

**HELPFUL TERMS**

| | |
|---|---|
| Posterior: back | Prone: facedown |
| Anterior: front | Supine: faceup |
| Proximal: close | Lateral: side |
| Distal: far | Medial: middle |
| Transverse: across | Superior: above |
| Ascending: upwards | Inferior: below |
| Descending: downwards | |

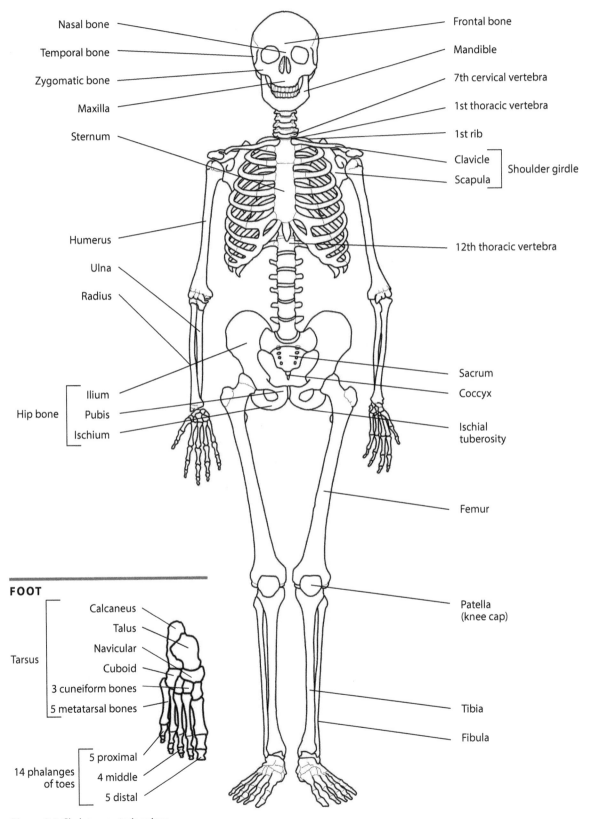

Nasal bone

Temporal bone

Zygomatic bone

Maxilla

Sternum

Humerus

Ulna

Radius

Hip bone

Ilium

Pubis

Ischium

Frontal bone

Mandible

7th cervical vertebra

1st thoracic vertebra

1st rib

Clavicle

Scapula

Shoulder girdle

12th thoracic vertebra

Sacrum

Coccyx

Ischial
tuberosity

Femur

Patella
(knee cap)

Tibia

Fibula

**FOOT**

Tarsus

Calcaneus

Talus

Navicular

Cuboid

3 cuneiform bones

5 metatarsal bones

14 phalanges
of toes

5 proximal

4 middle

5 distal

**Figure 2.4.** Skeleton, anterior view.

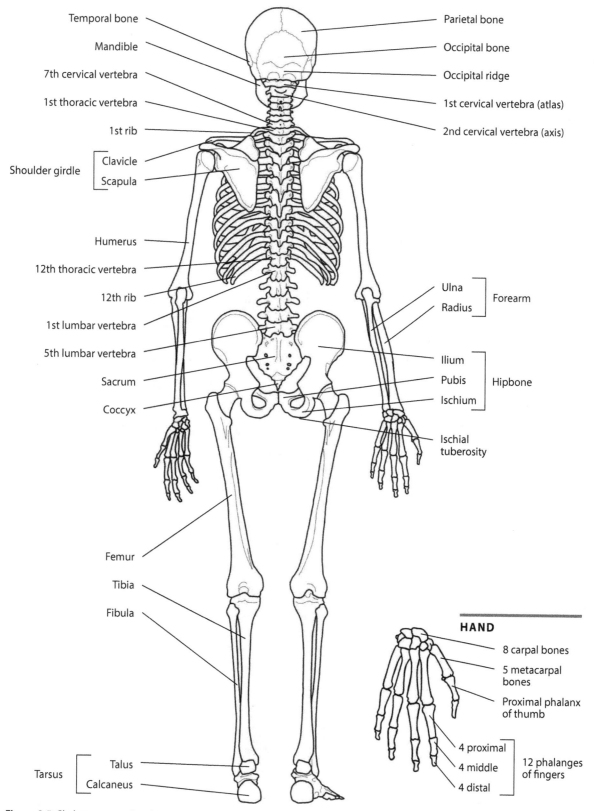

Temporal bone
Mandible
7th cervical vertebra
1st thoracic vertebra
1st rib
Shoulder girdle
  Clavicle
  Scapula
Humerus
12th thoracic vertebra
12th rib
1st lumbar vertebra
5th lumbar vertebra
Sacrum
Coccyx

Parietal bone
Occipital bone
Occipital ridge
1st cervical vertebra (atlas)
2nd cervical vertebra (axis)

Ulna
Radius
} Forearm

Ilium
Pubis
Ischium
} Hipbone

Ischial tuberosity

Femur
Tibia
Fibula

Tarsus
  Talus
  Calcaneus

**HAND**

8 carpal bones
5 metacarpal bones
Proximal phalanx of thumb

4 proximal
4 middle
4 distal
} 12 phalanges of fingers

**Figure 2.5.** Skeleton, posterior view.

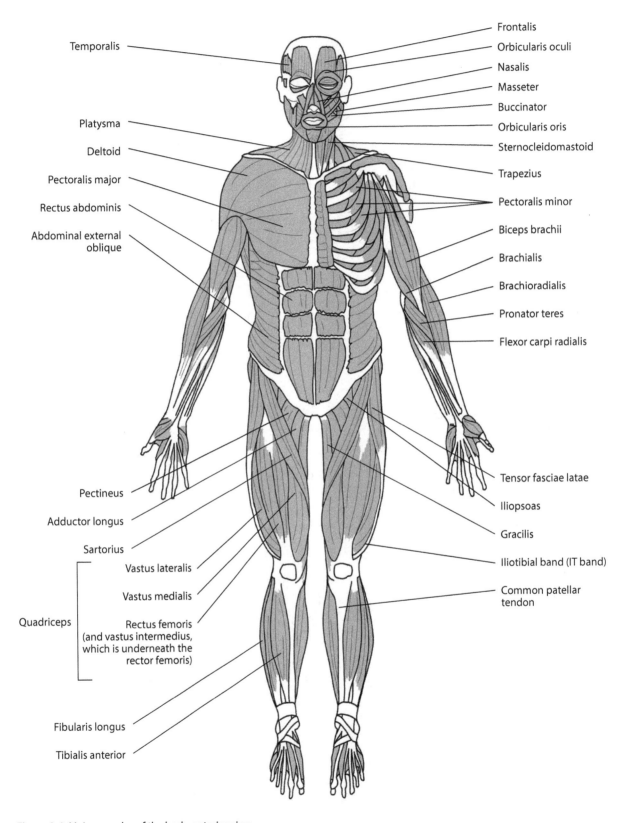

**Figure 2.6.** Major muscles of the body, anterior view.

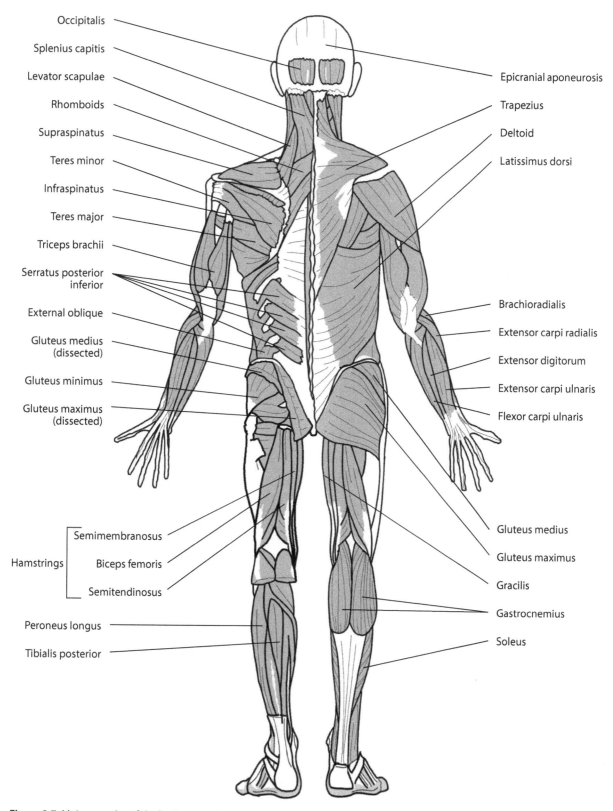

Occipitalis

Splenius capitis

Levator scapulae

Rhomboids

Supraspinatus

Teres minor

Infraspinatus

Teres major

Triceps brachii

Serratus posterior
inferior

External oblique

Gluteus medius
(dissected)

Gluteus minimus

Gluteus maximus
(dissected)

Epicranial aponeurosis

Trapezius

Deltoid

Latissimus dorsi

Brachioradialis

Extensor carpi radialis

Extensor digitorum

Extensor carpi ulnaris

Flexor carpi ulnaris

Gluteus medius

Gluteus maximus

Gracilis

Hamstrings

Semimembranosus

Biceps femoris

Semitendinosus

Peroneus longus

Tibialis posterior

Gastrocnemius

Soleus

**Figure 2.7.** Major muscles of the body, posterior view.

## Basic Palliative Massage Strokes

The common movements used in palliative massage include the following:

1. **Effleurage:** stroking movement
2. **Petrissage:** alternating pressure with wringing, kneading, and scooping
3. **Friction:** adaptive for patients and traditional techniques for the caregiving team
4. **Compression:** chest compression, chest pumping, and alternating digital compression
5. **Stretching:** thumb stretching, fingertip stretching, and palmar stretching
6. **Percussive tapotement:** cupping, adaptive single-handed pounding, beating, and hacking
7. **Vibration:** fine, coarse, static, and running
8. **Light reflex stroking:** longitudinal, circular, and backhanded

### Effleurage

*Effleurage* is a French term that means to cover or cloak. Fittingly, this stroke is most often used to cover or spread the body with oil. It is a warmup stroke with a gentle, double-loop shape. This is the introductory stroke I use most often to get my hands accustomed to my patient and the patient accustomed to my touch. With my palliative patients, this stroke can start to alleviate uncomfortable skin tension from extreme swelling or immediately create more warmth for those who are emaciated and skeletal. Effleurage also has its own stand-alone merits of promoting better circulation. The stroke encourages the congested circulation to move more effectively, helping to reduce swollen limbs, as well as reducing stress and inducing relaxation.

Introductory effleurage strokes are done at least three times on whichever part of the body you are going to massage: back, arms, legs, or chest and abdomen. The first time spreads the oil, the second time allows you to get comfortable with the stroke, and the third time establishes pressure and gets the circulation moving.

To begin a back massage, for example, put some oil or lotion on your hands. It is important to get the right amount of oil, which may take some practice. You want enough oil to provide ease of movement, but not so much that you make the person's back slippery. You want your hands to have good contact and not just skate over the surface. Start with just a few drops (not a dollop) and then add more as needed. You don't need to put on the total amount of oil you will use throughout the massage at the beginning. You can add lotion as the massage progresses. If you get too much, towel some off.

Place one hand on each side of the spine, applying firm, even pressure. Use the whole palmar surface of your hands, including fingers. Don't be dainty! Effleurage is a flat-handed stroke: keep your fingers together but flat, and make good contact with your entire hand, from the base of your palm to your fingertips.

Move your hands together from the shoulders down to the low back. At the base of the spine, loop your hands out to the outer back and sides and continue the pressure as you return along the length of the torso to the shoulders. Be firm, especially on the return stroke up the sides. At the shoulders, begin the stroke again.

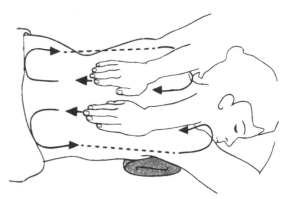

**Figure 2.8.** Effleurage from the lower back to the neck and shoulders or from the neck and shoulders to the lower back. Both directions work.

When effleuraging the arms or legs, use a technique similar to the one described above, but always push up toward the heart and never down toward the extremities. On the back, it doesn't matter—you can apply pressure in both directions, as the direction of massage pressure does not directly affect venous return.

Be sure to check the pressure of your touch. If the person is conscious and able to communicate, ask if you should apply more or less pressure. If the person is heavily medicated, you might not be able to get an answer, so just do your best. Most people are too light in their effleurage strokes and especially tentative with dying people. Indeed, everything I read about palliative massage suggests using a light touch. While I agree with gentle beginnings, I usually end up using the same pressure that I use on most of my healthy patients. Just because a person is skeletal, for example, doesn't mean they need butterfly pressure! Check in with the patient and, when possible, use their feedback to lean into the stroke and get the pressure perfect.

As this is the beginning of the massage routine, this stroke gives you lots of information about the part of the body you are going to accustom to your touch and get to know. As your hands warm up, you may be able to feel areas of tension or sensitivity on the person's body.

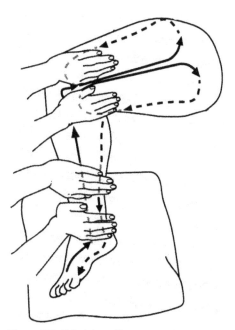

**Figure 2.9.** Side-lying effleurage to the leg. The solid line shows the direction of pressure, and the dotted line shows the return with a light touch.

As you effleurage a person who is very thin from extreme weight loss, you will find that the skin will bunch up as you push up or down the

back. Go slow and allow the skin to slide under your hands and smooth out again in the wake of your effleurage stroke.

I love this stroke. Effleurage is what to do in between other strokes. When you don't know what else to do, effleurage! With any palliative condition, this stroke is especially appreciated on the legs because of swelling and fluid retention. It offers a quick yet powerful way to improve circulation and reduce swelling.

### Petrissage

The next three types of strokes—wringing, kneading, and scooping—are collectively known as *petrissage*. If effleurage helps surface tension dissipate, petrissage strokes are more specific and deep-reaching in their therapeutic effect. I usually do wringing after effleurage, and then move on to the really focused kneading and scooping strokes.

#### WRINGING

In general, we massage in the same direction that muscle fibers run; wringing, however, is an exception. Wringing moves the muscles around more vigorously than effleurage. It moves the skin away from the underlying muscles to encourage the layers of the tissues to not adhere so tightly to each other. Wringing is another general stroke that helps establish or restore tolerance for more focused strokes from the thumbs and fingertips. Wringing lengthens muscles by working transversely (across) the tissue.

This stroke can never be overused. It is like the effleurage stroke that I use in between other strokes. It comes in really handy when someone is unable to turn or be arranged facedown. The patient can be in a faceup position and still get the backs of their legs massaged with a thorough wrap-around wringing.

I mainly use two kinds of wringing in my palliative massages: palmar wringing and thumb wringing.

#### PALMAR WRINGING

For closed palmar wringing, keep all five fingers beside each other. When massaging the patient's back, work at right angles to the spine and move your hands in opposite directions: one hand pushes the skin and underlying flesh away from you around the curve of the ribs, while the other pulls the skin toward you, from the other side of the back. Be sure not to apply any pressure directly onto the spine as you cross over it.

Your hands should be beside each other—close enough to touch—as they move in opposite directions back and forth across the muscles. If you are wringing with the correct technique, you can see the skin and tissues underneath your hands torqueing. Work up and down the whole length of the back. You will find you can move the skin and muscles quite easily. Go slowly and any loose skin that the patient has will not be a problem. All that skin torqueing might look awful, but it feels wonderful! Be sure to check the pressure of your touch with the person on the receiving end as you massage, if they can communicate.

Use a similar technique when massaging other areas of the body.

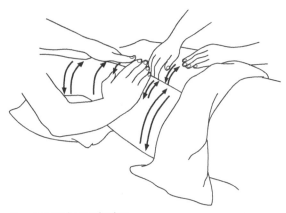

**Figure 2.12.** Leg wringing.

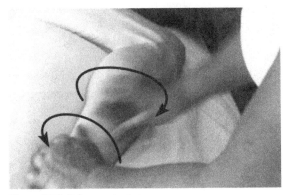

**Figure 2.13.** Palmar wringing.

**Figure 2.10.** Side-lying bilateral wringing. Work across both sides of the body at the same time.

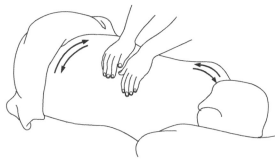

**Figure 2.11.** Side-lying unilateral wringing to back and shoulders. Work one side of the body at a time with hands side by side and close together.

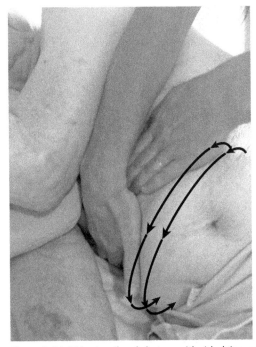

**Figure 2.14.** Wringing the abdomen with side-lying patient.

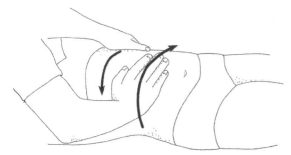

**Figure 2.15.** Wringing the abdomen, with patient supine.

This stroke is a favorite among my patients, both palliative and nonpalliative. There is something about the cross-fiber direction of the stroke that works on the nervous system differently from other massage strokes. Even the sleepiest and most relaxed of patients often make the effort to make a positive comment (especially when I'm working at the knee, a favorite spot for wringing).

### THUMB WRINGING

Although you most often use your whole palmar surface for wringing, you can also use your thumbs for smaller areas, such as around the knees or on the ankles. Thumb wringing works the same way as palmar wringing: move your thumbs in opposite directions across the muscle fibers.

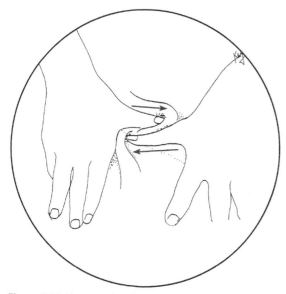

**Figure 2.16.** Use your thumbs to wring across the erector spinae muscles. Work up and down the back.

I use thumb wringing at the base of the knee, at the attachment of the quadriceps tendon to the lower leg, and also at the ankle, wringing the front of the ankle joint when the patient is prone (facedown), or at the Achilles tendon attachment when they are supine (faceup). When the patient is side-lying, I use thumb wringing at the head of the femur (hip joint) and the side of the thigh (iliotibial band).

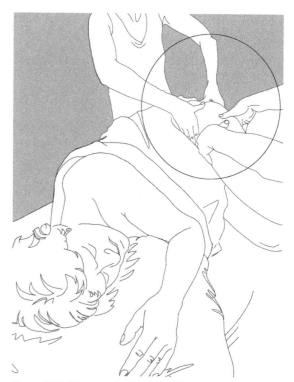

**Figure 2.17.** Thumb wringing at the hip joint and along the iliotibial band can soften tight spots and prepare them for more intensive work.

### KNEADING

Like a cat kneading your lap with its paws, kneading strokes involve the alternate squeezing and relaxing of tissues, applying and then releasing pressure. Kneading helps stimulate circulation and in turn promotes the natural healing of injuries, tears, and strains by bringing fresh blood to damaged tissue.

There are many kneading strokes to use with palliative massages. They range from big strokes using the entire palmar surface of your hand to nitpicky strokes using just the thumbs or finger-tips. Sometimes you might put one hand beside the other and move them in the same direction, alternately pushing the muscle and then releasing it, usually in a semicircular pattern. Other times, you might use one hand to knead while the other hand rests on or supports the patient's body.

Some of my most common kneading strokes are discussed briefly in this section.

### REINFORCED PALMAR KNEADING

Reinforced palmar kneading is when you put one hand on top of the other and make kneading circles. This helps you put the weight of your body into your strokes to really focus in on achy spots in large muscles, such as the hip or shoulders. On the back, the direction of pressure should always be up and away from the spine. On the legs or other extremities, the pressure always goes up toward the heart.

In my classes, I often see how people take the name "palmar kneading" literally. They use only the palm of the hand, sometimes keeping their fingers off the skin and just polishing with the heel of their hand. Palmar kneading is intended, however, to be more of a cupping movement that uses the entire hand. Give as much skin-on-skin contact as possible with the whole palmar surface of the hand, right to the tips of the fingers.

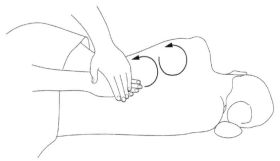

**Figure 2.18.** Reinforced palmar kneading.

### OVERHANDED PALMAR KNEADING

Overhanded palmar kneading is another stroke I use often, especially on the abdomen or hips in supine or side-lying posture. It is a circular stroke in which both hands move in circles, one hand (I usually use the right) staying on the skin the whole time and the other chasing it. Do a big circle around the abdomen, avoiding any tubes, drains, stoma, pouches, or tumors. When your

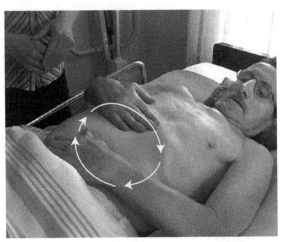

**Figure 2.19.** Overhanded palmar kneading to the digestive tract can be part of a self-massage routine. One hand stays on the abdomen the whole time, while the hand that follows hops over.

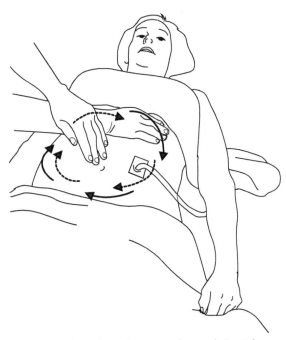

**Figure 2.20.** If your kneading passes by any drains, tubes, or stoma sites, just hop over and gently massage around it.

"chasing" (left) hand catches up to the right, hop your left hand over the right and continue around the circle.

When done in a clockwise motion on the abdomen, this continuous stroke is very thorough and effective for helping with digestive functioning. I also use it at the head of the femur when I am massaging the hip in side-lying positions. I often change back and forth between reinforced palmar kneading and overhanded palmar kneading.

When teaching someone else to do overhanded palmar kneading, get right beside the learner and put their hands on your hands so they can feel the rhythm and pattern. Do the circle three times so the imprint will carry into their attempts to do it on their own.

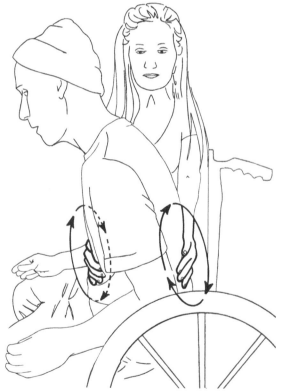

**Figure 2.21.** The same circular kneading used for overhand palmar kneading can be applied to alternating palmar kneading with the patient's body sandwiched between the hands. Move your hands in circles in opposite directions on either side of the patient's body. In this stroke, of course, there is no overhand "hopping" involved.

## ALTERNATE THUMB KNEADING

The thumbs and fingers are also excellent instruments for kneading strokes, especially in areas of the body needing focused attention. In alternate thumb kneading, the whole hand (including fingertips) makes contact with the skin, but the thumbs do the work. First one thumb and then the other makes small, half- to three-quarter-overlapping circles on the skin. If your thumbs get tired, give your hands a good shake to loosen up, refresh, and reset.

You want your thumbs balanced in their alternating rotations, pushing up and out along the direction of the muscle fibers. Always ensure that the pressure of each circle goes up to the heart. I encourage my students to talk out loud to get their thumbs into a rhythm, saying "up and out…up and out…up and out" or "right and left…right and left…right and left." I learned early on in my teaching that there is something about saying something three times that glues it into the brain the right way. I also often take my students for a "ride" on my thumbs so they can feel the momentum and balance of alternate thumb kneading.

Years ago, my students usually found that the thumb on their dominant hand would know what to do, but their other thumb would be clumsy and unable to accomplish full circles. Today, I find a shift as people are becoming naturally ambidextrous because of the use of electronic communication devices. Uncoordinated nondominant thumbs are becoming a thing of the past.

This stroke is a staple of my massage routine. I find that the tiny focus of this stroke really works to ease tension in muscles. I use alternate thumb kneading everywhere; probably the only place I don't use it is on the face. It tends to be particularly appreciated in the arms and legs, at the inner elbow and inner forearm, and around the knees and ankles, which are ideal spots to do long, relaxing sessions of alternate thumb kneading. Use this stroke, too, on the attachments of muscles, in the bulk of muscles, and in any knots or tight spots. I use this stroke after general strokes to the iliotibial band, head of the femur, or any other structures at the top of the leg.

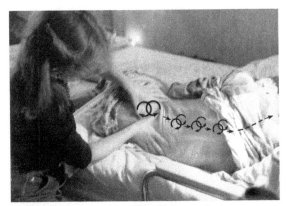

**Figure 2.22.** Alternate thumb kneading to the lower back, one side at a time, up and down the erector spinae. Negotiate around any folding or bunching of skin.

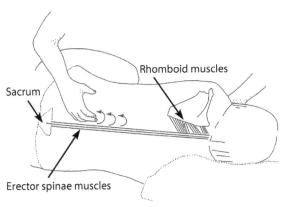

**Figure 2.23.** Fingertip kneading to the rhomboids and erector spinae.

Alternate thumb kneading always gets lots of calls for encores. This stroke is wonderfully designed to treat palliative aches and pains. Simply going over an area that is sore repeatedly with your alternating thumbs will slowly and steadily relax the tissues.

But don't wear out your welcome with too much alternate thumb kneading! Move back and forth between alternate thumb kneading and the more general strokes of palmar kneading or wringing. Use general strokes to smooth things out, effectively erasing the discomfort; then you can go back again to do another set of thumb kneading.

Single-handed thumb kneading is useful when you need to secure the person with one hand, especially in a side-lying position. I use one hand to hold on to the side of the person's hip and use the other hand to work away at the soreness in their hip muscles. I knead with a circular movement of my thumb on the muscle and then I switch hands and do the same with the other hand.

### FINGERTIP KNEADING

Fingers can also be used to knead, usually with reinforced fingertips: stack your hands on top of each other and keep your fingers straight and stiff. Then knead with a pivoting action of your wrist so your fingertips are like a soft drill. As with thumbs, you can also knead with one hand if you need to stabilize the person's body with your other hand.

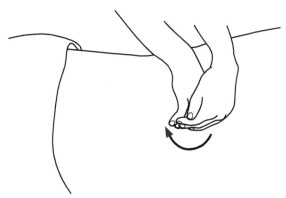

**Figure 2.24.** Reinforced fingertip kneading (both hands, fingers stacked).

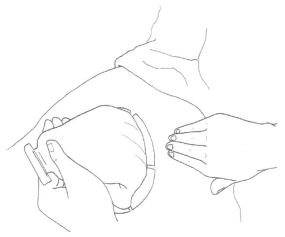

**Figure 2.25.** Single-handed fingertip kneading around a stoma site.

**Figure 2.26.** Side-lying, single-handed fingertip kneading to the occipital ridge with the head supported by the upper hand.

### LEVERED KNEADING

I will often refer to a "levering" technique throughout this book. While side-lying is the most common position you will see with palliative patients, you will see lots of people in the supine position. Often supine patients are highly immobilized, extremely weak, or paralyzed, but there are also occasions when side-lying patients, for one reason or another, cannot be moved either. For example, my patient Gaston had a huge thoracic and abdominal tumor on his side, so he was only able to stay on one side at the end. In any scenario where you are working with people who are always in one position, you can use a levering technique to massage the areas that are always underneath. The technique simply involves sliding your hands underneath the patient and then pushing up into the patient's body using the underlying surface as a pivot point for your fingers or hand and a resting surface for your forearm. For example, for levered palmar kneading, keep the forearm down on the massage surface and press up into the patient's back or the back of their legs and hips with your hand.

My experience with massaging palliative patients who are supine and unable to be turned or tilted began with my friend from high school, Dixie Allard. For years before she died of MS,

Dixie could not be moved an inch from her ideal position, so I was well trained by her to massage the underside of her body using this levering technique.

**Figure 2.27.** Dixie and me.

There are many reasons that could prevent a patient from turning or being turned, including being post-op, comatose, semi-comatose, or end stage; being in the ICU; having a spinal cord injury; or being in traction. However, once you master this technique, there isn't any situation where you can't give a full-body massage to someone in a supine position.

Levering techniques can also be used to your advantage in other, nonpalliative situations. As a person of small stature, I need all the leverage I can muster for working with my hockey players, sports enthusiasts, and IT career types with lots of head, neck, shoulder, and back tension to work out. With these nonpalliative patients, I use the levering technique to get more power into my therapeutic massage for the hips, back, or hamstrings. However, with palliative massage, the levering up technique is not for power, but for accessibility.

These underside massage techniques work best in a palliative setting when you lift the draw sheet (or other fabric), slide your hand underneath it, and then slide your hand under the patient. Although traditional skin-on-skin contact is always advantageous, it isn't helpful when working from underneath a person. You don't need to have skin-on-skin contact to be effective and make a difference in the blood or lymphatic circulation. You can have a draw sheet, a hospital gown, or clothing between your touch and the person's skin and still be able to improve the circulation that is challenged by the patient's constant weight on a particular area.

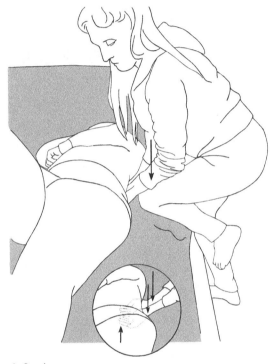

A. One knee up.

B. Stride.

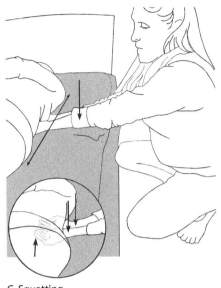

C. Squatting.

**Figure 2.28.** Three therapist postures to provide leverage.

KEY LOCATIONS FOR LEVERING

I use three kinds of levering—fingertip, palmar, and fisted—on three classic locations:

1. Hips with bent knee and stabilizing hand supporting the knee as you lever up into the hip muscles, gluteal muscles, and ischial tuberosity
2. Shoulder (back of the shoulder in the rhomboids)
3. Along the erector spinae, with single-handed fingertip kneading, alternating two-handed levering, and palmar levered kneading

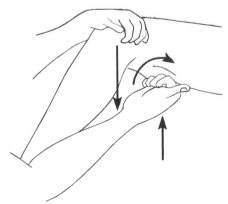

**Figure 2.29.** With a supine patient, I use a fisted kneading under their legs.

### LEVERED FINGERTIP KNEADING

Levered fingertip kneading is the best technique for massaging the underside of palliative patients who are unable to be turned. When doing levered fingertip kneading, be sure to keep your fingers straight and stiff so they act as one unit.

- **Single-handed fingertip kneading:** When the person is and can only be supine, I usually put one hand on top of their knee so that I can move their leg and easily access their lower back and hip. I can then gently rock their leg back and forth as I massage under their hips and back with my other hand. I find that the rocking motion makes it easier for me reach underneath and helps amplify the effects of my kneading into the gluteal muscles.

A. Single-handed palmar or fingertip levered kneading.

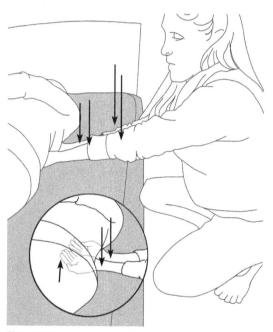

**Figure 2.30.** Levered fingertip kneading underneath the patient. It is the stroke I use most often with supine patients.

To reach the back of the shoulder girdle with a supine patient, I use the same technique with one hand on the elbow to allow me to slip my other hand onto the rhomboids between the scapula and the spine. I use a rocking motion with my hand on the patient's bent elbow as I knead the rhomboids with the fingertips of my other hand.

Ischial tuberosities

B. Single-handed levered fingertip kneading in wheelchair.

**Figure 2.31.** Levered kneading can help you massage a patient's gluteal muscles whether they are supine or in a wheelchair. You want to be sure to massage around the ischial tuberosities to prevent bedsores.

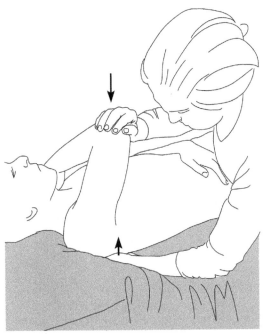

**Figure 2.32.** Levered fingertip kneading to the shoulder with elbow support.

- **Alternating fingertip kneading:** When using alternating fingertip levering, I have to change my posture from alongside and parallel to the bed to a right-angle stride position or a one-knee-kneeling posture. This helps me get both of my forearms pressed down on the surface of the bed so I can lever both hands at the same time or in an alternating rhythm up into the patient's underside.

Press the backs of the hands against the chair and press the fingers into the patient's body.

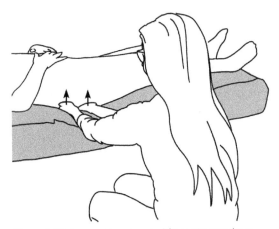

**Figure 2.33.** Levered two-handed fingertip or palmar kneading.

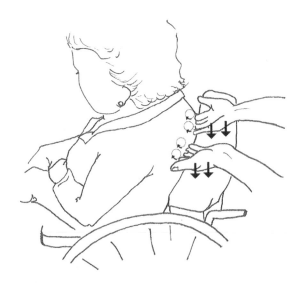

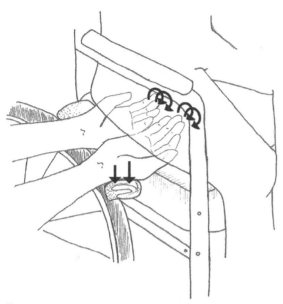

**Figure 2.34.** The levering technique is especially useful to massage people who spend a lot of time in their wheelchair. In this case, you might lever your hands or fingers against either the seat or back of the chair.

- **Side-lying adaptations**: Levering for a side-lying patient works basically the same as for a supine patient, but you might need to use one hand to massage and the other to stabilize. For example, when massaging underneath the hip that a person is resting on, you can slide your massage hand under them to begin levering and use your nonmassaging hand to stabilize their upper hip. Use the top hand to gently rock the patient as you lever up into the underside of their bottom hip and lower back.

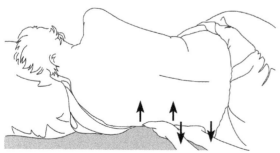

**Figure 2.35.** Side-lying levered fingertip underside massage.

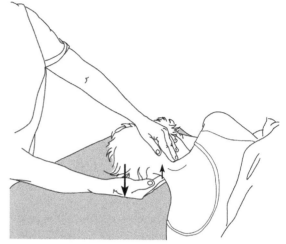

**Figure 2.36.** Side-lying bilateral fingertip kneading to the neck with levering from the lower hand.

### SCOOPING

Scooping is done with a closed-fingered, *C*-shaped hand like you would use to scoop a handful of water. In palliative massage, I use scooping primarily with breast and abdominal massage, but it can be used at the knees or on other large muscle groups. For example, I also use this stroke on the neck, scooping up toward the head, or on the back with my patient lying supine, scooping from the bottom of the shoulder blades up the neck with alternating hands.

For patients with breast cancer and lymphatic problems in the armpit and breast, I use this stroke gently. The scooping of the breasts is an upward, milking stroke performed by each hand in turn. It is as though each hand passes the breast off to the other hand in an alternating action.

Scooping to the abdomen is very helpful for digestion and can be effective even if the person has pouches, drains, a colostomy bag, or other obstacles; you can work around the obstacles with a modified scooping stroke.

**Figure 2.37.** Scooping with a wide-open, *C*-shaped hand. Alternate between your hands as you scoop.

## Frictioning

Traditional frictioning is a highly therapeutic, cross-fiber stroke used to wear down adhesions, which are areas of tissue that build up in response to injuries, infection, or postsurgical conditions. Tears or other injuries in the belly of muscles or their attachments to ligaments and other structures are healed by a glue-like substance called fibrin. Fibrin adhesions are inelastic, which can limit normal function, movement, and flexibility. If it is done properly, frictioning can break down adhesions and improve elasticity in muscles and ligaments, leading to decreased pain and increased function.

I use frictioning infrequently with my palliative patients, although those who have old injuries from childhood or adolescence that limit their hip mobility for walking can benefit from work done on their adhesions, even at a late stage of living. Sometimes the dying person can tell you where they've had an injury or where they have tight spots. You can feel the adhesion area as a thickening in the muscle. Your patient will give you feedback when you've found the right place.

In palliative care, frictioning can also be used gently at the back of the head on the occipital ridge, where there are strong muscle attachments. As your patient weakens in the natural process of dying, they may develop twists in their neck as the muscles atrophy from lack of use. Also, in the last days and hours of the person's life, there is the death grip stiffening—a shortening and flexing of these muscles. This, too, is an indication for gentle, cross-fiber massaging in this area.

To start the cross-fiber stroke, put your fingertips together. I usually use my pointer and middle fingers, but sometimes I use my thumb. Use the tips of your fingers to find the site of an adhesion. Once the person confirms you're at the right place (it's usually sensitive), start to rub your fingertips back and forth quickly, as though you are erasing the spot of the adhesion. Use pressure, but check in with the person on the receiving end so they can direct your pressure.

You are basically working to soften and stretch the tough adhesion under your fingers. You will have to use pressure to get this result but, as always, ask the person whether your pressure is too much, not enough, or just right. Usually if you have the right location—the place where the tension centers—the patient will find the stroke uncomfortable, but tolerable. Use this stroke in the middle of your treatment, not the beginning. Other, more general strokes will have "primed" the adhesion area for this focused treatment.

**Figure 2.38.** Use gentle, single-handed circular frictions to the occipital ridge. Use one hand to hold the head with the patient's face rotated to the opposite shoulder.

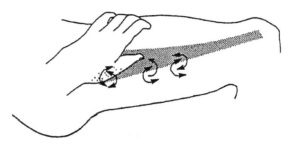

**Figure 2.39.** I sometimes use frictioning around the ankle joints and hands to create more flexibility and movement in end-stage phases, or I use gentle palmar frictions along the iliotibial band to loosen up stiffness.

I also include this therapeutic stroke in a massage for caregivers. Bedside, caregiver-on-caregiver treatments can often be very therapeutic. Caregivers learn to find each other's sore spots and help rid each other of shoulder or neck problems with daily mini-massages. The repeated work of volunteers looking after one another is the backbone of bedside health. As a caregiver, you can also use frictioning as part of your self-massage routine.

## ICE FRICTIONING

Ice can be used as a gentle, palliative frictioning tool. The cold has an anesthetizing effect while my fingers soften and break down hard muscle fibers. In a recent palliative experience, the patient, Di, insisted we keep frictioning and kneading her sore spots to lessen her muscle spasms. She specifically asked for ice frictioning because it gave her needed relief.

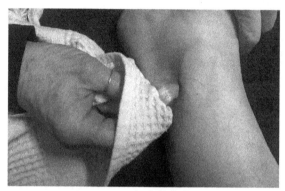

**Figure 2.40.** Ice frictioning around the knee.

## Compression

In massage, compression is steady pressure with no circular action. It is used in palliative massage primarily in the thoracic area to aid in expectoration after the respiratory massage. The pumping action of the compression helps to move the congestion up and out of the lungs. You will learn the details of this stroke in Chapter 5.

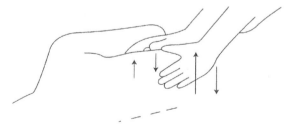

**Figure 2.41.** Costal angle pumping compression.

Compression is also used on many other areas of the body, usually with the thumbs repeatedly poking and releasing tight muscles.

## Stretching

Stretching is a continuous pressure stroke from beginning to end. The steady pressure increases the elasticity of the muscles because it stretches the muscle fibers. Palliative patients, because their joints and muscles are often constricted and increasingly fixed, tend to move into the fetal position. Slow stretching strokes can give patients better mobility and help ease the discomfort and pain of their constricting muscles.

Stretching strokes can be done with the thumbs (pads, tips, and sides), fingertips, and palms (reinforced and overhanded). It doesn't matter whether patients are side-lying, prone, or supine, nor whether it is a levered massage or a conventional massage. Ideally, stretching strokes are done very slowly, with the pressure adapted to the patient's tolerance and mobilization restrictions.

### SHORT-STROKE STRETCHING

Thumb stretching with short strokes is a little like alternate thumb kneading, but instead of the thumbs moving in overlapping circles, the thumb tips or sides move in short, overlapping, straight strokes of steady pressure to stretch out the tissue

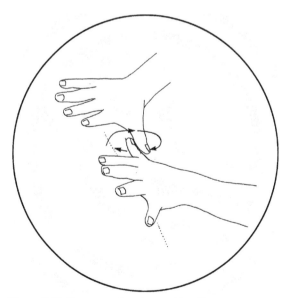

**Figure 2.42.** Transverse thumb stretching. You can use the same thumb pattern to run the stroke longitudinally along the muscle fiber.

underneath. Push your alternating thumbs ahead and away from you. Start with the thumb pads and move to the thumb tips for greater focus, pokiness, depth, and precision. This can also be a transverse stroke that can be performed using the side of the thumbs—not the tips—across the erector spinae muscles. Especially when people are spending long periods of time in bed, spinal strokes are very relieving.

## LONG-STROKE STRETCHING

Thumb stretching also works with long, continuous strokes. On the back, use a long, steady movement of the tips of your thumbs in the groove between the spine and erector spinae muscles. Move your thumbs slowly—very slowly—all the way up this groove. Moving slowly may help you find where muscles are bunched up, indicating a place to be worked on. I sometimes alternate this stroke with short, overlapping thumb stretching strokes in the same groove or right on top of the erector spinae.

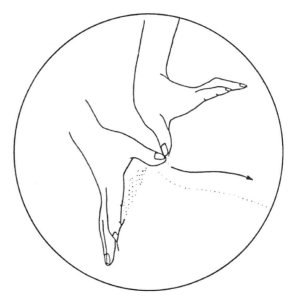

**Figure 2.44.** Longitudinal thumb stretching can single handed or two handed.

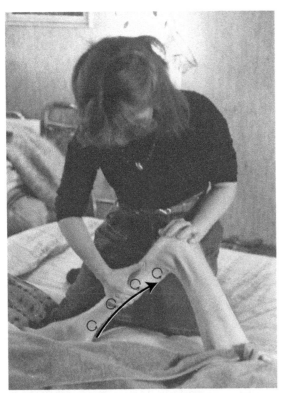

**Figure 2.43.** Fingertip stretching in a continuous stroke from the Achilles attachment to the back of the knee.

**Figure 2.45.** Thumb stretching, including the heel of the hand from the back of the knee to the ischial tuberosity. Bend the leg out slightly and support the side of the knee.

## PALMAR STRETCHING

Palmar stretching uses the whole surface of flat, palmar hands. The hands may be beside each other, reinforced (one on top of the other), or overlapping. I use palmar stretching on the full length of the back from the hip to the armpit, stretching the latissimus dorsi. This stroke can be done in a continuous, overlapping manner or with one hand starting as the other hand finishes. It can be done in either direction, up or down the back.

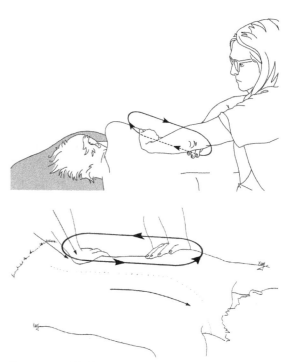

**Figure 2.48.** Side-lying and prone overhanded palmar stretching.

### Percussive Tapotement

Tapotement is a percussion movement. It is a category of massage stroke that includes cupping, pounding, hacking, and beating. In palliative conditions, tapotement is used primarily for respiratory relief or for lower back discomfort. Although I don't use the full range of tapotement strokes with palliative patients, I always use cupping all over the thorax to aid in expectoration and help the lungs. I also use a gentle pounding tapotement on the lower back of patients. This has an anesthetizing effect and eases back pain. With patients who are thin or skeletal, I always put a padding of towels over the area where I am using tapotement strokes. You can also administer tapotement strokes on top of blankets, sheets, or hospital gowns.

Keep your tapotement strokes on the front or back of the body, not the sides. The exception to this rule is cupping, which works nicely along the angle of the ribs at the side of the body to treat respiratory conditions. When massaging a weak and palliative person, adapt your pressure and choice of strokes.

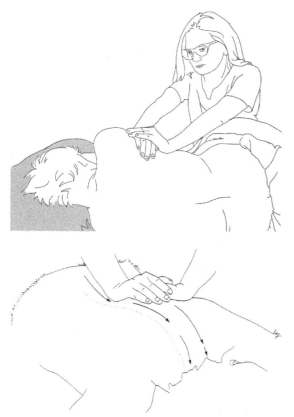

**Figure 2.46.** Side-lying and prone reinforced palmar stretching.

**Figure 2.47.** Side-lying, side-by-side palmar stretching to the latissimus dorsi.

Although tapotement strokes other than cupping and pounding aren't often used with palliative patients, I provide them all here since they are an important part of my "care for the caregivers" lesson for head, neck, and shoulder massages in Chapter 9. Tapotement can bring relief to family members and friends of the patient, especially if they have any back problems or head, neck, and shoulder issues, or simply to give them a positive ending to a long caregiving shift!

> **Use a towel to cushion tapotement strokes for palliative patients.**

### CUPPING

Cupping is a traditional treatment for respiratory conditions, such as shortness of breath, congestion, coughs, or end-stage lung saturation. The stroke helps dislodge congestion in the lungs and aids in expectoration. Cupping is usually done only on the back and the ribs. In side-lying, you can apply cupping to the upper aspect of the ribs, which is more accessible in this position than in any other.

Cupping is my favorite tapotement stroke, and for palliative conditions with congestion in the chest, this stroke is a godsend. Before modern medications for drying up mucus in the lungs, traditional cupping tapotement was the most effective way to aid in expectoration. It was even part of nurses' training! Helping to get junk out of the lungs helps people breathe better, taking pressure off the heart and maybe allowing them to live better and longer.

Cup your hands and bring them down in a fairly fast drumbeat, which should create a hollow sound. The most common mistake students make is keeping their fingers straight; be sure to keep the curve of your palm extending all the way out to your fingertips. The sound of cupping done properly is distinctive: the hollow sound differs audibly from the slapping sound made when the hand starts to flatten out. If the sound is not hollow or if your patient says the stroke stings, cup your hands more. When you soften the stroke by cupping your hands properly, you will hear the difference immediately. I always use a towel to insulate the stroke and check in with the patient about the strength of my impact.

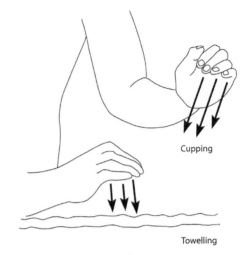

Cupping

Towelling

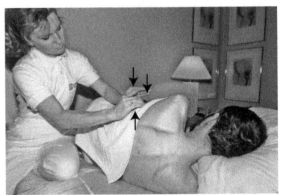

**Figure 2.49.** Cupping.

When you apply this stroke fast, it becomes very superficial in effect. When it is slowed it down, it has a chance to reverberate throughout the thorax and loosen the expectoration from the lung wall to be coughed up and out.

### POUNDING

For the patient, the pounding stroke is like a local anesthetic: it numbs areas that feel the discomfort of bedrest, usually the lower back. I use a rolling pounding style of tapotement on the sacrum for this purpose. This rolling tapotement is the same stroke I use when mountain climbing to relieve low back tension from backpacks or prolonged hiking. About one minute of rolling tapotement on the low back will erase the achiness of the hike and freshen the low back for another few hours of hard work.

Make tight fists, thumbs tucked in. This makes a cushion on the ulnar border (little finger side) of the hand that makes contact. A tight fist has a softer impact than if the hand is loose, which can feel bony. You don't want the stroke rebounding off the back; instead, use a rolling application where the fists make a circular movement between impacts. The result is a sort of pounding caress.

If the patient is very thin, use the stroke on top of folded towels and clothing; it doesn't need to be skin to skin. You can even do the rolling pounding on top of a soft ice pack that conforms to the body's shape.

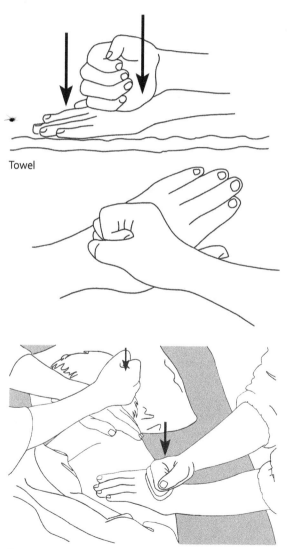

Towel

**Figure 2.50.** An adaptive style of pounding uses one hand to cushion the pounding stroke of the other.

Pounding is also a caregiver favorite! This stroke, when applied to the low back and sacrum, will expand someone's tolerance for being the massager or the sitter. For caregivers, the pounding can be done when they are changing shifts and are reporting in about the time spent with the patient. If the person is seated, stand close at the side of them looking downward to their lower back. From this position the percussive stroke will roll up towards you, which is easier than trying to work across the back. Two minutes of steady pounding can relieve lower back achiness.

### LOOSE FINGERTIP HACKING

Fingertip hacking is great for caregivers' upper shoulders. It can be done for someone sitting up if their arms and shoulders ache from either massaging or from sitting and sleeping in awkward positions while caregiving. Take both hands and put them in a prayer position close to each other. Alternate lifting each hand and making contact with the person's back in a hacking motion. Your fingers should be loose, so your fingertips will flick against each other. Only the little finger side of the hand will make contact with the person on the receiving end of this invigorating stroke.

Once you get a rhythm, speed it up so your hands are a blur of activity. The trick is to keep your hands from tangling up with each other. Most people find that one hand will keep a steady rhythm, while the other will be all over the place. But the more you practice, the better you will get at keeping your hands balanced and even in tempo and strength.

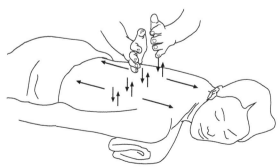

**Figure 2.51.** Loose fingertip hacking can be performed on a person lying prone or sitting up.

Shake out your hands when your hacking gets lopsided or your hands get tangled up. The shake will help you reset. Ask your recipient about pressure. On bony people, use a lighter pressure than on those who are more padded. Remember, though, when checking in that the person you are massaging always has the right answer about pressure.

### STIFF FINGERTIP HACKING

This stroke is similar to loose fingertip hacking, but instead of keeping your fingertips loose, you keep them glued tightly together. The action of the hand lifting up and down is also more controlled in this stroke. The fingers do not flick against each other, but hold tight to each other as the hand moves in a chopping motion.

Both hacking strokes are used on the upper shoulders and the entire back in either a facedown or seated position.

### BEATING

Beating sounds terrible but feels wonderful. Tuck your thumbs into your hands to make fists. Then flatten out the fists into monkey paws. Make contact with the person's skin using the knuckled surface of the hand in a palms-down posture. Beating is a movement of the hands up and down from the wrists, not the whole arms. The hands alternate up and down with loose wrists. Your whole flattened fist, not just the fisted fingers, will make contact with the person.

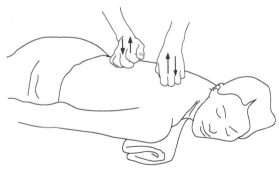

**Figure 2.52.** Beating.

## *Vibrations*

Vibrations have a fast, shaky quality, like getting "nervous" with your hand. Using bent or straight arms, produce fine, trembling vibrations with your palms or fingertips. Stiffen up the arms and quickly bounce up and down on the skin or make a side-to-side vibration movement. Palmar vibrations can be made with the palms stacked (reinforced) or side by side. I use a couple types of vibrations:

- **Fine:** Move your hands as if you have a light tremor.
- **Coarse:** Move your hands side to side and up and down with more activity behind them. The movements are larger and more obvious than with fine vibrations. I use these after an application of fine vibrations.
- **Static:** Picture your hands as a jackhammer, with the hands angled down on a specific spot and moving up and down without changing location on the body. Drill in one spot, then move to the next location and repeat. Both fine and coarse vibrations can be done in a static way.
- **Running:** Either coarse or fine, these vibrations move. They can go in any direction, although an excellent spot to use them is down the descending colon as a fix for constipation. See page 157 for details.

Vibrations are useful for respiratory and digestive blockages, and very light, fluttering types of vibrations can work along nerve routes for neurological soothing. Most North American massage therapists use electronic vibrations, but European massage therapists commonly use a bent elbow or stiff, straight arm to apply this traditional massage stroke. These strokes were the most difficult for me to master. Most people will have one hand that vibrates more easily, while the other is less skilled. I like to use reinforced hands (i.e., one hand on top of the other) to accomplish these fine movements, where the hand that vibrates better helps its partner.

In my early instruction, I was taught not to apply pressure with this stroke, but today I use firm pressure, copying my experience on the receiving-end of vigorous vibrations in Germany. My massage therapist there, a Roman Catholic nun wearing a full black and white habit, drilled away with running and static vibrations with a huge tremor quality. I had a deep relaxation response, sleeping two rejuvenating hours immediately after that massage session.

With palliative patients, vibrations can be delivered even over areas that might be bandaged or tumorous. Because it can be applied in just one spot, it is easy for the person receiving the vibrations to get used to and sink into them.

For the person delivering the massage, this stroke requires some endurance. After years of practice, I can out-vibrate anyone, but years ago, I would be good for short bursts only. Practice this stroke for two minutes and you will see that it is easy for the first 30 seconds, and then it gets more difficult to maintain. If you shake out your hands and start fresh again, you can develop more stamina and endurance.

When receiving this stroke, organize an experiment in which someone will tell you when one minute is up and then two and then three and four and five. Experiencing the effect at two minutes is nothing like the effect at five minutes, when there is often a numbing reaction and a diminishment of pain.

Just as it can take minutes for the stomach to tell the brain it is full, the body takes time to register the strokes throughout the nervous system. It takes time for the skin to register the pressure of the stimulation and get the message to the brain to turn off the pain. The vibrations work by overstimulating the skin, which eventually overtakes any painful sensations—there just isn't room for them. This effect has a common link with our final stroke: light reflex stroking.

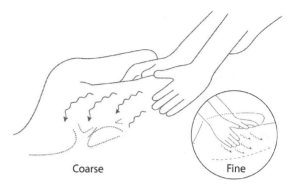

**Figure 2.54.** Side-lying running vibrations in both directions.

Coarse Fine

### Light Reflex Stroking

A good stroke to finish the therapeutic section of any massage routine is light reflex stroking: moving your hands with a light touch over the body. One variation uses the back of your fingers for the stoke away from you and then the palmar side of your fingers as you move toward you. When stroking away, start with the knuckles closest to your palms, then gradually move to the middle knuckles, and then the fingertips.

On the back, simultaneously glide your fingers along each side of the spine from the neck down to the lower back. Then, switch to overhanded stroking with your hands moving like a conveyor belt of continuous movement: as one hand lifts off at the low back, the other hand makes contact at the neck. After this, switch back to both hands

**Figure 2.53.** Vibrations can be with a side-to-side or up-and-down movement.

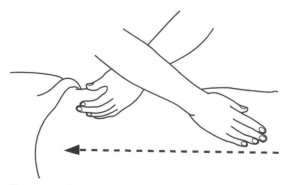

**Figure 2.55.** Continuous overlapping light reflex stroking from the neck to the sacrum/lower back.

at once. Whatever combination you use, keep the flow going for at least five or six strokes. Make each stroke lighter or slower than the last so you finish with your hands hovering over the person's skin.

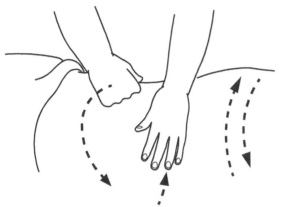

**Figure 2.56.** Back-of-the-hand variation of light reflex stroking.

Light reflex strokes, applied continuously over minutes at a time, create an anesthetizing effect, a numbing accompanied by relief. It is a genuine "neurological eraser." When I am teaching this stroke, I demonstrate this by asking my audience to find a sore spot on their forearm and press on it with their thumb going back and forth for 10 to 30 seconds while I am explaining the phenomena of this neurological eraser. Then I ask them stop pressing and see how they can still feel the sore spot when they are no longer touching it. With a focus on the discomfort, I ask them to then lightly stroke the area with their fingertips and with the back of their hand, making it as light as a caress. When they finish and they are hands-off, there is no sensation of that uncomfortable thumb print.

> **Always end any massage treatment with soft strokes.**

This is a useful stroke to help people (and animals) get to sleep. Some people cannot sleep no matter how medicated they are, but they get easily hypnotized by light reflex stroking. The length of time that you can deliver the stroke is usually in direct proportion to the depth of sleep or relaxation achieved.

## The Finale

For all massage routines, try to back out of the massage the same way you went in. The three strokes of effleurage, wringing, and reinforced palmar kneading are used as the final bookends when I am finished with the more focused massage strokes that make up the middle of any massage sequence. I start with these three strokes and usually end with the same three strokes.

All you need to do is remember to always finish by smoothing out with wringing, then reinforced palmar kneading, and finally effleurage. Light reflex stroking is a nice finish if you're ending the massage or moving to a new body part.

In tandem massage, we often finish with "the wave." We start at the head of the patient with two team members, in perfect unison, lightly stroking down the patient's whole body with their fingertips, restarting again and again and again, lighter and lighter each time until they are barely touching the patient's skin. When it is a team of four to six people, the wave is longer and bigger, but it is still deeply relaxing, soothing, and fun at the same time.

## Postmassage Treatments

All your massage work will generate warmth in the patient's body by increasing their circulation. Take advantage of this warmth by covering them up and allowing them to just lie peacefully still. This is an excellent time for meditation, prayer, or visualization. The patient can use the massage as a vehicle for a deeper experience of letting go. An Epsom salt bath (described on page 17) can deepen the relaxation effects of the massage and help the patient get more mileage out of your treatment.

You might also use hot-water bottles, Tiger Balm for the hands or feet, cold cloths, or an alcohol rub to finish, depending on whether the person is feverish or cold. I like to put a cool eye pack on the patient and tell them to rest for a few minutes. I coach them to keep breathing deeply, like in yoga class, and I'll just tiptoe out to my car, leaving them to drift off to sleep.

## My Finishing Routine

Everyone develops their own finishing routine. When I was first a student of massage, I used to get a headache when I worked to get rid of someone else's headache. This was clearly going to be a problem if I wanted to pursue this career! By practicing different closing rituals and detox endings, I came up with a solution for cutting down on energy transference: I now end the massage by washing my hands and then rinsing with cold water (the colder the better!) This helps ground me and cut down on the possibility of energy transference from the person I've been massaging. Simple, yet effective.

# 3

# Full-Body Palliative Massage

With the basic strokes you learned in Chapter 2, you now have all you need to give someone a palliative massage. If I have 20 minutes or more, I always do a full-body massage. But even with restricted time constraints, I will briefly move around all the bases of a full-body routine, trying not to leave any parts out.

From my experience receiving massages, I find that my nervous system has a greater relaxation response when the therapist gets to everything, including my anterior trunk (abdomen). A full body massage also gives me feedback about how my body is doing. It's the same with palliative patients. Your massage will help them feel the places they can no longer touch themselves: as we massage, we provide them with needed tactile feedback, something rarely thought of in the context of palliative care.

## Key Features of Palliative Massage

Each palliative patient is different, and there is no one-size-fits-all routine that will work for all patients. Sometimes routines have to be changed on a daily basis because of changes in the patient's condition. You have to adapt to the palliative patient; you can't expect them to be able to adapt to your massage routine. For instance, you can't always say, "turn over now" or "turn to your other side" as you would with a healthy patient because often the patient cannot.

Palliative full-body massage differs from non-palliative full-body massage in other ways, too. Differences include the following:

- **Areas of focus:** In palliative massage, I always include special massages for digestion and the upper respiratory tract. Extremities are also always massaged because of swelling.

- **Patient position:** The most common position for massaging healthy people is the prone position, which is the least-used posture for palliative patients. The most common position in palliative massage is the side-lying position; supine (faceup) and seated positions are also common. Palliative massage can be a challenge because often patients are unable to move easily. They may also have tubes, drains, and pouches that you will need to work around. Your basic routine can be adapted to the position or positions in which the person is most comfortable. The patient may need to change position part way through the massage, in which case you will need to change your approach as needed.

- **Massage team:** Palliative patients sometimes have intense family involvement and caregiving. A good way to harness people's concern and sense of helplessness is by giving them a role on the massage team. Like maternity massage, the best way to treat a person in palliative care is with massage teams made up of family, friends, and volunteers.

- **Massage frequency:** Massage is much more frequent in a palliative setting. Ideally, increasing the massage frequency to two or three times a day is best for palliative patients. Morning and evening are good times: morning to prepare the body for movement, and evening to help with sleep. A midday massage helps the patient prepare for an afternoon sleep.

- **Swelling:** Swelling in the extremities is very common in palliative patients as the organs shut down or the person becomes unable to walk. Extremities will need elevation in order to counteract some of the effects of swelling. Whether short and focused or long and thorough, massage can be an effective way to reduce swelling and make the patient more comfortable. While you massage other body parts, just propping the legs up above the heart with pillows can be an effective form of postural drainage.

### Bedsore check

Bedsores (also called pressure ulcers or pressure sores) range from small discolorations of the skin to open sores that go all the way to the bone. Critical areas to watch are the points of the coccyx (tailbone) and anywhere along the spine and back, shoulder blades, elbows, heels, and the back of the head. If the patient habitually lies on their side, watch the sides of the ankles, knees, shoulders, hips, and ears.

All palliative massages are an important opportunity to check on general skin condition. Be alert for early signs of bedsores. Bedsores first appear as reddened areas on the skin at a point of body pressure on the surface. A red mark should be massaged in a circular motion to restore circulation in the area. This massage should be done several times a day for several minutes at a time, and repeated as long as the mark persists. If the red mark disappears while you are rubbing, even though it reappears when you stop, the damage is still minor and healing should be swift. You will learn more about bedsores and their prevention in Chapter 4.

> **At the first sign of a potential bedsore, take action immediately!** *Do not neglect them.* **Pressure marks can rapidly develop into ulcerated sores that are difficult to heal.**

If a red mark persists and develops into a bedsore, keep in mind that the sore may be more severe under the skin than is first apparent on the surface. The wound will need to be treated by cleaning, debridement, iodine sterilization, and exposure to air or sunshine. Sometimes a dressing is required. Such a wound needs frequent attention and is a real setback to the patient. Seek the advice of a medical professional to deal with pressure sores as soon as you detect one.

## Full-Body Massage Routine

The basic full-body routine I outline here is in the following order:

1. Arms
2. Legs and hips
3. Back and neck
4. Digestive and respiratory tracts
5. Face and scalp

However, you can mix things up and switch the order if you have a preference or if you need to spend more time in certain areas. Just try to touch all these areas, even if some are only massaged briefly.

This section will first cover massage techniques for a supine patient. You will find adaptations for side-lying patients on pages 87 to 93.

### Arms

1. EFFLEURAGE THE ARM

a. **Stand in a stride position.** Stand beside the patient with one foot in front of the other.

b. **Glide palms up the arm.** Place your hands side by side on the patient's fingertips. Lean forward as you move your hands up the arm to the shoulder. Use palmar pressure, keeping your fingertips in contact with the arm and

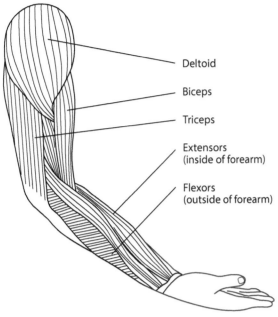

**Figure 3.1.** Arm anatomy.

Deltoid

Biceps

Triceps

Extensors
(inside of forearm)

Flexors
(outside of forearm)

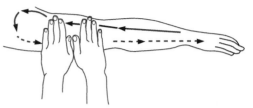

B. Two hands effleurage as one unit.

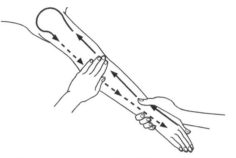

C. Effleurage up the outside of the arm, loop around the shoulder, and return to the wrist without pressure.

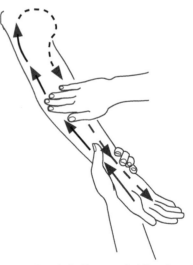

D. One-handed effleurage, holding the wrist with the other hand. Effleurage up the inside of the arm to the armpit and return to the wrist without pressure.

**Figure 3.2.** Arm effleurage can be done with two hands together or one hand at a time.

conforming your hands to the shape of the deltoid muscle at the top of the arm. Remember that pressure should move up the arm towards the heart, one hand beside the other until they reach the shoulder.

c. **Slide your hands around the shoulder.** Move right around to the shoulder muscles in the back, pressing from front to back. Then lightly glide back down the arm with no pressure, just light reflex stroking.

d. **Repeat three or four times.**

A. Tandem two-handed effleurage.

### 2. KNEAD THE SHOULDER

a. **Palmar knead the deltoid.** If your patient is lying supine, hold the arm by the wrist and knead the deltoid muscle at the top of the shoulder with the palm of the other hand. If your patient is sitting up, you can palmar knead both deltoids at once from the front. Reinforced palmar kneading to the deltoids is another great way to open up circulation to the whole arm.

**Figure 3.3.** Single-handed palmar kneading to the deltoid.

b. **Palmar knead the trapezius.** Wrap around the deltoid muscle to the trapezius in the back for some single-handed palmar kneading, alternating palmar kneading, and reinforced palmar kneading.

c. **Knead the back of the shoulder.** I use lots of single-handed fingertip kneading (with stiff, straight fingertips) and thumb kneading on the back of the shoulder on the rhomboids and erector spinae muscles. I alternate this with palmar kneading to smooth things out. Keep repeating this combination for the entire back of the shoulder girdle.

d. **Knead the front of the shoulder.** Use palmar kneading, fingertip kneading, and thumb kneading on the front of the shoulder girdle where the pectoralis muscles and deltoids attach.

### 3. TRICEPS AND BICEPS

You can knead the biceps and triceps with one hand or two, but be sure to work all along the length of the muscles. Pay special attention to the

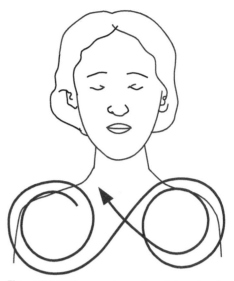

**Figure 3.4.** With one palm on top of the other, knead the pectorals in a figure eight with pressure pushing from the front to the back.

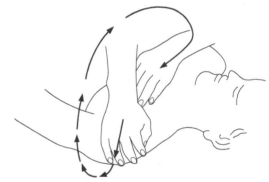

**Figure 3.5.** Another method is to knead the pectorals away from you using overhanded palmar kneading.

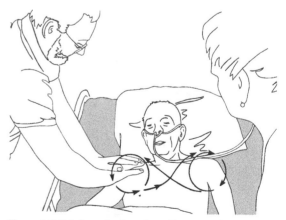

**Figure 3.6.** Reinforced palmar kneading around the shoulder and in a figure eight over the other shoulder.

attachments of the triceps and biceps at either side of the elbow.

a. **Scoop and release the triceps.** Hold the wrist with one hand and, with your other hand in a small *C*-shape, scoop up and release the triceps.

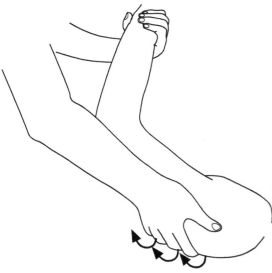

**Figure 3.7.** Scoop and release the triceps.

b. **Thumb knead the triceps (single-handed).** Still holding the wrist with one hand, use the thumb of the other hand to knead the length of the triceps.

c. **Thumb knead the biceps (alternating hands).** Let the forearm lie down straight or rest up against your body while you knead the biceps with your thumbs.

**Figure 3.8.** Work on the biceps with alternate thumb kneading.

## 4. ELBOW

Massage for the elbow is especially important on palliative patients to prevent tissue breakdown and pressure sores. If the IV is an issue at the elbow, you don't have to avoid the arm, even if the arm is bruised. Use your best judgment. In most cases, you can massage around an IV and very gently massage over any discolorations, which can help heal them faster.

a. **Palmar knead the elbow.** With the hand that is closest to the patient, hold the wrist and bend the arm. Cup the olecranon (elbow bump) with your other hand and knead it with a circular motion.

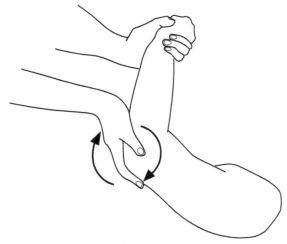

**Figure 3.9.** Palmar kneading to the elbow.

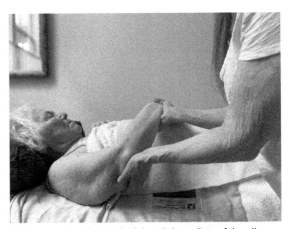

**Figure 3.10.** Single-handed thumb kneading of the elbow.

b. **Perform alternate thumb kneading on the inner elbow.** This is a delicious part of the arm massage. The inner elbow is very sensitive and often a favorite spot for you to linger, especially among those who are strong enough to push their own chairs. The inner elbow is an important feature of palliative massage because the body naturally flexes in on itself as the person weakens. Massaging this area will prevent the elbow from becoming fixed and stiff. Spend lots of time at the inner elbow with slow alternate thumb kneading and possibly some thumb wringing.

c. **Perform single-handed thumb kneading around the elbow.** While holding the wrist with one hand, knead all the way around the elbow with the thumb of the other, massaging the attachments of the biceps and triceps. Lift the arm for easier access to the back of the elbow joint.

## 5. FOREARM

Similar to the inner elbow, the forearm is an important area for palliative massage. Massaging the forearm will help to prevent the hand from permanently contracting.

a. **Knead the forearm flexors (inside of forearm).** You can rest the patient's arm against

you or hold it away from you while you perform alternate thumb kneading to the forearm flexors. Bend the elbow to encourage postural drainage from swollen fingers and wrists.

b. **Knead the forearm extensors (outside of forearm).** Hold the wrist with one hand and knead the forearm with the other. Work slowly and firmly toward the hand. Repeat three times up and down the entire length of the forearm, extending beyond the wrist to the hand. Remember that the pressure of each individual stroke is toward the heart, even as you move down toward the hand.

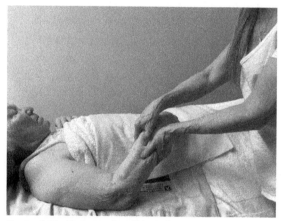

**Figure 3.12.** Alternate thumb kneading to the forearm extensors that lead through the wrist and onto the back of the hand and fingers.

## 6. WRIST AND HAND

The hand massage need not only be part of a full body routine. It can be performed as a stand-alone massage and is the ideal visitors' massage.

a. **Perform alternate thumb kneading to the back of hand.** Bend the wrist with the upper arm resting on the bed and the elbow bent at a right angle. Use alternating thumbs to knead on the back of the hand (the dorsal surface). Massage the muscle attachments at the wrist with tiny strokes. This is usually very relaxing for the patient, so I spend a lot of time teaching families and friends to massage the patient's hands from the wrist to the fingertips.

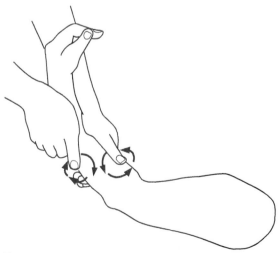

**Figure 3.11.** Alternate thumb kneading to the forearm flexors.

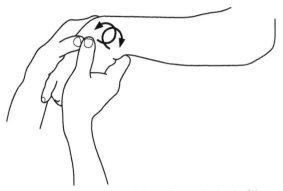

**Figure 3.13.** Alternate thumb kneading to the back of the hand. Start at the wrist for some focused attention.

b. **Thumb wring the wrist.** Use tiny wringing movements on the wrist with your thumbs.

c. **Perform alternate thumb kneading to palm.** Flip the hand at the wrist so the palm is facing you and knead it with your alternating thumbs, focusing on the base of each finger and the heel of the hand.

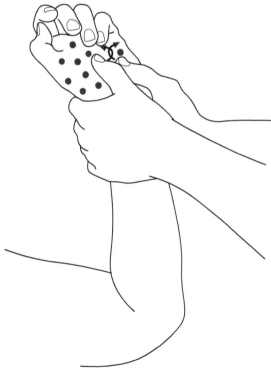

**Figure 3.14.** Alternate thumb kneading to the palm of the hand. You can also do some digital compression.

d. **Perform alternating digital compression to palm.** Using the tips of your thumbs, alternate pressing each into the palm of the hand, especially the heel of the hand. Move the compressions around the palm to cover the area from the wrist line crease to where the fingers start.

e. **Perform dorsal-palmar stretching**. This is a two-movement stretching stroke that works the transverse arch (base of fingers) of your patient's hand. With both your hands, arch and relax the patient's hand to stretch it out.

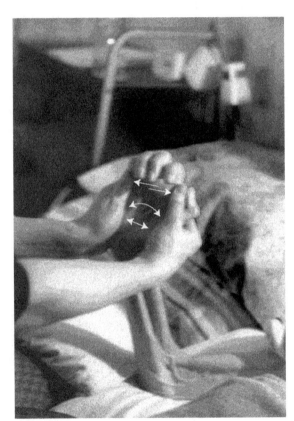

**Figure 3.15.** Use your fingers and thumbs to arch and relax the hand, especially across the base of the fingers.

f. **Thumb wring the palm and back of hand.** Although I have instructed that all pressure be upward towards the heart, for the hand I change things. Tilt the patient's hand so it is in a "halt" position. Grasp the wrist with both hands and, with your thumbs, massage the heel of the hand and work towards the base of each finger with teeny-weeny alternate thumb wringing.

g. **Corkscrew each finger.** You can do this move at three levels: the base, middle joint, and last joint. Use extra time at the base of the fingers. Secure the joint of the finger closest to the main body of the hand between your thumb and your pointer finger. With the other hand, corkscrew individual fingers by twisting them in a direction away from the center finger. The middle finger can be corkscrewed either or both ways. Massage each finger three times in this twisting motion. Don't worry about remembering which direction to twist: it will feel natural to do it in the right direction and *un*natural to do it in the wrong direction!

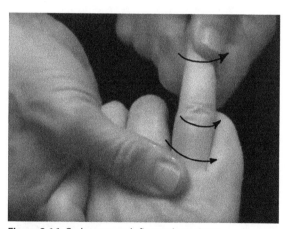

Figure 3.16. Corkscrew each finger three times.

h. **Finish.** If it is a short massage (only the hand) finish with light, overhanded stroking from the forearm to the fingertips. If it is a full-body massage, move to the next step.

### 7. WHOLE ARM LIGHT REFLEX STROKING

a. **Stroke the entire length of the arm with your fingertips.** Use light pressure. For a supine patient, massage both sides of the arm, with one hand on the top of the arm and one hand underneath. Both hands should be at the same level at the same time. Stroke from the back of the shoulder girdle to the palm of the hand. Try to make contact with all of the areas you massaged.

Figure 3.17. Light reflex stroking to the arm.

b. **Repeat four or five times.** The last stroke should have the lightest contact.

### *Legs and hips*

Supine or reclining patients are particularly susceptible to pressure sores and unusually swollen extremities. When you are working with these patients, it is extremely important to massage places vulnerable to pressure sores, such as the sitting bones (ischial tuberosities). You will also use massage to stimulate the patient's compromised circulation. The farther down the leg (lower leg, ankles, and feet), the slower and more involved the massage must be to remedy the swelling and circulation challenges caused by immobility and end-stage weakness.

### 1. WHOLE LEG EFFLEURAGE

a. **Effleurage the leg, starting at the foot.** Sandwiching the foot at the toes, slide the hands side by side up the foot and across the leg, effleuraging up the leg to the hip. Pressure should move up towards the heart, with light reflex pressure back to the foot again. At the hips, glide up and around to the back of the hip, contacting the entire gluteal area. This is a wider effleurage than you would perform when massaging a patient who will later flip over to a prone position.

b. **Repeat three times or more.**

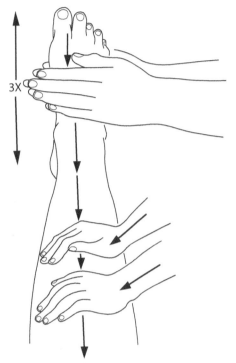

**Figure 3.18.** Anterior leg effleurage.

## 2. HIP AND GLUTEAL MUSCLES

On your last effleurage up the leg, stay at the hip and prepare to massage it and the gluteal muscles to "uncork the bottle" and open up circulation to the leg. Remember: you can massage with your hands under the draw sheet or skin on skin.

a. **Knead the gluteal muscles.** Slide a hand underneath the patient's gluteal muscles and lever up into the gluteal muscles and coccyx using single-handed palmar kneading and fingertip kneading. Rest your other hand on the thigh or the head of the femur.

You can also work underneath the patient with both hands using alternating fingertip kneading and alternating circular palmar kneading.

Step back in a stride position and rest your elbows and lower arm on the bed in order to lever up into the posterior hip muscles. Be sure to work all around the ischial tuberosity attachments of the hamstring muscles.

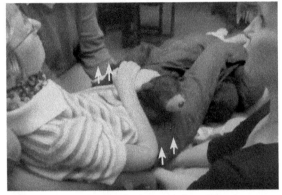

**Figure 3.19.** Massage for the lower back and hips in tandem. Levered fingertip kneading to the gluteal muscles and ischial tuberosities.

**Figure 3.20.** Levered fingertip kneading to the hip. Fingertip kneading is shown here in two styles: single-handed under the draw sheet on the right and with both hands on the left. This stroke is ideal for opening circulation to the leg and preventing pressure sores at the sacrum and ischial tuberosities.

b. **Knead the head of the femur.** Stand in a stride position to get the right angle to do some single-handed thumb kneading and alternate thumb kneading to the head of the femur.

c. **Palmar knead the hip.** Finish your focused work with palmar kneading to the hip.

**Figure 3.21.** Reinforced palmar kneading to the head of the femur.

## 3. THIGH

**a. Wring the thigh.** Take care to wrap underneath the thigh as far as you can reach, lifting the leg slightly with pillows to gain easier access to the back of the thigh.

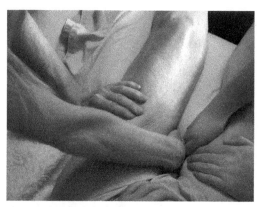

**Figure 3.22.** Thigh wringing.

**b. Knead the quadriceps.** Use alternate thumb kneading on the quadriceps in three lines to cover the inner, middle, and outer muscles.

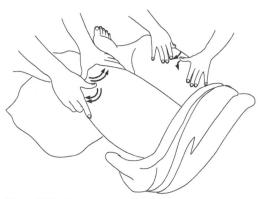

**Figure 3.23.** Alternate thumb kneading to the quadriceps.

**c. Knead the iliotibial band.** Do some alternate thumb kneading to the outer thigh along the iliotibial band from the lower knee to the head of the femur. Move along the length of the band with your hands working across the muscle fibers, as shown in Figure 3.25. You can also knead with your thumbs working along the length of the fibers from the hip to the knee.

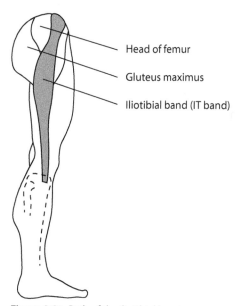

Head of femur

Gluteus maximus

Iliotibial band (IT band)

**Figure 3.24.** Path of the iliotibial band.

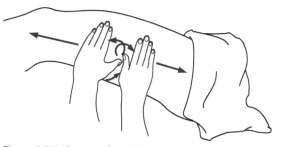

**Figure 3.25.** Alternate thumb kneading to the iliotibial band. Massage from the hip to the outside of the knee.

**d. Thumb stretch the hamstrings.** Lift the knee with one hand. Run the heel of your hand and thumb from back of the knee (popliteal fossa) to the ischial tuberosity in a stretching stroke.

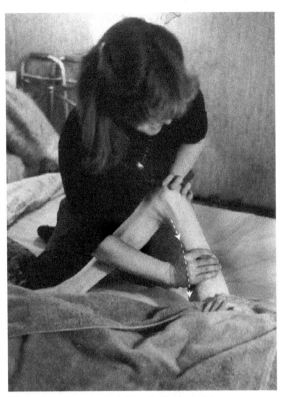

**Figure 3.26.** Thumb stretching to the hamstrings.

## 4. KNEES AND LOWER LEG

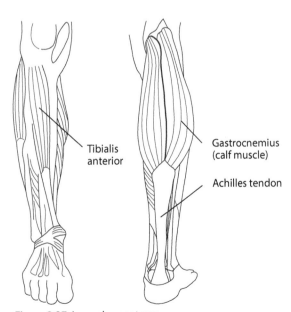

Tibialis anterior

Gastrocnemius (calf muscle)

Achilles tendon

**Figure 3.27.** Lower leg anatomy.

a. **Wring and thumb knead the knee.** With one hand above and one hand below the kneecap (patella), wring around the knee. Be slow and be thorough. This stroke is usually a favorite of patients and highly relaxing.

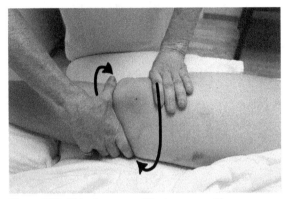

**Figure 3.28.** Wringing around the kneecap with an open, C-shaped hand.

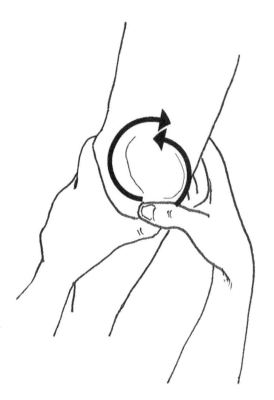

**Figure 3.29.** Alternate thumb kneading around the perimeter of the kneecap.

**b. Wring the lower leg.** To reduce swelling in the lower legs, release the surface tension with wringing to the entire lower leg from knee to toes.

**c. Knead the tibialis anterior.** Use small alternate thumb kneading strokes on the tibialis anterior muscle along the outer ridge of the tibia. You can also use your palms to knead on either side of the shin bone.

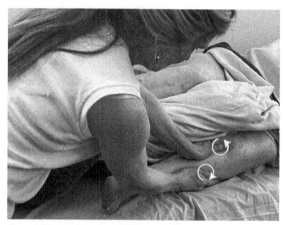

Figure 3.30. Palmar kneading to the shin.

**d. Massage the calf.** Bend the knee and secure the foot in place (sometimes I sit on the bed and wedge the foot underneath me) while massaging the calf (gastrocnemius) muscle. I use a "splitting stroke" to separate the gastrocnemius from the Achilles tendon attachment at the ankle to the back of the knee. Cupping each side of the heart-shaped calf muscle with your

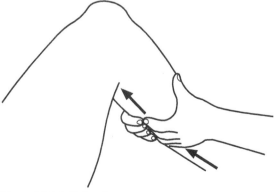

Figure 3.31. Splitting the gastrocnemius.

curved fingertips running up the middle, pull upwards with your fingertips. On the way back down to the heel, wring across the calf muscle to knead it back together.

**e. Thumb stretch the tibialis anterior.**

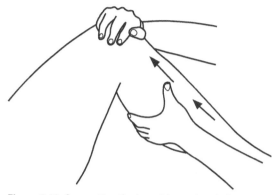

Figure 3.32. Supporting the leg with one hand, do some single-handed thumb stretching to the tibialis anterior.

**f. Palmar knead the heel.** The pressure site at the heel is one of the fastest breakdown areas. Pay special attention to massaging the entire heel with fingertip and palmar kneading. Put the heel of your hand to the heel of the foot.

**g. Wring the ankles.** The ankles can be another potential site of pressure sores. Use both hands to wring around the ankles and then out to the toes. By wringing right around, front to back, you can also increase flexibility at the ankle joint.

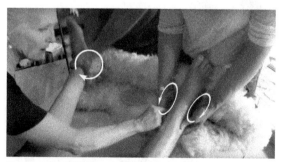

Figure 3.33. Kneading the heels and wringing around the ankles can keep these areas healthy and free of pressure sores. If your patient lies mostly on their back or a particular side, pay special attention to whatever part of the body touches a surface most of the time. Notice the sheepskin under the foot, which also helps in the prevention of pressure sores.

Intermittent effleurages throughout the lower leg massage can help move fluid up the leg and drain the peripheral swelling.

## 5. FEET

Foot massages can be used as a stand-alone massage or as part of the leg massage. The foot massage is easily taught to grandchildren and visitors as a mini-massage and is a favorite with patients.

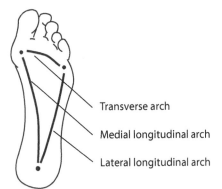

Transverse arch

Medial longitudinal arch

Lateral longitudinal arch

**Figure 3.34.** Arches of the foot.

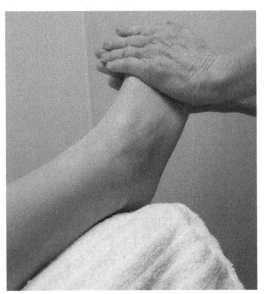

**Figure 3.36.** Make a "prayer sandwich" with your hands and effleurage the foot from toes to ankle.

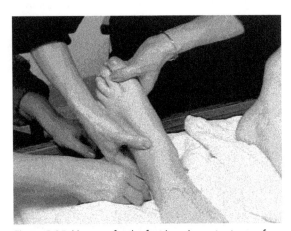

**Figure 3.35.** Massage for the feet is an important way of reducing the swelling many palliative patients experience in their lower limbs.

a. **Effleurage the foot.** Place the foot between your palms and effleurage the entire foot and ankle. Do this at least three times.

b. **Knead the ankle bones.** Knead the ankle bones (malleoli) with the heels of your hands and your thumbs.

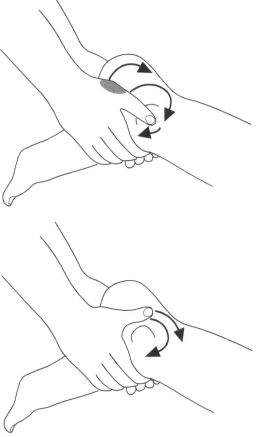

**Figure 3.37.** Knead the ankle bones with your thumbs and the heels of your hands.

c. **Thumb knead the top and bottom of the foot.**

d. **Thumb wring the top and bottom of the foot.**

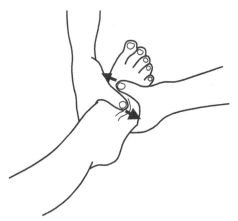

**Figure 3.40.** Dorsal thumb stretching to the foot.

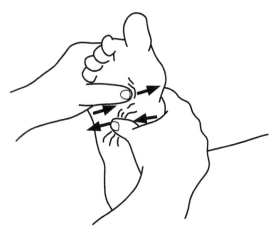

**Figure 3.38.** Thumb wringing the foot.

e. **Corkscrew each toe three times.**

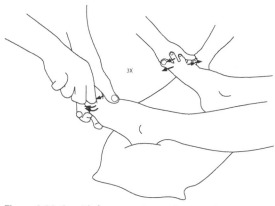

**Figure 3.39.** As with fingers, wring each toe to the nearest edge of the foot. The middle toe can go either or both ways.

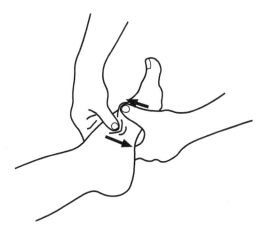

**Figure 3.41.** Medial thumb stretching to the foot.

f. **Thumb stretch across the top of the foot.** (Figure 3.40)

g. **Thumb stretch the medial longitudinal arch.** (Figure 3.41)

h. **Thumb stretch up the top of the foot.** Stretch all along the groove between the long bones. (Figure 3.42)

i. **Mobilize the transverse arch.** With both hands, hold a foot at the base of the toes where they join the foot. Your thumbs will be on the bottom of the foot and your fingers

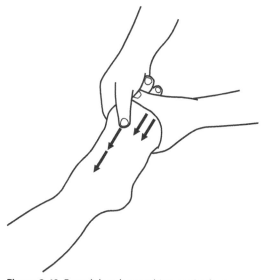

**Figure 3.42.** Dorsal thumb stretching up the foot.

on top. Working from toe joint to toe joint along the transverse arch, move one hand up and one hand down to mobilize each joint. (Figure 3.43)

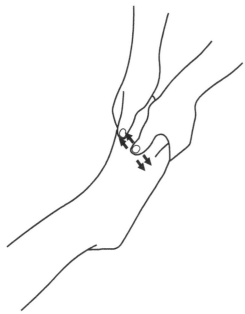

**Figure 3.43.** Transverse arch mobilization.

**j. Perform digital compression to the sole of the foot**. Alternate left and right thumb tips to apply pressure slowly and firmly all over the sole of the foot. Treat the sole of the foot like a

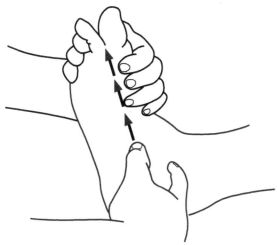

**Figure 3.44.** Gentle frictioning to the medial longitudinal arch.

series of trigger points, with the patient breathing into the steady pressure of each thumb. Digital compression is always the favorite stroke in this routine. Be sure to ask for lots of feedback to be sure your pressure is right.

**k. Deliver gentle friction to the medial longitudinal arch.** (Figure 3.44)

**l. Deliver gentle friction to the joint at the base of the big toe.**

**Figure 3.45.** Gentle frictioning to the base of the big toe.

**m. Perform eversion and inversion**. Twist the foot inward then outward, holding the foot with one hand and the ankle with the other hand.

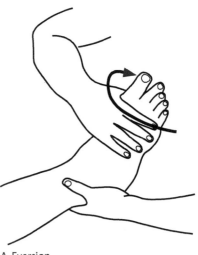

A. Eversion

B. Inversion.

**Figure 3.46.** Eversion and inversion.

**n. Stretch the transverse arch.** Slide your hands from the ankle to the toes like you are squeezing the foot through your hands to make it longer. When you get to the base of the toes, bend the toes downward. Thumbs are on the top of the foot, fingers on the bottom.

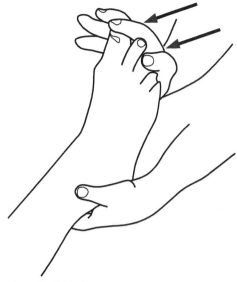

**Figure 3.48.** Flexion.

**p. Mobilize the toes.**

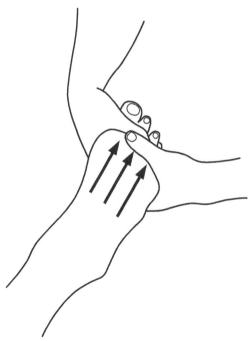

**Figure 3.47.** Transverse arch stretching.

**o. Use your palm to flex the toes at the transverse arch.**

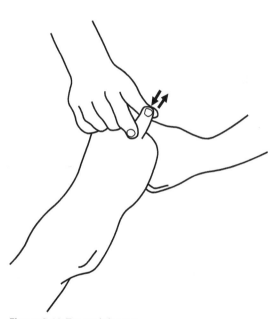

**Figure 3.49.** Toe mobilization.

**q. Mobilize the ankles.** Mobilize the ankle joint while flexing the foot. Rotate the ankle three times in one direction, then three times in the other. (Figure 3.50)

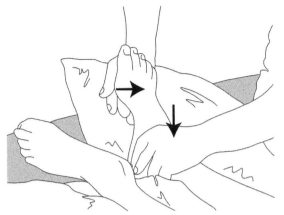

**Figure 3.50.** Mobilizing the ankle joint while flexing the foot.

**r. Effleurage the entire leg.** Perform this effleurage stroke three times.

**s. Deliver light reflex strokes to finish.**

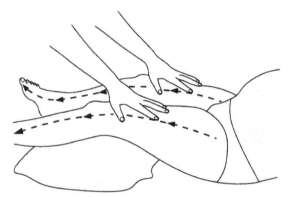

**Figure 3.51.** Light reflex stroking to the legs from feet to hips.

After the hip, leg, and foot massage, patients are ready for more specialized work, depending on their condition, need, and desire. Leg pumping is done after the hips are thoroughly loosened up. It is an excellent treatment for digestive issues. Turn to pages 148 to 150 for instructions. This is also an excellent time to do try some hydrotherapy techniques, such as ice massage or foot baths with Epsom salt and warm water.

## Back and neck

The primary purposes of the back massage are contact, comfort, circulation improvement, and relaxation. With a back massage, however, you also have direct contact with the central operating systems of the body: all major organs are housed in the torso and are fed and cleansed by the arteries and veins that work their way through it; nerves running from the spine connect with these organs and affect their smooth operation. Back massage will benefit this important network of activity. (For example, lower back massage can help relieve intestinal distress such as diarrhea, and can assist the absorption of nutrients through intestinal walls.) In fact, a full back massage can benefit the whole body through the nervous system.

With the levering technique I covered in Chapter 2, you can deliver an effective back massage even if the patient cannot lie on their stomach or turn to both sides. In this section, I cover back massage for both a supine patient and a sitting patient, as well as a brief outline of prone massage. Side-lying back massage, which is very common, is covered in the adaptations for side-lying full-body massage starting page 87.

**To review the levering technique, turn to pages 45 to 49.**

SUPINE BACK MASSAGE

**a. Effleurage the back.** Standing at the patient's head in a stride posture, slide your hands underneath the patient's back as far as you can reach. Then, with one hand on either side of the spine, pull up the length of the entire back from the iliac crest and sacrum to the occipital ridge. Use a wide stride posture to protect your back. An alternative method is to effleurage each side of the back separately, with both hands working one side at a time.

**b. Palmar knead the back.** Starting anywhere along the back, move your hands in sweeping palmar strokes with an alternating pattern, levering up from the surface of the bed.

c. **Fingertip knead, stretch, and lift the back and neck.** Move up and down the back from the neck to the sacrum, usually along the erector spinae, slowly levering up into the back muscles. Be sure to get feedback from the patient about favorite spots and extra sensitive places. Sometimes I have had to dodge around tumor sites carefully and use foam donuts to ease pressure on the tumor and make it easier to massage around the site.

**Figure 3.54.** Bilateral fingertip kneading to the sides of the neck up to the base of the skull.

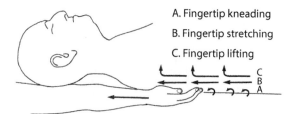

A. Fingertip kneading

B. Fingertip stretching

C. Fingertip lifting

**Figure 3.52.** Slide your hands as far as possible under the patient's back and use the massage surface to lever your fingers up.

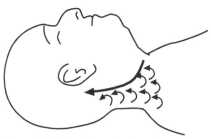

**Figure 3.55.** Deep fingertip kneading to the trapezius and neck muscles up to the base of the skull.

d. **Effleurage and knead the neck.**

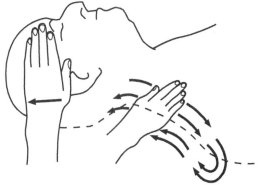

**Figure 3.53.** Modified effleurage to the neck. Use one hand to press the head gently to the side to give a little more space for the other hand to effleurage along the side of the neck.

**Figure 3.56.** Light fingertip stroking with pressure from the head down.

e. **Scoop the back and neck.** Slide your hands under the patient's body and scoop them toward you to work the erector spinae, rhomboids, and trapezius muscles. Alternate your hands, scooping diagonally across the patient's back as you pull toward you. Be sure to avoid any pressure on the spinal column itself.

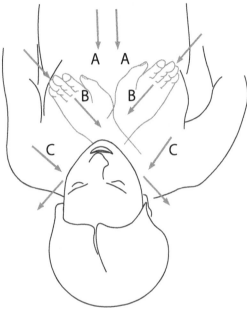

**Figure 3.57.** Scooping to the rhomboids, erector spinae, and trapezius. Slide your hands under the patient's body and scoop them toward you to work the erector spinae (A), rhomboids (B), and trapezius muscles (C).

f. **Massage to prevent pressure sores on the back.** Massage the spines of the scapula, spines of the sacrum, and tail bone (coccyx). Alternate between fingertip kneading and palmar kneading interspersed with mini-effleurages to the area.

g. **Perform bilateral lifting**. Facing the patient, reach around the patient's body to their back with one hand on either side, fingertips meeting at the spine. Lift your hands very slowly up and around the patient's body until the heels of your hands meet in the center of the body with very light contact. Lift three times at three levels: the diaphragm, the waistline, and the lower back. Be

sure to stabilize your posture when performing this lifting stroke by putting one knee on the bed or wedging up against the bed.

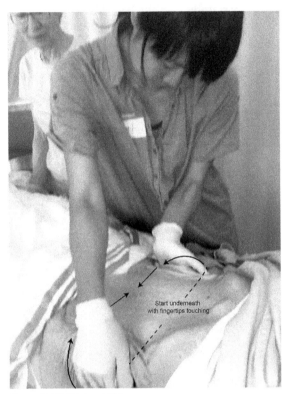

Start underneath with fingertips touching

**Figure 3.58.** Bilateral lifting.

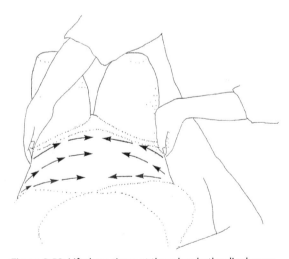

**Figure 3.59.** Lift three times at three levels: the diaphragm, the waistline, and the lower back.

**h. Finish with effleurage and light stroking.**
Finish your back massage routine with effleurage up or down the back and light reflex stroking down the sides.

### SEATED BACK MASSAGE ADAPTATIONS

A seated backrub is a good choice when the person receiving the massage cannot lie down—if, for example, there is no table or bed, if the person receiving the massage has difficulty breathing when reclining, or if a medical apparatus becomes an obstacle between a massager and a reclining recipient. Remember, too, that a seated backrub can be easily adapted for public occasions: sitting at a picnic table, waiting for a movie to begin, or traveling for any length of time by train or bus.

Make sure the person you're working on is supported and doesn't have to hold themselves up in a seated position. You want their back and shoulder muscles relaxed and receptive to your touch. My patient Jim and I worked out a method in which he sits up in bed and leans forward onto his hospital eating table, atop a comfortable pile of pillows (usually three). At the top of this pile, I place a small rolled towel that supports Jim's head, his face turned to one side. I brace the table so it won't move. This position ensures that he won't get a crick in his neck.

You'll also want to make sure that the person you're massaging is within easy reach of you. I find I can safeguard my own back against strain by moving throughout the massage from one side of the bed or chair to the other. Moving around will also ensure that you work both sides of your patient's back.

Use the stride position to get power and pressure with one foot in front of the other. Follow the same basic routine as a prone back massage (see Prone Position, page 81). As always, modify the strokes to suit your posture and the patient's tolerance for pressure.

Here are some suggestions for adaptations of a prone back massage routine for the seated position:

**Figure 3.60.** Effleurage in an adapted seated position with the patient leaning on the hospital tray. Use pillows on the tray for added comfort.

**a. Use a one-knee-up, one-knee-down posture.** With one knee up and one knee down, perform alternate thumb kneading and fingertip kneading along the erector spinae muscles between the occipital ridge at the base of the skull down to the lower back and sacrum.

**b. Make use of single-handed strokes and levering.** In some seated positions, your patient will need to lean on one of your arms (across their chest) to fully relax, leaving you just one hand to use for massage. You can also use two-handed levering techniques with the patient seated against a back rest.

**c. Put on the brakes!** Seated massage includes, of course, wheelchair massage. If massaging someone in a wheelchair, make sure you put on the breaks so the chair doesn't roll away from you with the first pressure.

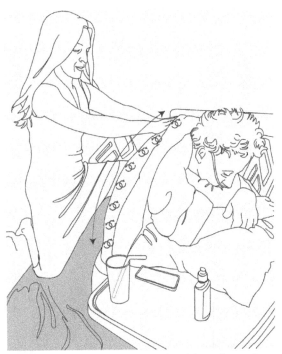

**Figure 3.61.** Performing alternate thumb kneading and fingertip kneading with one knee up and one knee down.

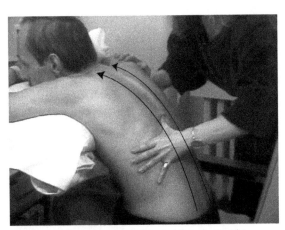

**Figure 3.62.** Try some single-handed thumb stretching between the erector spinae and the spine from the sacrum to the occipital ridge. In this photo, the patient is resting on pillows, and my hand is resting on his opposite shoulder. If you have both hands available, you can also use both thumbs at the same time, at the same slow speed.

**Figure 3.63.** If the patient can lean forward onto pillows or your supportive arm, that gives you single handed access to the back. Otherwise, slide both hands down the back between the patient and the chair back and use the levering technique.

## PRONE POSITION

The traditional position for a back massage is with the patient prone since that gives you easy access to the whole back at one time. However, this classic massage position is rarely seen in palliative circles because most patients have trouble lying on their stomach due to difficulties breathing or tumor sites. However, tumor sites may be anywhere, and may therefore be the reason why someone might *only* be comfortable facedown. In these cases, you can put pillows under the ankles and abdomen for support. Uncover only the patient's back; tuck the sheet into their underwear.

The routine for a prone back massage is also largely the same as the one used for a seated back massage (described in the previous section).

a. **Effleurage the back.** Move hands down the back from the shoulders to the waist on either side of the spine, and then come back up close to the sides of the body. Do this three times.

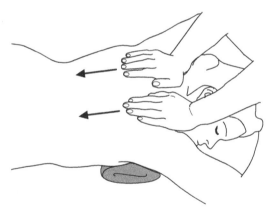

A. Place palms on shoulders.

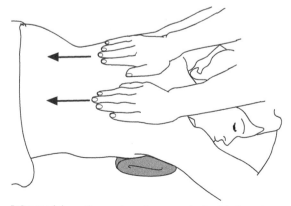

B. Proceed down the erector spinae muscles beside the spine.

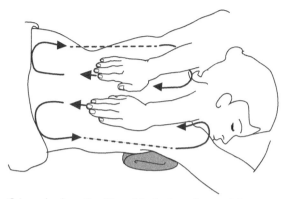

C. Loop back up the sides of the body and around the shoulders to the starting position at the top of the trapezius muscles.

**Figure 3.64.** Effleurage on the back. You can use firm pressure both ways.

b. **Perform bilateral wringing.** Wring across the entire back, including the sides as far as you can reach, then wring over the top of each shoulder (trapezius).

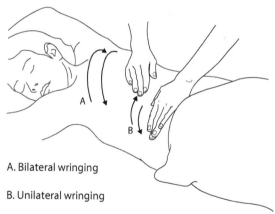

A. Bilateral wringing

B. Unilateral wringing

**Figure 3.65.** Wringing the back.

c. **Perform reinforced palmar or fingertip kneading.** Knead the erector spinae muscles on each side of the spine. The pressure of your circles is always up and away from the spine as you massage up and down the length of the spinal muscle. Don't move too far away from the spine—it will be too pokey!

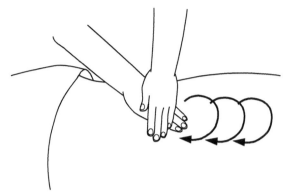

**Figure 3.66.** Two-handed reinforced palmar kneading.

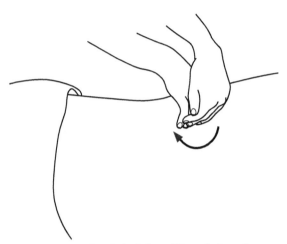

**Figure 3.67.** Two-handed reinforced fingertip kneading.

d. **Perform alternate thumb kneading and wringing.** Knead down the muscles on each side of the spine. Repeat three times, followed by wringing across the back.

**Figure 3.68.** Alternate thumb kneading.

e. **Finish with light reflex stroking.** Light reflex stroking is a nice finish to massage. For butterfly stroking, add a flicker movement to your fingertips. You can also use the back

of your fingers for the stroke away from you and the palmar side of your fingers for the stroke towards you. When stroking away, start with the first knuckle of your fingers and then gradually move to the middle digits and then the fingertips.

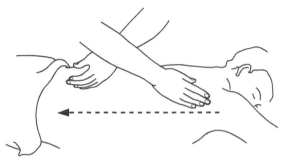

**Figure 3.69.** Light reflex stroking.

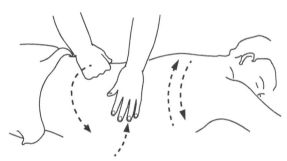

**Figure 3.70.** A variation of light reflex stroking using the back of your fingers for the stroke away and then the palmar side of your fingers as you move toward you.

### Circulatory, respiratory, and digestive system massage

When you are working with palliative patients, the circulation, digestion, and respiration systems are routinely compromised. You will, without a doubt, often find yourself massaging to remediate problems stemming from the failure of these systems. This is a good spot in the full-body routine—after the back massage—to add in some special treatments.

Chapters 4, 5, and 6 provide detailed explanations, diagrams, and illustrations about massage techniques to use to promote circulatory, respiratory, and digestive functioning. In those chapters you will learn how these systems work and the best ways to use massage for these systems to make your patient more comfortable.

### Face and scalp

When the person is faceup, add to their comfort by tucking them in securely from the arms to the feet. Remember, too, that the body starts to cool down and the heart rate slows after five minutes of being horizontal. The patient might not feel any need to be covered when you start, but they may be chilly five minutes later.

The face and scalp massage is often a patient favorite, but some people find it gives them a headache. Take some precautions. Have the back of the head slightly elevated so the patient's neck is semi flexed. This will help them avoid getting sinus congestion during the massage. A cool cloth on the forehead is another comforting technique.

Although I include a face and scalp massage in all full-body massages, it is particularly important as part of palliative care. In addition to helping respiration, it also leads to overall relaxation and pain management, and it can help patients clear some of the brain fog they experience due to medications. You may want to repeat the face and scalp massage a few times during a full-body massage routine: at the beginning, in the middle, and at the end.

To begin the massage, your patient should be comfortably lying faceup.

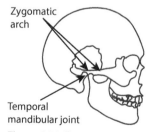
**Figure 3.71.** Face anatomy.

Zygomatic arch

Temporal mandibular joint

**a. Perform head flexing.** Standing at the head of the bed, lift the patient's head three times very slowly, chin to chest, a bit further each time. Coach your patient to relax the weight of their

head in your hands, and not to help you lift the head.

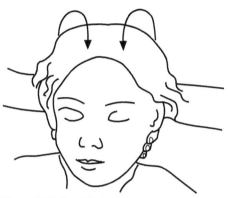
**Figure 3.72.** Head flexing.

**b. Knead the scalp.** Make a claw shape with your hands so you can massage the scalp with your fingertips. Then, slowly and firmly knead the scalp. You should be able to see your patient's forehead wrinkling as you do this. Keep moving to a new location and get a new grip, but do not rub back and forth or you will wear out your welcome! Hook onto the scalp and move it without frictioning back and forth. Check in with the patient about your pressure frequently. This stroke is particularly helpful for palliative patients experiencing brain fog.

**Figure 3.73.** Scalp kneading with rotated head.

Slowly turn the head to one side with a hand under one ear. Use your free hand to slowly and deliberately knead the scalp at the back of the head on the occipital ridge. Slowly turn the head to the other side, again holding a hand under the ear, and use the other fingertips to firmly and slowly knead along the base of the skull with small, circular kneading strokes and upward traction in each stroke where the skull meets the neck. This will help lessen tension in the neck.

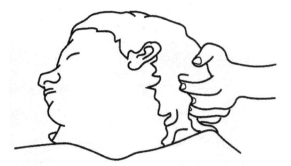

**Figure 3.74.** Fingertip knead the base of the skull along the occipital ridge.

c. **Rotate ears and apply pressure to pressure points.** Grasp an ear in each hand. Give slight traction by pulling outward, and rotate the ears with steady pulling in one direction three times. Then reverse and pull in the other direction. Now use your pointer finger and thumb to slowly and firmly squeeze around the outer perimeter of the ear. Work as slowly as possible; because this gives the patient time to digest the stroke.

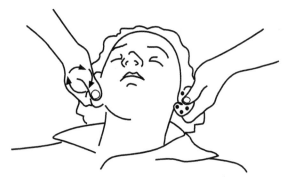

**Figure 3.75.** Ear rotations and pressure points.

d. **Knead ear attachments.** Use your fingertips to knead all around the attachments of the ear to the face. Be fairly firm but also check the

pressure with your patient. After kneading, repeat ear rotations.

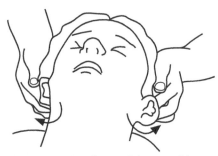

**Figure 3.76.** Knead around the ears with your fingertips.

e. **Temporal kneading.** Press the tips of your three middle fingers together on the temples, right on the hairline where the skin and scalp meet. Keep your fingers straight and allow your wrists to pivot. Move all along the temples down toward the mandibular (jaw) area. You might ask your patient to open and close their jaw to fully feel the effect of the stroke. Repeat the temporal kneading, but slow it down a little.

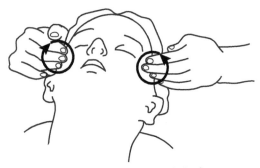

**Figure 3.77.** Temporal kneading with the fingers.

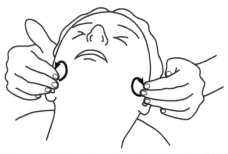

**Figure 3.78.** Kneading at the temporal mandibular joint in front of the lower earlobes.

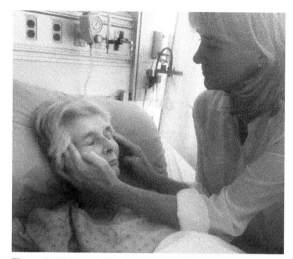

**Figure 3.79.** Face-to-face kneading at the temples.

**Figure 3.80.** Two seniors learn to give each other a face massage.

**f. Stroke facial contours.** Be sure your nails are really short because this stroke uses the tips of the fingers to contour the face.

- **Lower contour stroking:** Line your fingers up together so they will act as one unit. Start from the chin with both hands and firmly stroke the face from the center to

the ears. Next, move your hands up to just below the lips and stroke the face. Then place both your hands above the lips and stroke. Now move your hands to the flare of the nostrils and stroke along the jaw and out. The last stroke starts between the eyes and moves out along the lower border of the eyes.

**Figure 3.81.** Lower contour stroking.

- **Upper contour stroking:** For the upper contours of the face, use your thumbs, not your fingers. Place your thumbs on top of the eyebrows and stoke firmly along the line of the eyebrows. Continue this same action but each time place the thumbs just a little bit higher on the forehead and stroke firmly until you reach the hairline.

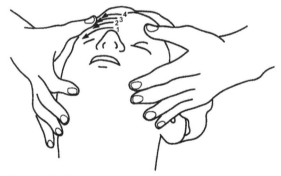

**Figure 3.82.** Upper contour stroking.

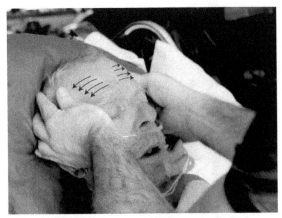

**Figure 3.83.** Richard gets his forehead massaged.

**g. "Shampoo" stroke the scalp.** Vigorously, but lightly, massage the entire scalp at top speed. Make the fur fly, but don't irritate the hair follicles. You can rest your patient's head in one hand and turn the head while you stroke with your other hand.

**Figure 3.84.** The shampoo massage.

**h. Knead the scalp.** Because the back of a patient's head is often a critical site for pressure sores, do a second round of scalp kneading.

**i. Butterfly stroke the face.** Use very light pressure to gently stroke all the contours of the face, especially down the nose and cheeks. Use your fingertips and the back of your hands for two different sensations.

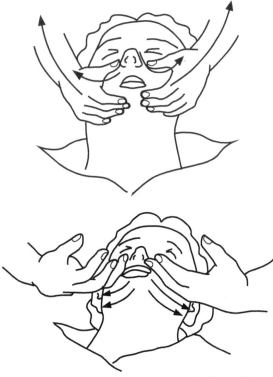

**Figure 3.85.** Light fingertip stroking with the front of the fingers and then the back of the fingers.

**j. Apply hot cupping to the face.** Rub your hands together quickly and firmly to warm them and then place the hands on your patient's face, slowly and gently. Take at least three slow, deep breaths with your patient to finish.

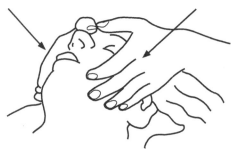

**Figure 3.86** Hold your warmed hands to your patient's face as they breathe deeply.

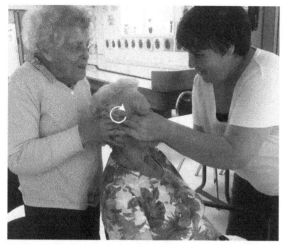

**Figure 3.87.** Teaching facial massage.

## Full-Body Massage (Side-lying)

Side-lying is the most important patient posture to perfect when you are doing palliative massage. I tend to also use this position with my nonpalliative patients for better accessibility to their hips and shoulders.

Side-lying is a wonderful way to adapt your massage when negotiating tumor sites, drains, or pouches, whether you need access to the front or the back of the patient.

Follow the same massage routine as for supine full-body massage. Ideally, the patient will change sides halfway through the massage so you can massage both sides equally. However, because everyone tends to have a favorite side to lie on, this can become a contentious issue; you may not be the most popular person when you encourage equal massage time for both sides. Ideally, patients should turn or be turned periodically to avoid pressure sores developing at the head of the femur. However, if turning just isn't an option, you can massage the underside of a person using the levering technique.

### Arm massage adaptations

If the patient can't turn and you need to massage the bottom arm, start by massaging the deltoid with single-handed strokes—palmar kneading,

single-handed thumb kneading and single-handed fingertip kneading. Adjust the supporting pillows to give you room to maneuver as you work to open up the circulation to this extremity. The rest of the underside of the arm is easy to massage after the deltoid is finished.

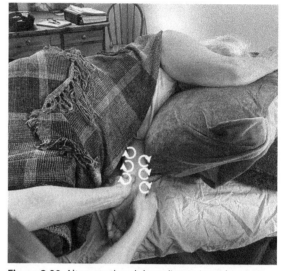

**Figure 3.88.** Alternate thumb kneading to inner lower arm.

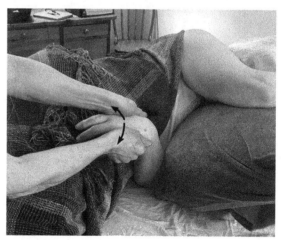

**Figure 3.89.** Transverse stretching to the dorsal surface of the hand.

### Back massage adaptations

You can use the same back massage sequence that applied to the supine patient only with the

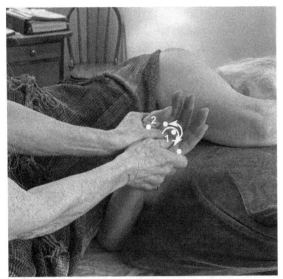

**Figure 3.90.** Alternate thumb kneading and digital compression to the palm of the hand of the underneath arm.

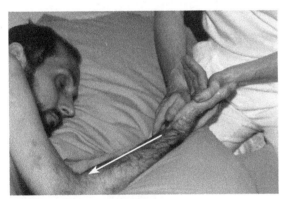

**Figure 3.91.** Forearm effleurage.

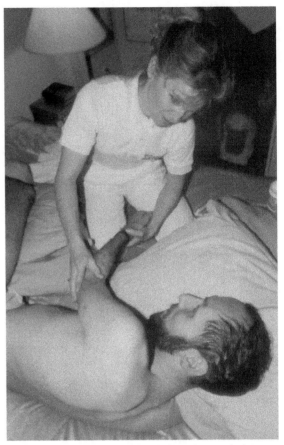

**Figure 3.92.** Single-handed thumb kneading to the biceps.

emphasis being on one side first, and then the other side once the patient has flipped over.

If you are massaging someone in a hospital bed, use the side railing to your advantage. Instead of dropping the railing, you can use it to support your lower back. Lean against the railing to brace yourself when doing the back massage from a standing position in front of the person.

It isn't always easy to move around the bed, especially if your patient is at home (and not in a hospital bed). Don't forget that you can massage the back by reaching over the patient's body from the front. Become adaptable and practice from both sides.

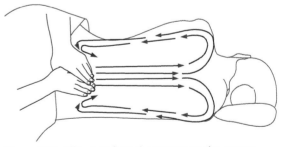

**Figure 3.93.** Effleurage from the sacrum up the erector spinae.

If it's too difficult to reach all the way around a patient for bilateral wringing, you can do unilateral wringing for the back and shoulders. Just

**Figure 3.94.** Synchronized and alternating tandem effleurage.

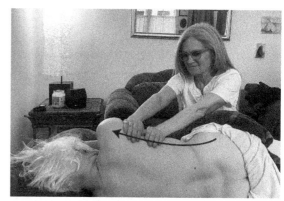

**Figure 3.97.** Palmar stretching to the latissimus dorsi.

be sure to balance these unilateral strokes on the other side once the patient has turned over. If they are unable to turn over, remember to massage the side of the back that rests on the bed with your well-practiced levered fingertip kneading, palmar kneading, and effleurages!

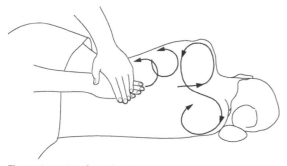

**Figure 3.95.** Reinforced palmar kneading.

## Hip and leg massage adaptations

The side-lying posture is ideal for hip work, so I use it even with my nonpalliative patients. The opportunity for pressure sores on the head of the femur is greatly reduced as long as you massage the underside of the leg on the bed, either by having the patient turn, or by using the levering method. Don't leave anything untouched! The series of images that follow take you through various options for side-lying hip and leg massage.

**Figure 3.98.** Levered fingertip kneading to the hip to prevent pressure sores at the head of the femur.

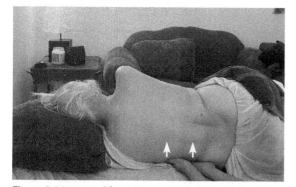

**Figure 3.96.** Levered fingertip kneading on the patient's underside. Massage from hips to shoulder.

**Figure 3.99.** The half-crooked leg position gives you access to both the inside and outside of each leg.

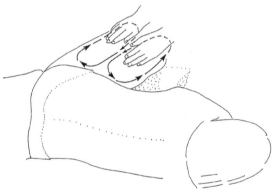

**Figure 3.100.** Begin with effleurage. Try to reach as much of the leg as you can.

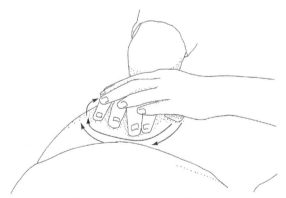

**Figure 3.101.** Reinforced palmar kneading to open the hip. You can also use overhanded alternating palmar kneading.

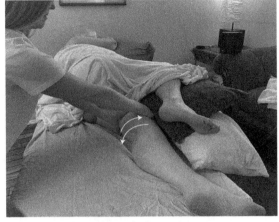

**Figure 3.102.** Wringing on the hamstrings.

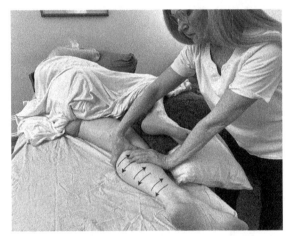

**Figure 3.103.** Wringing to the calf from the front of the patient.

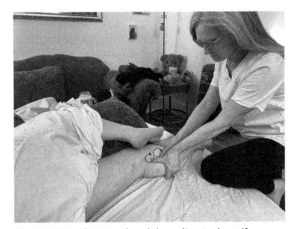

**Figure 3.104.** Alternate thumb kneading to the calf.

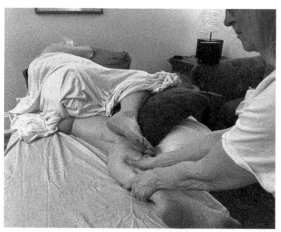

Figure 3.105. Alternate thumb kneading to the lower leg.

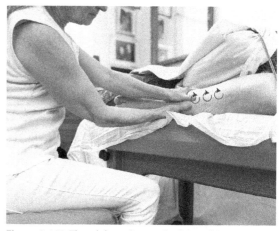

Figure 3.108. Thumb kneading to the front of the lower leg.

Figure 3.106. An optional position for massaging lower leg from the front of the patient.

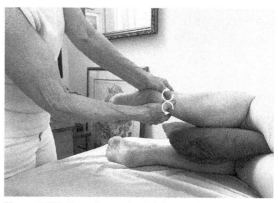

Figure 3.109. Kneading to the Achilles tendon where it attaches to the calcaneus.

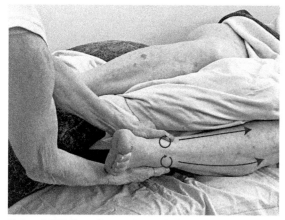

Figure 3.107. Kneading to the ankle followed by a stretching stroke up the shin.

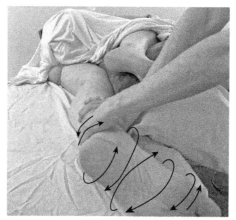

Figure 3.110. Wringing to the ankle to finish off the lower leg massage. Bring the stroke right down to the toes so the whole foot is involved.

**Figure 3.111.** Thumb kneading to the calcaneus (heel bone) for pressure sore prevention and to reduce swelling.

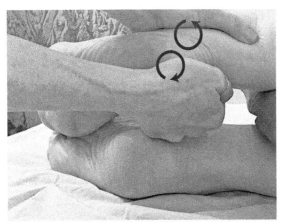

**Figure 3.112.** Kneading to the calcaneus with the heels of your hands. Switch back and forth between kneading with the thumbs and the heel of the hand.

### Face and scalp massage adaptations

Don't leave out the face and scalp massage, even if your end-stage patient's stiffening muscles prevent them from turning their head and body to allow a supine face massage. As with other side-lying adaptions, just slide your hands underneath the side of their face on the pillow and massage in a balanced bilateral manner.

Be sure to include the ears as this is vital to preventing pressure sores that can be quickly acquired, even in the last two or three days of a person's life. Use all the strokes: ear rotations, ear tip compressions, and fingertip kneading around

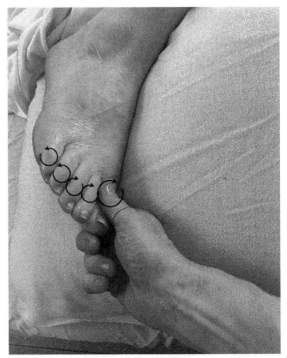

**Figure 3.113.** Corkscrew the toes to maintain mobility, release surface tension, and reduce swelling.

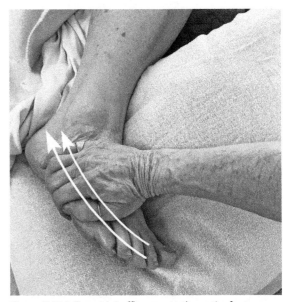

**Figure 3.114.** Do a mini-effleurage to the entire foot repeatedly from the tip of the toes to the ankle.

where the ear attaches to the side of the head. The face massage in side-lying can be awkward, but it's excellent for allowing the person to relax and ease the facial tension of end stage breathing and spasticity.

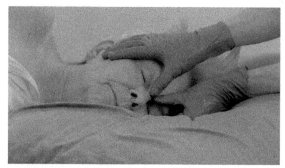

**Figure 3.115.** Side-lying thumb stroking to the forehead, and fingertip kneading to the temples and mandibular joint. Also include the facial contour stroking as you would do if the person were supine.

### GENERAL TIPS

- Be flexible and creative in your set-up, making sure that both you and the person you are massaging are comfortable. You should be able to reach your patient's back without straining. Make sure you have easy access to both sides of the body, if possible.
- If you're doing a bare-skin massage, you'll want to use oil and lotion as a lubricant.
- Feel complimented if the person you are massaging falls asleep under your touch; these catnaps can be deeply relaxing and restorative.
- Do not forget to continually solicit feedback on the pressure of your touch. This is particularly true when massaging someone whose illness may increase sensitivity to touch (such as lung lesions or intestinal distress).
- If your hands get tired, shake them out and take a deep breath or two before continuing. After giving a massage, I find washing my hands in cold water soothing.
- Work up and down the back beside the spine, but never work directly on the spine itself.
- When you're finished the massage, cover the person you've been working on to conserve warmth and offer comfort.

## Online Classroom

Visit brusheducation.ca/dying-in-good-hands to watch these videos:

Arm massage – supine

Hand massage

Corkscrewing fingers and toes

Levered fingertip kneading to the gluteals

Legs and hips – supine

Supine back massage – levered

Fingertip kneading to the back

Back massage – sitting

Back massage – wheelchair

Neck, face, and scalp massage

Neck, face, and scalp massage – seated

Scalp kneading

Occipital ridge kneading

Fingertip kneading and ear rotations

Temporal kneading

Facial contour stroking

Butterfly stroking

Hot cupping

Side-lying – turning your patient

Side-lying – arm massage

Side-lying – back and hip massage

Side-lying – levered fingertip kneading to the hip

Side-lying – leg massage

Side-lying – face and scalp massage

General tips – how to ask for feedback

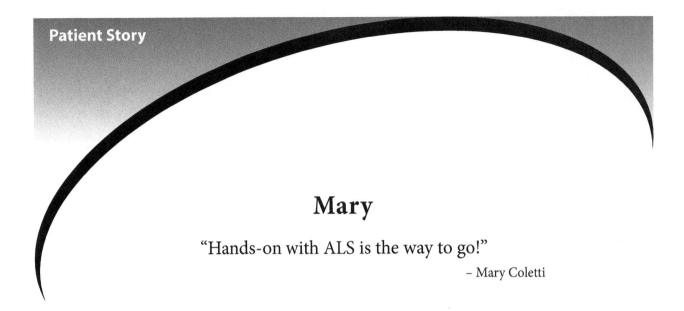

# Mary

"Hands-on with ALS is the way to go!"

– Mary Coletti

In the spring of 2009, I was asked to build a massage team to work in palliative care with a woman with ALS.

In Nelson, the Coletti family name was synonymous with ALS. Mary Coletti, who ran the local branch of the ALS Society, gave herself an early diagnosis of the disease. She had an intimate relationship with ALS: her dad had died of the disease when Mary was four years old, and her mother-in-law had died of ALS shortly before Mary's diagnosis.

I had been brought on board to teach Mary's team massage techniques for the early symptoms of muscle weakness in Mary's arms—an effect of ALS. The workshop, organized by Mary's friend, Laura Torrens, was set up next door to Mary's house at her father-in-law's place. Mary was there with a gathering of seven people ranging from relatives to ALS Society volunteers. Many faces at that original teaching session stayed on the massage team to the end of Mary's life.

The most important person at that meeting was Mary's best friend, Lorraine. She and Mary had made a pact that Lorraine would keep massaging her even when Mary could no longer ask her for massages. Mary Coletti had more people wanting to learn to massage her than any other person I had worked with in my entire career of teaching palliative massage. This team—fluctuating between 10 and 12 members—lasted from that first spring through summer and autumn of 2009 and on to the following spring.

At first, Mary's hands could move, but as her arms stilled, home support and other hospice and summer school volunteers got involved. In fall 2009, my summer school palliative massage student Melissa was keen to continue to massage Mary on a regular basis. Melissa became the backbone of our massage team. She was dedicated to Mary, making time every week to come down to Mary's lakeside house from her mountain-top home miles away by walking, riding, or borrowing vehicles. Melissa's early morning massage appointments were unusual for a nineteen-year-old's natural body rhythms.

Mary had managed to avoided pressure sores, and I wanted to help her keep it that way. I had originally encouraged Mary to keep resting on her side after massages, taking her weight off those pressure sites and making it easier to massage her back. My good idea did not get a positive response. It was simply too uncomfortable for Mary to use the side-lying position.

Still, I was determined that Mary's health was not going to be compromised or her time here shortened by succumbing to dangerous pressure sores. This meant that it was very important for everyone on the team to learn to massage Mary's back when she was lying faceup. I worked hard to make sure all volunteers were confident about massaging Mary's underside—one of the most awkward parts of massaging someone who cannot turn over comfortably. If we could keep her free of reddening, thinning, or any other early warning signs of skin breakdown, this massage project would be a success in my mind.

Mary's breathing quickly became a focus of our massages. Her wish to not move onto a ventilator made it important to keep her lungs clear and her breathing as comfortable as possible. Ideally, a person like Mary, whose lungs cannot expel, would be encouraged to move into different upper body positions to help drain each of the lobes of her lungs. The best drainage position is side-lying with the person's head below their waist. Tilting and other postural positioning can help with this. As her illness progressed, however, Mary became increasingly uncomfortable in any horizontal position, and began sitting more and more upright. This upright posture was not the best drainage position, especially for the lower lobes of her lungs, and the threat of pneumonia was always there. Although it was compromising her lungs, this was, ironically, still her best breathing posture, day or night.

Mary's upright position made our massages, with all their respiratory strokes, from rib raking to cupping, all the more important. I worked on having everyone learn to massage the areas of Mary's ribs that would afford the greatest relief for her lung congestion. I taught rib-raking, costal angle thumb stretching, and bilateral long strokes along the edge of the ribs where the diaphragm muscle attaches, combined with careful chest compressions.

Although the entire massage team was taught all the respiratory techniques, Mary still had a hard time coughing up any sticky phlegm. Her coughing was tugging at her diaphragm, making her whole tummy sore. We delicately massaged around the diaphragm attachment along the costal angle of the ribs. Tiny fingertip kneading along the angle of the ribs loosened up this painful tension and helped her to breathe more deeply.

The massage for Mary's back was also very important to help Mary's lungs stay clear. Within minutes of massaging Mary's back from the neck down to the lower back, she would begin to cough. This was a compliment to anyone massaging her.

As Mary became weaker and more compromised, she started developing a reddening where one foot was rubbing up against the other one. We kept those feet well massaged, using sheepskin against her internal ankle bones, and the redness disappeared. If Mary had developed a pressure sore or ulcer that needed bandaging, she would not have been able to move her feet so easily, which would be a problem in more ways than one. These feet were important communication device for her.

Mary's ALS made speech difficult, and eventually impossible, but that didn't stop her from communicating. I had known Mary before her diagnosis as a talkative person in the antique store on Baker Street. She was funny, quick, and inquisitive. Now, in Mary's non-speaking life, she was still very communicative. Indeed, she was, perhaps, even more emphatic. You could feel her eyes on you: a silent intensity. She would raise her eyebrows, squint her eyes and dramatically nod in agreement or shake her head with disapproval. Mary could let me know what she thought of my massage, using her eyebrows to answer my questions about the pressure of my touch and if I had missed anything. We all looked into her face for direction to know what she wanted or how she felt.

Beyond body language, Mary's ALS didn't even stop her from using words. She ran a talking machine with her right foot. She had a foot pedal—a big, round, yellow button—that she used to spell out words for us to read. When she finished a sentence, a mechanical voice would tell us what she was saying. It sounded like Hal, the mechanical voice in the movie *2001: A Space Odyssey*. She was independent by nature and the talking machine suited her needs. Sometimes, when the machine was nearby, she would quietly formulate a sentence when I was massaging her, and I would always be surprised by the mechanical voice suddenly talking to me.

Mary had been an elementary school teacher. Now she wanted to educate other ALS families and friends to learn to massage. So, she organized me to film her last year with her massage team. Her husband Lou appeared one day with a camera to record the tandem massages that Melissa and I were doing in the garden. From that moment on, we recorded Mary's story on film. We made instructional documentaries and a variety of classic documentaries for different audiences. We made films for youth, for friends and family, for hospice workers and volunteers, and for ALS Society volunteers. In this way, Mary helped—and continues to help—others in virtual and live classrooms learn hands-on massage techniques for other people with ALS.

Looking back on our film directorship, Mary and I had a pattern. I would get an idea and pass it on to Lou, who would in turn discuss it with Mary. Mary would have a concern and pass it on to Lou, and he would check it out with me. Lou was our assistant director and more. He ironed out timing issues, organized details and equipment, set up ladders, and recorded great footage with his little high-definition camera. We were a great team!

By winter, despite being permanently congested in her lungs, Mary continued to outlive everyone's expectations. She enjoyed the New Year's party that arrived by surprise at her house, living room concerts, Valentine's Day, and the Winter Olympic Games. As winter turned to spring, she enjoyed the snow melting, the robins coming out in full force, and the first flowers of the year.

The massage team now needed more people to come on board. We had gotten Mary this far without a fever, an infection, even one pressure sore, or pneumonia. It was an amazing team effort that saw Mary gently into the departure lounge waiting for lift off. We all knew that she was preparing to leave and that she was in control; she knew what she was doing. She was fully aware of her precarious position and the preciousness of each breath.

In Mary's last days, our focus gently changed. She found it difficult to get her breath. Now we tried to not stimulate her breathing or clear her lungs with cupping or any vigorous massage methods. We massaged simply to soothe her panic and

struggle to breathe. Every time we massaged her, she calmed down and could breathe more easily. She was now upright all the time in the best posture to catch her breath.

She got a full body massage in the morning. This got her chest loosened up, making coughing and suctioning more productive. However, we didn't want to encourage coughing in the evening because it was so stressful and unrestful for Mary. To calm her at night, then, we only massaged her extremities, including her neck and face. This helped her sleep better. She still loved her feet being massaged and it seemed that a small foot massage went a long way to relax her, no matter what the level of discomfort she was experiencing.

When the family moved Mary to the hospital, the massage team continued with hands-on massages every day. One day when I arrived at the hospital, Mary opened her eyes, looked at me, and then at her legs: she was telling me she wanted me to massage her legs. After I'd massaged her legs, I moved up and began working on her arms. When Mary started to spasm in her breathing, I ran for her nurse, Paul. He quickly started deep suctioning and worked steadily to try to ease the pressure in her chest. I kept my hands moving in an attempt to calm her, continually talking to her about what a good job she was doing while her friend Norma held her feet. Mary was using tremendous effort to breathe and was starting to sweat.

Then she left us. Her breathing had the end stage rhythm, but she was not there. Her eyes became fixed, unblinking, and unseeing. I ran my hand over her heart. It was slowing down. Mary wasn't breathing, but my hand on her pulse told me she was still in the land of the living. I leaned forward and whispered loudly in her ear, "Come back here, Mary." Nothing.

"Mary, your family is not here with you. Come back. They would want to be here. Come back."

She blinked! With a sigh of relief, I kept massaging. We powdered her back and put dry towels under her gown to soak up the sweat. This exertion was not a fever, but the fight to live a little longer. So far, Mary was winning that fight. Before I left, I commented to Mary that she was having some test runs, looking over the edge, and that I was glad that she had come back.

When I arrived in Mary's hospital room on the morning of her last day, Michael, her son, was sleeping on the hospital couch with the family dog, Casey. That was the first time I had seen a dog in the palliative ward. With Lou asleep on one couch and Michael asleep on the other, Mary was safe to go.

I left an hour later, after massaging Mary for the last time, and knowing that Nik and Lorraine would be arriving soon. Around noon I got the call that Mary had died peacefully, with Lorraine and Nik massaging her.

Mary had worked hard to leave a platform of change to outlive her. She was determined to make change happen and did this by filming the final chapter of her life. She felt she could effect change through her film and her story, *Massaging Mary: Hands On with ALS*.[16] She gave herself a powerful voice that would be heard long after her last breath. She made a living legacy of change, a recipe book for the best way to die. And when Mary first asked Lorraine to massage her arm, she gave her best friend—and, eventually, a whole community of family and volunteers—a great gift: the opportunity to help her die, saying her final goodbye through that ancient and everlasting power of touch.

Mary.

# 4

# Circulatory Massage

Keeping the flow going is one of our most important goals when massaging those who are dying. Dying people are often too weak to move their bodies by themselves, so they lack circulatory stimulation. Massage can replace this lack of movement and act like a passive form of exercise.

Massaging the body as it fades in function is good for keeping the person warm, moving fresh blood to the cooling extremities, preventing bedsores, reducing swelling, and taking away the achiness of lying for hours in different horizontal positions.

There are two distinctly different circulatory systems. The first one is the lymphatic system, which takes clear fluid, our infection-fighting equipment, around the body. The second is the cardiovascular system, which takes blood, carrying cellular food, to the hungry cells and collecting garbage from our muscle metabolism to be filtered out by our digestive and respiratory organs. Optimizing blood and lymphatic circulation is our aim when we massage those who are dying.

---

**THE THREE S'S OF CIRCULATION**

My focus when massaging both circulatory systems—lymphatic and cardiovascular—is manifold. My overall objectives are to massage the skin to stimulate it and help it keep its resiliency; to reduce the swelling from the patient's challenged lymphatic and cardiovascular systems; and to stretch the limbs and muscles to make them more elastic and, in turn, make the joints more mobile.

## 1. Stroking

Massage strokes for circulatory palliative care run the gamut from effleurage and intensive petrissage strokes to light stroking with the gentlest touch. The overall goal is to help the immobile or partially immobile patient get their circulation systems moving, preventing both swelling and pressure sores.

## 2. Swelling

The reduction of swelling helps the limbs move more freely and the body feel physically more relaxed. Reducing the taut surface tension results in an overall lessening of pain and discomfort.

## 3. Stretching

The objective of stretching is to counteract the contractions of fetal positioning that palliative patients begin to assume near the end of life. These contractures are natural, but are a fast track to aging in palliative scenarios. Always stretch out the arms, hands, legs, feet, and trunk of the body after massage.

---

## Principles of Lymphatic and Cardiovascular Palliative Massage

The basic objective of working with the two circulatory systems through massage is to stimulate circulation and mechanically help the body flush

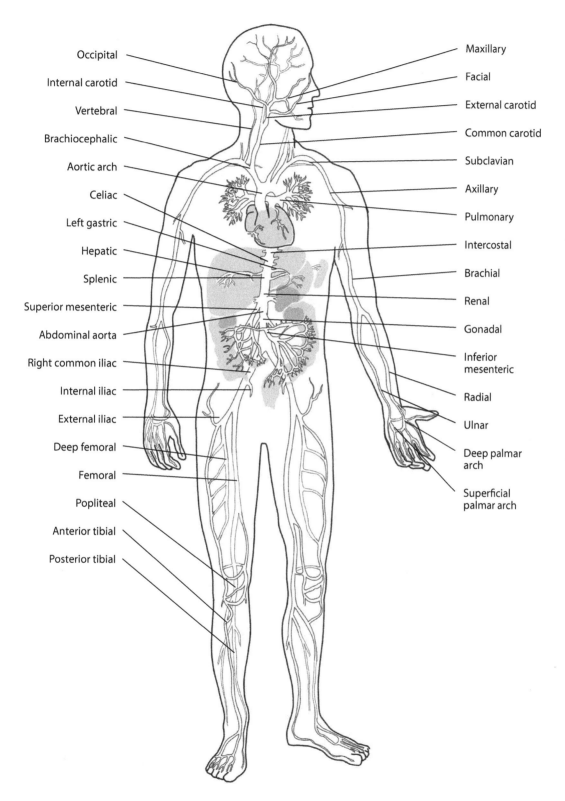

Occipital

Internal carotid

Vertebral

Brachiocephalic

Aortic arch

Celiac

Left gastric

Hepatic

Splenic

Superior mesenteric

Abdominal aorta

Right common iliac

Internal iliac

External iliac

Deep femoral

Femoral

Popliteal

Anterior tibial

Posterior tibial

Maxillary

Facial

External carotid

Common carotid

Subclavian

Axillary

Pulmonary

Intercostal

Brachial

Renal

Gonadal

Inferior mesenteric

Radial

Ulnar

Deep palmar arch

Superficial palmar arch

**Figure 4.1.** The cardiovascular system: arteries.

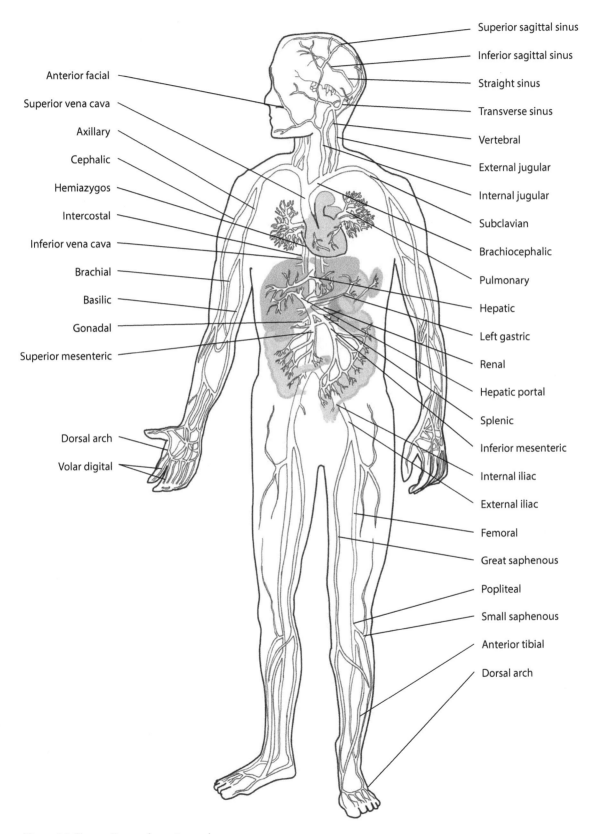

**Figure 4.2.** The cardiovascular system: veins.

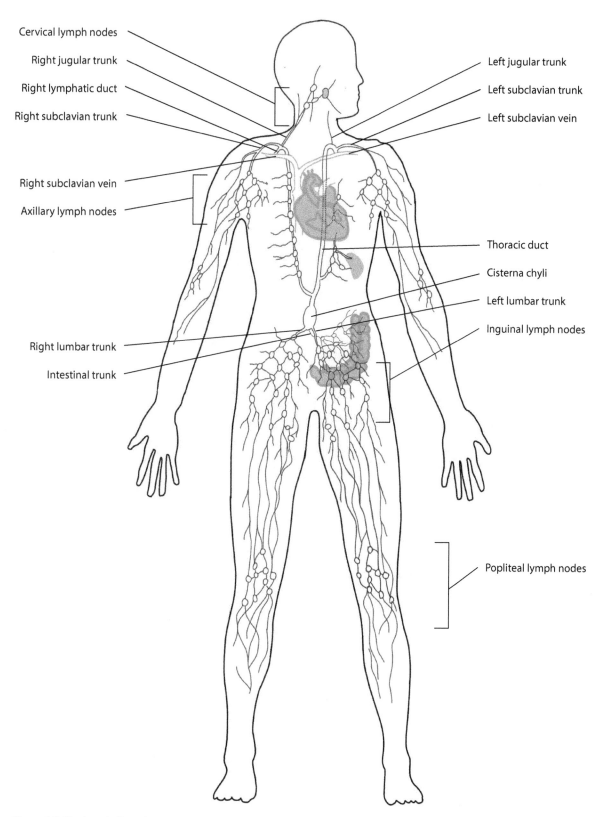

Cervical lymph nodes

Right jugular trunk

Right lymphatic duct

Right subclavian trunk

Right subclavian vein

Axillary lymph nodes

Right lumbar trunk

Intestinal trunk

Left jugular trunk

Left subclavian trunk

Left subclavian vein

Thoracic duct

Cisterna chyli

Left lumbar trunk

Inguinal lymph nodes

Popliteal lymph nodes

**Figure 4.3.** The lymphatic system.

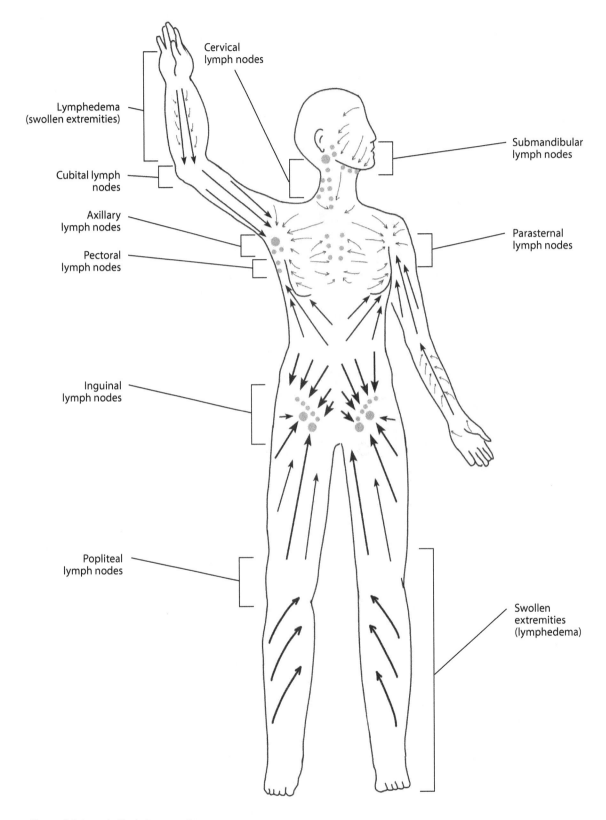

**Figure 4.4.** Lymphatic drainage system.

fluids from the systems naturally. In palliative care, lymphatic and cardiovascular massage therapy is particularly important because failure in these systems, if unattended, can result in extreme discomfort, pain, infection, and immobility.

While you don't necessarily need to know the complexities of these systems, it is important that you know their flow patterns. In both the lymphatic and cardiovascular circulatory systems we want to help fluids drain from the extremities toward the trunk of the body. Always start by "uncorking the bottle," as you learned in Chapter 3 (see page 32), moving from the trunk of the body out toward the tip of the extremity, applying pressure in the opposite direction, toward the trunk of the body. For example, begin an arm massage at the shoulder, then move down the upper arm, and then the lower arm, all the while aiming your pressure up towards the shoulder. It's the same with the legs: massage the hips first, then thigh, and then the calf.

While in the extremities, all circulation comes from the trunk of the body, within the trunk of the body itself, the sources of the two systems are different. The lymphatic system has no pump source, while the pump source for cardiovascular system is the heart. Still, massage can help both systems by promoting venous return and lymphatic flow.

A key difference in massaging the two systems is that lymphatic massage is specific to the locations of the lymphatic nodules while cardiovascular massage is used all over the body. Another difference is that lymphatic massage strokes are always light and gentle in pressure, whereas cardiovascular strokes can be firmer.

Another difference is in how we use our hands. For lymphatic massage, the strokes typically use the fingertips and thumb in a brushing action. For cardiovascular massage, the strokes use more pressure, usually with more contact and broader movement. I find using the back of my hand is best for the lightest stroking action to encourage lymphatic return. In cardiovascular massage, you can use a heavier stroke.

## Lymphatic System Massage

Lymph is a clear fluid that aids the body's immune system and helps clear waste. It moves from body tissues through lymphatic vessels and various nodes toward the center of the body, where it eventually intermingles with blood returning to the heart from the extremities.

The lymphatic system relies on muscle movement to move lymph toward the trunk of the body for filtering and renewal. In massage for the lymphatic system, you start at the thoracic duct located in the torso and move out toward the extremities while brushing toward the lymph collection sites at the top of the extremities.

### Rhythmic stroking

When working with lymphatic swelling (lymphedema), I use fingertip stroking and apply the same principle I use with venous blood return: massage toward the heart. Lymphatic massage strokes, however, are modified to gently break up surface tension and help the lymph fluid along its route up and out of the legs and arms into the trunk of the body.

I use a rhythmical stroking pattern of "short, short, long," alternating short fingertip strokes with long palmar effleurage strokes. This can be modified to be two short fingertip strokes and a short palmar effleurage. I also use the "short, short, long" stroking pattern to reduce swelling in joints and lower limbs.

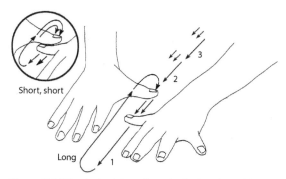

**Figure 4.5.** "Short, short, long" lymphatic thumb stroking.

## Pumping

Pumping is another massage technique used with both the lymphatic and cardiovascular systems. When I use pumping, I stand at the top of the table (at the patient's head) and gently grip both armpits at the wing of the pectoralis muscles. I then pump the armpits, alternately pressing in and then releasing out. This pumping opens up the circulation to the area, increasing the blood flow and the movement of lymphatic fluids.

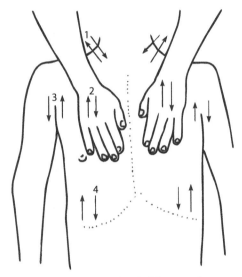

**Standing at the head of the person:**
1. Fingertip pumping
2. Upper thoracic palmar pumping
3. Armpit (axilla) whole-handed pumping

**Standing at the side of the person:**
4. Bilateral palmar pumping with an open C-shaped hand

**Figure 4.6.** Bilateral lymphatic pumping for the upper body.

These massage strokes—pumping and rhythmic stroking—can be done using the entire palmar surface of your hand. I incorporate the lymphatic drainage sequence as part of my general cardiovascular massage. I alternate pumping and rhythmic stroking with more classic massage strokes as I move up the leg, arm, or sides of the body with a gentle-yet-firm pressure. My lymphatic therapists recommend that lymphatic strokes be repeated at least 10 times.

## Pressure Sores

Pressure sores are a circulation problem. Our circulation naturally slows down as the body weakens. Bed sores are also due to extended periods without movement. As unmoving muscles atrophy, there is no protection for the body's bony protuberances; these bony bumps get red from the pressure of the body's weight against a surface. If not stimulated by movement or massage, the redness turns white. This is a warning sign of a bedsore. It is also a sign that is easily overlooked by the untrained eye.

In palliative care, where patients bodies are weakening and they are mostly sedentary—sometimes palliative patients have long periods of no movement at all—bedsores are one of the most common problems. Most bedsores develop on the tailbone, hip, and heel, but they can appear almost anywhere. They can be complicated by pain and infection, and may even result in an earlier death.

### Pressure sore prevention

The best prescription for bedsores is, of course, prevention! A suitable lying surface is most important. An egg-crate mattress can be helpful, as can sheepskin or special pads and mattresses such as the Silicore Pad and the Roho Pad. An alternating pressure pad can also work. These are almost essential for long-term use, though some people find a waterbed is also excellent for home use.

Sheepskin is fantastic. Each wool hair has a spiral shape, like a miniature spring. These hairs provide a cushion that doesn't flatten out, supporting and evenly distributing body weight and taking pressure off limbs and pressure points. Putting sheepskin down on wheelchairs, beds, couches, car seats, park bench, or anywhere where the palliative person sits or lies down will help pressure points and general circulation.

Sheepskin is also excellent for wicking moisture away from the skin and for regulating body temperature. Both properties help prevent bedsores and other skin conditions. Sometimes I put a plastic bag under the sheepskin so it is easier to slide the patient over a surface.

**Real sheepskin pads can help optimize the circulatory effect of massage.**

Traditionally, caregivers have used a foam donut, rolled towel, or something similar to distribute the body weight around the area of a pressure sore, thus reducing or eliminating pressure on that point. A homemade donut made out of a foam sleeping mat can help prevent ulcerations as need develops. The foam should be soft and can be found at many retail stores, thrift shops, or even yard sales; often people find what they need in their own garage. Foamies can be cut to fit the person's rear end or whatever site is causing the problem.

**Figure 4.7.** Brian's caregivers taught me to use donuts to prevent pressure sores. Here you can see the traditional type of blow-up donut hanging around the toy owl's neck. This was typical of what we used in the 1970s and 1980s, although we also had many homemade versions constructed of foam and various other materials.

Blow-up donuts are another option: they allow for a variety of air levels so you can create different pressure. Less air in the donut means less pressure around the site of potential pressure sores or ulceration and less chance of circulation blockage.

Many caregivers have stopped using donuts because the pressure of the circular donut can sometimes cause its own set of problems, including new pressure sore sites. I think they are still useful if managed properly and used along with—not instead of—frequent turning. Switching the patient's position is really the key to preventing pressure sores.

**Figure 4.8.** Medical sheepskin at work.

The need for turning and repositioning varies from person to person quite dramatically, but the nursing norm is to turn a person every three to four hours. I advocate turning a patient every two hours, but sometimes even I have to remind myself of the importance of this point of care. As I write this, for instance, I am thinking about last night, when I was giving my patient Florin a massage in his chronic care facility. I used my levering technique for his back massage because I didn't want to interrupt his rest to turn him. I realized then that the reason most of us don't turn our palliative person often enough is simply because we don't want to disturb them. I needed to remind myself that, even if it disturbs him momentarily, frequent turning will benefit Florin, as it will other palliative people, with both an easier back massage and a decreased chance of developing pressure sores.

*OTHER CAUSES OF BEDSORES*

- **Clothing**: check for wrinkles and folds, tightness, bands, thickness, or hard objects
- **Braces and splints**: check for rubbing and for pressure points on the skin
- **Linens**: watch for harsh-textured bed linens, or linens washed in harsh laundry soap
- **Scented soaps and creams**: use only glycerin soap and nonallergenic, pure soaps and creams

In all cases, having the body parts rest on sheepskin rather than regular sheets and pillowcases will help alleviate pressure sores and avoid damage to hair follicles, which causes hair loss.

### Massage for pressure sore prevention

Massaging a person's skin will improve circulation and help to prevent pressure sores and skin breakdown. The skin will keep healing itself right to the end if given the opportunity to regenerate. I am amazed how my patients with wounds, postsurgical incisions, and pressure sores will keep healing at these breakdown sites and rebuilding new growths.

When my mom was dying, she was very thin, but only near the end did pressure points become an issue. She seemed more comfortable resting on her right side so she could see people more easily. I didn't notice we were letting her stay on that side more than the other until I was massaging her hips and saw reddening on the head of her femur. This alerted me that I needed to be more conscientious about turning her from side to side more frequently.

Massaging patients at pressure points, like I did for both of my parents, will relieve skin breakdown and thinning and will help the person protect their immune system by keeping the skin intact. The more we can prevent pressure sores, the more comfortable we can make our loved ones' final days.

To massage pressure points, work in a circular motion around the site with larger strokes, then use small alternate thumb kneading and fingertip kneading strokes. Then move to broad palmar single-handed or reinforced kneading strokes for about one minute per location. I try to do all 10 classic pressure sites with both traditional massage and ice massage.

---

### THE 10 PRIMARY SITES OF SKIN BREAKDOWN

*ACCESSED WHEN PATIENT IS SUPINE*

1. Scalp (occipital protuberance, where the head touches the pillow)
2. Shoulder blades (spine of the scapula)
3. Elbows (olecranon process)
4. Tailbone (coccyx)
5. Heel bone (calcaneus)

*ACCESSED WHEN PATIENT IS SIDE-LYING*

6. Ear (auricle)
7. Hip bone (head of the femur)
8. Knees (sides)
9. Shoulder tips
10. Ankle bones (malleoli)

---

If there is any indication of pressure sores, alleviate the pressure! If patient must be in a supine or side-lying position, then use medical donuts or another support to protect the site.

#### 1. SCALP

The back of the head is often overlooked as a potential bedsore site. The following scalp massage directions are for upright or side-lying patients.

When I massage the scalp, I use my fingertips to move the underlying scalp muscles. A light, superficial shampoo stroke (vigorous-but-light massage of the entire scalp with the fingertips at top speed) will still get the circulation going, but the most effective types of scalp massages are very focused, with the fingertips working deeply and thoroughly.

Rather than rubbing back and forth, "hook" onto the scalp to move it against the skull; this allows the patient's blood to get more nutrition to the skin and saves the hair follicles from irritating pressure and resulting hair loss. Support the neck

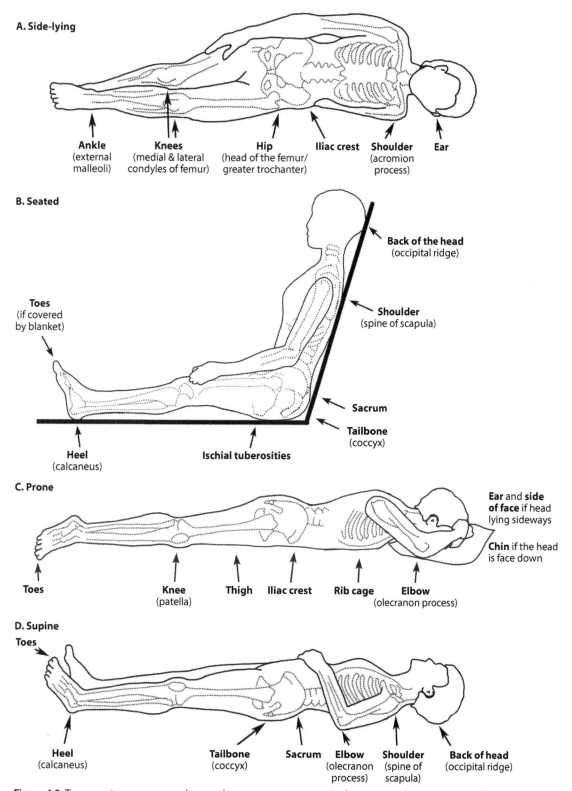

**A. Side-lying**

**Ankle** (external malleoli)  **Knees** (medial & lateral condyles of femur)  **Hip** (head of the femur/ greater trochanter)  **Iliac crest**  **Shoulder** (acromion process)  **Ear**

**B. Seated**

**Back of the head** (occipital ridge)

**Shoulder** (spine of scapula)

**Toes** (if covered by blanket)

**Sacrum**

**Tailbone** (coccyx)

**Heel** (calcaneus)  **Ischial tuberosities**

**C. Prone**

**Ear** and **side of face** if head lying sideways

**Chin** if the head is face down

**Toes**  **Knee** (patella)  **Thigh**  **Iliac crest**  **Rib cage**  **Elbow** (olecranon process)

**D. Supine**

**Toes**

**Heel** (calcaneus)  **Tailbone** (coccyx)  **Sacrum**  **Elbow** (olecranon process)  **Shoulder** (spine of scapula)  **Back of head** (occipital ridge)

**Figure 4.9.** To prevent pressure sores, keep a close eye on pressure point hot spots and massage at the first sign of redness. Get professional medical attention as soon as possible.

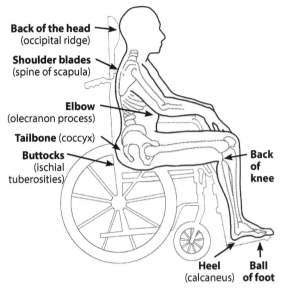

Back of the head
(occipital ridge)

Shoulder blades
(spine of scapula)

Elbow
(olecranon process)

Tailbone (coccyx)

Buttocks
(ischial
tuberosities)

Back
of
knee

Heel
(calcaneus)

Ball
of foot

**Figure 4.10.** For patients who spend a lot of time in a wheelchair, be sure to target these hot spots.

to free the back of the head from the pillow in order to massage thoroughly.

### 2. SHOULDER BLADES

When the patient is seated, start by massaging the muscles attaching the head and neck to the back. Stand to the side with one hand on the front of the patient's shoulder to stabilize them while kneading with fingertips from the top of the neck to the attachment of the rhomboid muscles on the spine of the scapula. The spine of the scapula is that upper ridge of the shoulder blade that you instinctively reach for when attempting to ease the tension out of your shoulders.

The bony spine of the scapula gets more obvious as a dying person shrinks in body mass. Though this ridge causes problems with redness and potential breakdown less frequently than the other sites listed here, it is still important to get at it with your fingers from a side-lying massage position, a faceup position with your hands underneath the person, or the traditional massage position, facedown in the bed. It is also easy to work this area when the patient is in a seated position.

If the person is upright, stand at their side and place a supportive hand on the front of their shoulder. Use the other hand to fingertip knead all around the scapula (shoulder blade), not just at the muscular attachments of the rhomboids and subscapularis, supraspinatus, and teres minor but also on the spine of the scapula itself since it is pressed against the flat surfaces where the person is sitting. I use very specifically placed fingertip kneading along this ridge and alternate with broader strokes of thumb kneading and palmar kneading. I work over the entire shoulder for about five minutes on each side.

### 3. ELBOWS

Pressure sores can quickly develop on the elbows because they are one of the boniest parts of our bodies. Even when we are healthy, the elbow is particularly vulnerable to bumping and bruising. There is just no padding at all to protect it. Elbows can experience skin problems in the first 48 hours of immobility. People in the ICU who can't be moved are very prone to elbow tissue breakdown.

When you are massaging the elbow, hold the patient's arm at the wrist, bend their arm at a right angle, and then cup the elbow with your other hand to apply circular palmar kneading, then fingertip kneading, and back again to palmar kneading. Keep repeating the strokes to massage all the tiny nooks and crannies of this important joint. The whole arm can be included in the massage, of course! Rubbing in some serious oils like Bag Balm and Udder Ease can also help the skin stay strong.

### 4. TAILBONE

The tailbone (coccyx) is tricky. It is the most important pressure site to keep intact because pressure sores here provide an open-door opportunity for diaper-related infections to go looking for trouble. The lower back, sacrum, and coccyx are perfect sites for breakdown and infections. I have my students practice diaper changing so they are not intimidated or inexperienced in changing a full or damp diaper if needed.

Usually, massaging someone's tailbone is contraindicated in professional massage protocol for a healthy person getting a massage. But with palliative patients, this is the most important place to include in the massage routine and should be taught to families. Like the elbow, there is little to no padding on the tailbone. This is a bony part of the body on everyone, but it is usually at least partially protected by the gluteal muscles. When closer to death, however, gluteal muscles tend to atrophy and leave the tailbone at risk. Its surrounding tissues will break down quickly and easily if not watched carefully. People who are changing diapers are in the best position to watch for developing sores and to rub this area.

Using single-handed fingertip kneading, run your fingers all along the sides of the coccyx. Work right over the tailbone, moving across it as well as up and down the sides. Use lots of oils as well as exposure to air or the sun.

## 5. HEEL

The heel is padded, but it is still delicate and easily affected by pressure. Reddening can happen quickly; sheepskin booties are a good remedy for long periods of supine, faceup convalescence.

Use the heels of your hands to massage the heels of the patient. Include simultaneous bilateral thumb kneading, alternate thumb kneading, and wringing on the top and bottom of the foot itself. End with a prayer-position effleurage, with the foot sandwiched between the hands. Replace booties immediately after massaging the heels—it can be risky to forget them.

If the patient doesn't have booties, or before you replace them to work elsewhere on the body, raise the patient's heels off the bed by putting a roll under the ankles. This airs the heels and allows the skin to breathe. If the patient is chilled, cover the feet in this raised and supported position.

## 6. EAR

The ear is a side-lying pressure spot, and since most people like to lie on their sides, it's a common place for pressure sore development. Turn patients from side to side and rub the ears carefully, whether they are faceup on their backs or lying on their side with one ear exposed. You can reach underneath the person to massage the other ear and get both done while keeping the person in their favorite side-lying posture. The ears respond well to warm oils and lots of massage. They are made of cartilage, not muscle. While they are often sinewy and tough, they are always very sensitive—so sensitive, in fact, that you have to be careful about how you touch them, and may have to get past ticklishness on the part of the patient. See page 84 for ear massage instructions.

## 7. HEAD OF THE FEMUR

The head of the femur is often the first place we see reddening when a person has been lying on their side for a long period. My process is to massage around the hip and then work my way into the reddening to reduce or completely erase it. I begin by massaging the lower back and then work into the gluteal muscles using palmar kneading and alternate thumb kneading. I then move to the reddened areas, going back and forth between general and specific strokes. Ice massage can also help stimulate this site.

## 8. SIDES OF KNEES

The outside edges of the knees have bony protuberances that are attachment sites for our upper and lower leg muscles. When a patient is usually side-lying, the pressure between the knees can cause problems, so use a pillow or sheepskin to keep the knees from touching each other. The outer aspects of the knees also are possible sites for pressure sores from resting on the mattress. Be sure to check the inside *and* outside of the knees and cushion them preventively or as needed.

## 9. SHOULDER TIPS

The acromion process of the outermost aspect of the shoulder, or the shoulder tips, can be a potential pressure site if the patient is left too long on their side. Inadequate pillow support for the head can put too much pressure on the shoulder and lead to bedsore problems in this area.

## 10. ANKLE BONES

The bony bumps on a person's ankles are called malleoli. The tibia—the largest lower leg bone—has its bony bump on the inside of the ankle, while the fibula—the smaller bone of the lower leg—has its bump on the outside. These two bumps are the endpoints of the lower leg bones. They are also the most compromised site of the whole body, as they are at the tail end of our circulation system.

The malleoli are often overlooked because there can be a lot of excitement around activities in the trunk of the body. Ankles rarely cause problems that can be felt by the patient. But even though the skin breakdown that occurs in this area often does not cause much sensation or discomfort, it is as dangerous as anywhere else. It is one of the most important areas to preserve because it is so hard to heal once it has opened up. Its peripheral location on the body causes particular circulatory challenges because it takes more effort for the heart to pump blood to the region.

Visually, the ankle bones have very little to show, without much skin surface to observe. Elderly people have lots of discoloration of the lower leg in their normal, nonpalliative life due to aging and inactivity. They often do not show signs of skin breakdown because the pink color of the skin is permanently discolored in shades of blue, purple, or red, and breakdown on the ankles can be easily missed.

The ankles will not easily heal on their own without the help of massage. Patients can even lose their legs if they have other conditions, such as diabetes. Diabetes already puts patients in danger of losing a limb; add a pressure sore, and the patient is in a predicament that could unduly shorten their life.

Often, patients cannot move their legs at all when they are weak and close to death. We want to keep them as comfortable and well-preserved as possible, and to this end we must massage their legs—especially their lower legs—every day, or preferably a number of times a day: in the morning when washing them, in the evening when washing them, and probably another time in between. This will also lower the chance of ankle bedsores, keeping the ankles well fed with blood and lymph.

## Other treatments for bedsores

### ALOE VERA

Aloe vera has been used in healing for about 3500 years, but there are few scientific studies supporting its use. However, one study has shown that aloe vera is an antioxidant that has complex chemical properties that promote healing. The study also shows that it's an antibacterial agent that inhibits infection, reduces inflammation, and hydrates the skin.[17]

A recent study focuses specifically on the use of aloe vera for pressure ulcers. The results have been positive. In a clinical trial on 80 patients in Iran, researchers compared aloe vera with other treatments for pressure sores and found there were significant differences in pressure ulcer occurrence in the two groups. Aloe vera, they concluded, was "much more effective and less costly in preventing and healing the ulcers compared to current treatments."[18]

### SUNBATHING, MOONBATHING, AND AIR BATHING

Air bathing is an old-fashioned palliative treatment that simply means exposing the skin to the air in order to let it heal faster. While there aren't scientific studies to prove it, I've seen air bathing, moonbathing, and sunbathing be quite effective. In my experience, the skin usually does better uncovered, whether it be in sunlight, moonlight, or indoors. If indoors, keep the room warm to let your patient's skin breathe as much as possible. In the fifties, people used metal caging to keep bedcovers from touching a patient. You can achieve the same result by rigging up tenting so the skin can have lots of air exposure while still providing discreet covering, even in public settings.

This process is a lot like airing a baby's skin to prevent or treat diaper rash. Going without diapers in palliative conditions helps the person's skin to heal faster. Disposable bed pads make it easy to keep the skin exposed for extended periods of time instead of being confined in diapers.

Exposure to the sun has an added benefit: sunlight stimulates the skin to protect itself. Sunlight makes the skin hardier, kills bacteria with ultraviolet rays,[19] and stimulates the body to make vitamin D, which builds the patient's overall health. Careful exposure during outdoor massage in the afternoon sun can be an enjoyable experience. The

**Figure 4.11.** I watched Brian's pressure sore on his lower back and tailbone become tougher with sun exposure. His caregivers put him out in the sun every day, regulating the exposure carefully to prevent sunburn. His backside healed up faster than any open sore I had seen heal under bandaging.

patient gets a daily dose of vitamin D and warm relaxation—with the added benefit that fungus, infections, wounds, and incisions are able to heal faster.

Most palliative skin disturbances respond well to carefully managed sun exposure. Other less dramatic conditions, such as skin irritation, hypersensitivity, bruising, and deterioration, also respond well to the right touch and to the positive addition of sun and air exposure. I suggest air bathing every day before and after a morning massage, and sunbathing every day with increasing levels of exposure.

Sun therapy, known as heliotherapy, has long been used to help heal a wide variety of conditions—from bone problems like rickets to skin diseases like impetigo or eczema. I used to pore over old medical textbooks for information about physiotherapy, and I remember seeing pictures of sanitariums with balconies set up for heliotherapy. In these sanitariums, the patients were moved around the building according to the angle of the sun at different times of day, and the length of their exposure was monitored. Patients were carefully graduated up the scale of ultraviolet exposure. Through this process, their skin healed up quickly. One of my first patients was getting ultraviolet exposure every day for some postsurgical skin problems.

Her wound healed up in record time and she looked like she had been going to a beauty parlor rather than to physiotherapy.

I caution my patients to use the sun sensibly when assisting their skin in healing itself. The ultraviolet rays stimulate the cells to proliferate, which is what we want in order to close up an opening or tone a weakening area of skin. However, too much sun and they will get a burn. I recommend starting with five minutes of exposure and building it up by a couple of minutes each day. You can cover the person with a sheet and rotationally expose different parts of their body, or you can completely uncover them and expose their entire body in a private location. Be careful not to exceed the appropriate amount of sun exposure and make sure the patient stays hydrated.

A study led by Canadian researchers at the Women's College Hospital and Baycrest Geriatric Health Care System in Toronto, reported that an average of one in four patients across Canadian healthcare settings suffers from a pressure ulcer.[20] I can't overstate the importance of paying attention to pressure areas and pressure sores: they can affect anyone, and can quickly become deadly. For example, the actor who played Superman, Christopher Reeve, who became quadriplegic after a horse riding accident, died of complications from a bedsore.

## JIM ST. JAMES

Jim St. James was Canada's longest-living AIDS patient when I met him in the early 1980s in Toronto. He was a popular speaker and helped me teach others about massaging people with AIDS at my massage school. Jim was predeceased by many of the people he helped: about three hundred people died before him as the AIDS epidemic swept the city. What a shock to see so few at his funeral. What a reality check about the devastation of this disease.

In the five years that we worked together, Jim helped me make *Massaging People with AIDS*, a film to encourage families and friends to massage their loved ones suffering from the disease. Filmed at St. Michael's Hospital in Toronto, our film taught the lessons that Jim and I had learned together over the years. We taught how to massage in hospital chairs and hospital beds. We also showed folks how to massage with surgical gloves on and how to massage those places that seem untouchable— including Jim's ulcerated, bandaged leg.

Jim's healthy leg looked fairly normal to the eye, but it was a whole different experience to the touch. Tough and rigid, it felt more like tree bark than skin. Yet he felt everything: all temperatures, textures, pressures, types of touching. That untouchable leg was fully feeling.

His bad leg had weeping ulcers that had become gangrenous. Jim's ulcers were not on any of the usual pressure sites of the body; they were on the front of the lower leg where the skin is very transparent and thin. His foot was wrapped with white bandaging to the ankle. When massaging Jim, I would put a few pillows under his knees and lower legs to elevate them. Due to his circulatory disfunction, the entire leg was dark blue, distended, and hot to the touch.

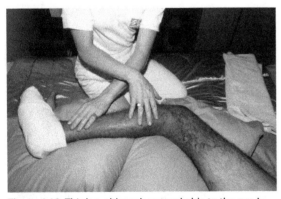

**Figure 4.12.** This leg, although untouchable to the eye, is massageable! Jim responded to the massage on his legs with a big sigh of relaxation. He loved being touched.

I taught people to wear gloves if they were at all nervous about touching him. In those days, there was still a lot of public misinformation about the transmission of HIV. I wanted Jim to have as much hands-on care as possible. His grandmother, for example, was a hands-on type of person, but she was scared to touch him. With surgical gloves, however, she felt more secure and safe.

Jim's ulcers were difficult to control. In one case, what started as a single sore quickly became a raging opening that couldn't be closed. Then gangrene set in. When they decided to try to save his leg instead of amputating, it seemed like a vote for life. He was pleased to avoid surgery and was hell-bent on going out with all of his parts!

I put signs up around Jim's bed: "Touch me"; "Massage my legs, please"; "Massage me anytime." My idea was that this would encourage his friends to get the massage oil and rub him, even if he was asleep. He tended to sleep a lot during this stage of his life, but the massage signs plastered around his bed let the public, his family, his friends, and AIDS supporters know that they could get hands-on with him.

## Swelling

Swelling is often a problem for palliative patients. Overall swelling due to the shutting down of the kidneys is often concentrated in the arms and legs and is often present during the last stage of life. The person may look like they are putting on weight and returning to their former healthy appearance. In fact, they are filling up with fluid that the kidneys are unable to filter and drain from the body. When we have been used to someone looking emaciated for months, this sudden filling out and return to them looking like they did before they were ill or dying brings a sweet sadness because it is an indication of approaching death. Other times, however, the swelling continues, leading to the person looking bloated or disfigured.

### Passive drainage positions

Passive drainage positions are an easy way to combat swelling, both during massage and when the patient is resting. Adjustable medical beds also give the patient wonderful opportunities for postural drainage simply by adjusting the angle of the foot or head of the bed.

A. Prone, lower leg elevation.

B. Prone, full leg elevation.

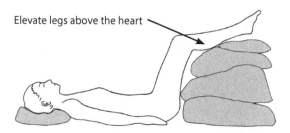

Elevate legs above the heart

C. Supine, legs above the heart. Support legs enough for the lower back to be flat against the surface.

**Figure 4.13.** Lower extremity passive drainage positions.

### Massage for reducing swelling

Through massage I have seen dramatic changes to swollen arms and legs: we can reduce the swelling mechanically, stroke by stroke. I believe it is important for dying people to get their extremities "reduced" with massage on a daily basis. Massaging palliative patients' legs, and especially their ankles and feet, can release skin tension and that terrible associated "skin headache." Massage can allow the whole body to relax until the fluid tension builds up again.

With some people, we are not always able to keep the swelling at bay. As the patient continues to fade, swelling continues to occur. But with others, the swelling does stay away (or is at least kept in control) with frequent effleurage and constant elevation.

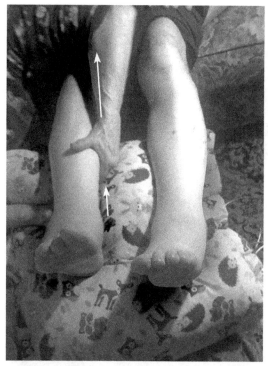

A. Reduce swelling in the lower leg with palmar scooping to the calf up past the knee.

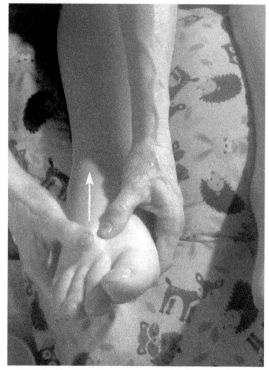

B. Stroke upward with the thumbs to reduce swelling in the foot and ankle.

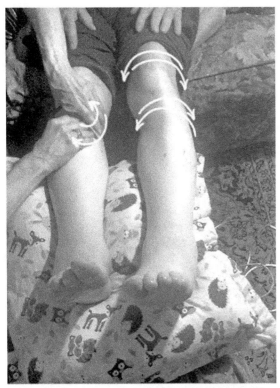

C. Open up circulation to the lower leg by wringing the knee above and below the patella and by scooping the patella with an open, C-shaped hand.

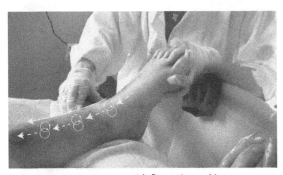

D. Promote venous return with fingertip stroking alternating with fingertip kneading.

**Figure 4.14.** The lower leg is a common spot for swelling and a great spot for massage.

## AUNTIE LIL

My Auntie Lil was feisty and independent in her life and in her death. Yet the gift of touch that I had to offer in her last few days of life helped her to tolerate the inflating of her body as it weakened and as her kidneys backed up. I used massage strokes up her back to smooth out the impressions of the wrinkles from the bedsheets and to help move the fluid that had formed like a mattress underneath her skin. With each stroke, the buildup of fluid was expelled through her skin and the bed became soaked. As the tension in her skin surface lessened, it seemed to cry with tears of relief.

As I massaged her, I quietly cried with the memories of her effect on my life. When I was a teenager, she was my mentor, my favorite aunt. But in the last 10 years of her life, she had become hardened and distant; there was no reaching her. Now, with such pressure of physical discomfort, she allowed me back into her life to help. The release of fluid during that one and only back massage gave her enough relief that she also let me massage her puffy legs. She proudly complimented me and my professional accomplishments when introducing me to her attending physician.

After I finished up and applied dry pads underneath her back, she was pain-free and looking rested and cheerful as she said that she was now going to visit with my dad.

The massage that day to ease her overall skin tension was like waving a magic wand over a snarly creature, making it soft and amenable. It was the last time I saw my aunt alive. I was glad to be able to touch her, comfort her, and give her some emotional stamina to greet her brother and make her last amends.

The most satisfying benefit of circulatory massage is relieving this overall body swelling and dramatically reducing skin tension. In this way you improve a person's well-being up until the end of their life, helping them to spend precious time with their families. The most basic amateur massage can transport the grumpiest of relatives happily into the next dimension.

### Swelling due to breast cancer

Palliative swelling can also come from tumors that cause a logjam in the lymphatic or blood circulation systems. In particular, breast cancer patients who have had diseased lymph nodes extracted often get swelling. Elephantiasis (extreme swelling) may occur in the arm where cancerous lymph nodes have been removed. Patients' arms can be so swollen they look like they are going to burst.

Repeated small, short, and light massage strokes, directed upward towards the trunk of the body, will help to return the arm's lymphatic flow and reduce the swelling in the arm. This swelling can also be treated with ice massage.

OPENING CIRCULATION TO THE ARM

The following five-step technique opens circulation to the arm. It follows the basic arm massage that is part of the full-body massage you learned in Chapter 3, but it has a bit more focus on small, short, light strokes.

1. **Uncork the bottle at the shoulder.** Repeatedly apply palmar kneading to the whole shoulder, with big circles from the front around to the back, stretching the pectoral muscles that run from the breast bone to the armpit as you push away from yourself to the top of the shoulder, then to the armpit and back up and around. I use small fingertip kneading and single-handed thumb kneading around the shoulder to get the whole area stimulated. This opens up circulation to allow the swelling from the arm to travel into the trunk of the body where the kidneys can expel the buildup of lymphatic fluid.

2. **Massage from the top of the arm to the elbow.** Start massaging the top of the arm in the shoulder area using small, more focused strokes like thumb kneading (single-handed and alternate) and fingertip kneading. Be slow and meticulous.

Work down the arm towards the elbow with short strokes in a continuous upward direction of pressure. Massage the inside and outside (biceps and triceps) of the upper arm with lots

of thumb work and effleurage. This works the swelling up to the open waters of the shoulder, where your massage has already removed congestion.

3. **Uncork the bottle at the elbow.** Now bend the arm and work all around the elbow as though you are polishing it. Cup your hand to the shape of the elbow and wrap your palm around it. Repeat the same "uncorking the bottle" principle you used on the shoulder at the elbow joint so the swelling and congestion in the lower arm can travel up toward the trunk of the body. The elbow is a bit like a dam on a river; we need to open it up so the flow can go through and move upwards with the venous return, those little veins that take deoxygenated blood back up to the heart and lungs to be replenished with oxygen.

4. **Massage down the forearm.** Work with small, repeated upward strokes, starting closest to the edge of the swelling in the elbow. Work down the forearm using the same massage strokes that we applied to the upper arm. Always keep the pressure of the strokes directed towards the heart. I use lots of alternate thumb kneading along the front and back of the forearm.

5. **Massage the hand.** Massage the hand and carefully attend to each finger one at a time. Pretend each finger is an extremity of its own. Starting where the finger attaches to the hand, move toward the tips of the fingers, directing each tiny massage stroke towards the heart. Use focused, small massage strokes. Then corkscrew each finger, twisting toward the nearest side of the hand (with the middle finger going either or both ways). Include lots of firm thumb kneading and any other intuitive massage movements to work the fingers, hand, and wrist.

## Bluing

The circulatory changes in the final stages of life are pretty predictable. Most people experience a blue discoloration—also called cyanosis—that starts at their fingertips and toes. Often this can go undetected if the dying person is covered up. The progression is not always predictable; for example, a person's legs can go blue overnight, while the arms and upper body still look pink.

Sometimes, cyanosis, doesn't appear at all. In some cases, a person's breathing quits before their circulation. For example, my mom never showed any bluing of her body anywhere. Instead, her departure signs were in her altered breathing patterns.

When "bluing," or cyanosis, does occur, however, it is not going away; the person is going away. It is an accurate indication that they are close to dying that day or within the next couple of days. My patient and friend Cec turned blue from his toes to his thighs by the time he passed away. Cec's legs at his death were very dark blue, perhaps the darkest shades of blue that I had ever seen. This change in body color is the result of a lack of oxygen to the blood. This same lack of oxygen works as a barometer for the shutdown of the rest of the body's functions. When the circulatory system shuts down, the nervous system shuts off the switch and breathing quits.

However, the blueness does not mean that you should stop massaging. Regular massage routines for the legs and arms are useful in end stage, because we still don't know if the person's death will come in minutes, hours, or days. As we massaged Cec on the day of his death, his bluing increased along with the coldness of his extremities. His nose was cold to the touch and his face became white and ashen. Before he finished breathing, it seemed like no more oxygen was being pumped into his blood at all, as he was rapidly turning from pink to purple. Because we were right beside him, we registered his dramatic change in temperature. He was now cool all over, except for the arm that his wife, Joni, was stroking. She had stroked this arm continuously for the last hours of his life while singing to him. This one arm was the only pink part left.

## Joint Movement

When Cec died, Joni noticed that the arm she was stroking was warm for more than an hour afterwards, and it remained pink and moveable, demonstrating the power of massage to increase joint movement. Massage keeps the joints of dying people more supple and loose, making them easier to wash and move. Their joints will not be fixed in place if they have been massaged in the last 24 hours.

During the massage routine, move the legs and arms through their full range of motion (ROM). Just move the limbs like the person would have done when they were stronger. Either of the following techniques is beneficial:

- **Active assisted ROM,** in which the dying person helps you move their limbs
- **Passive ROM,** in which the dying person does not assist in moving their limbs, and the therapist alone moves the joints through their possible ranges

Even if the limbs are moved by other people, the movements will bring fresh blood into sleepy extremities and move stagnant circulation back into the trunk of the body. Concentrate on movements of the hip, knee, ankle, shoulder, and elbow. These movements will help keep the patient mobile and independent. It will also elicit reflex responses in the digestive system and the respiratory system, providing better bowel movement and breathing until the last breath. Massaging before and after moving the joints will help the dying person maintain this mobility.

---

Massage can affect the whole body. The process of moving the patient's blood and lymphatic fluid around as though the person were still able to walk, swim, or run can greatly enhance a patient's comfort and well-being at the end of life. With just 20 minutes a day, we can help prevent pressure sores and swelling, give comfort, and perhaps even extend life.

## Online Classroom

Visit brusheducation.ca/dying-in-good-hands
to watch these videos:

Pressure sites

Pressure sores and sheepskin

Head wedging – pressure sore preventative

Pressure site massage – ischial tuberosities

Pressure site massage – occipital
protuberance (scalp)

Pressure site massage – olecranon process
(elbow)

Pressure site massage – coccyx (tailbone)

Pressure site massage – ear (bilateral)

Ulcerations in the legs

Massage for reducing swelling – legs

Opening circulation to the arm

Peripheral cyanosis – bluing

# Bill

"The heart that has truly loved, never forgets."

– Thomas Moore

In 1980, a phone call from Nelson to my home in Toronto woke me. My dad, Bill, was hospitalized. He had suffered a stroke.

He was pronounced to be suffering from arteriosclerosis, a vascular disease. He was encouraged to change his diet and lifestyle. To give him support, I changed my diet along with him and lost 10 pounds.

The next hospitalization occurred about a year later. This time, it was more serious—he was diagnosed with cancer of the bladder. I arrived in Nelson the day of my dad's surgery.

Out of surgery, my father had an artificial bladder attached to him. He was delirious and not himself. I massaged him to help him stay in the moment, in the room. One night when I left the hospital, I got a call around midnight to come back. My dad had pulled out all his tubes and was calling my name. As I ran into his hospital room, the crowd around his bed parted like the great sea, their faces looking toward me with pure relief. My dad was wide-eyed, terrified, and in a straightjacket to keep him from pulling out his tubes again. He was determined to get out of the hospital.

"Chris, get me out of here," he said.

I placed a hand on his chest and said, "Dad, I'm here. You are okay. You are in good hands. These people have saved your life!"

The staff left us alone. Initially he pressed against his restraints, trying hard to get out of the bed. He was a big man of big strength. His weakness of the past days had been replaced by the return of his Herculean power. He was going somewhere, but going nowhere at the same time. Gradually he calmed down; I had finally rubbed him into submission. As long as my hand was on his chest he could breathe easily. When I took my hand away, he would wake up and start to struggle against his restraints. Around four in the morning, he went to sleep. I had massaged his extremities and worked my way under his back in his tied-down apparatus. He was snoring loudly; the staff, by then, were my best friends. In the morning I realized I had not even taken my coat off from the night before.

For the next few days, he lingered near death. I found this out accidentally when one of the night nurses answered my call about my dad's lack of urinary output. The nurse said that my dad's kidneys were failing. No one had mentioned death. I kept massaging him and slept in brief spurts in a chair next to his bed.

Despite his prognosis, my dad survived his cancer, and a month later I brought him home to his wife, my stepmom Valerie. I then taught her everything I knew about how to cope with the crisis hands-on. She had a real interest in learning massage. She was great with her hands and sacrificed her long fingernails to work the areas that required therapeutic pressure and focus. We worked together on clearing my dad's lungs and improving his circulation. He returned to health, but our hands-on teamwork would be needed again, years later.

---

The first winter I spent back home in Nelson after living away, several years after my dad's stroke and cancer survival, he broke his hip outside the city medical clinic. Although his surgery was the very next day, his heel broke down within 24 hours of hospitalization, resulting in painful pressure sores.

In my previous experience with my dad in hospitals, he'd never had a skin breakdown. This time his heels opened up and looked raw. I asked my friends to help me massage him to prevent further damage to any bony protuberance. Immediately, we put his feet on sheepskin and massaged his extremities around the clock. We managed to prevent skin breakdown in the other heel, despite his confinement to one position in bed for an entire week in order for him to stay in traction for his broken hip. I used my well-tested techniques for massaging underneath his back and hips since he could not be turned. My dad was a redhead and had very fair skin, which made it easy to monitor blood flow. We learned that, just by looking for redness, we could see where massage was needed to prevent pressure sores and skin breakdown. I made sure that we massaged every pressure site on his body a number of times a day until he was able to be turned. However, in his seven days of traction, there was one hidden pressure site that I missed: the back of his head. He developed a bald patch here as a result.

Once he was out of traction, we needed to turn my dad frequently, about every two hours, from side to side as his hips became reddened at the head of the femur. Of all patients I have ever treated, he was one of the most sensitive to skin breakdown. By the time he left the hospital, we had sheepskin under his entire body. Keeping his skin intact was a major accomplishment. I was glad that I was able to do for him what I had been successful at doing for others.

Shortly after returning home, Dad became very ill and again his kidneys collapsed. This time he was seriously failing. He was not allowed to move or turn, a perfect set-up for pneumonia. We slid sheepskin underneath him, and I perfected my neutral spine back massage, with him lying faceup so the traction for his hip was lined up the right way. Although he was very congested, our massages to clear his lungs helped him to avoid pneumonia.

The skin on my dad's back was in immediate danger of breaking down, just like his heels had done. I levered my hands underneath him and massaged him from one end to the other, pushing down with the back of my hand on the sheepskin. As I leaned over with my elbows on the bed, my hands under his back, my posture was a lot like praying at the bedside. I asked any other visitor who was present to join me on his opposite side and we would tandem massage up and down his back. We managed to keep his skin healthy by simply rubbing it.

Although my dad's hip did heal, his condition continued to deteriorate. He was 77 and he was heading down a steep slope. He slept more and needed constant attention. Valerie and I started taking shifts. If she was away for some reason, I slept over.

When my dad fell out of bed one night, I called the ambulance to have them help me get him back into bed. He was permanently unsteady on his feet and needed a wheelchair at all times. One night when I was looking after him, he fell again. He had been looking to "have a dram," as he said—hoping to get to the kitchen and have a drink without anyone knowing. My daughter, Crystal, who was 14 at the time, helped me roll him onto a blanket and drag him into his bedroom, but we could not get him into bed. We again called the ambulance and waited on the floor, curled up around him until they arrived.

That weekend, my dad became incontinent. Now in diapers, we realized that he was too weak to go anywhere. But he knew that Christmas was coming and he wanted to buy his Christmas gifts in person. His last outing was to the jewelry store to buy Valerie a ring and to buy his granddaughter a crystal sculpture. He became bedridden at the end of that day.

At Christmas, I brought Dad a model sailboat that his sea captain uncle had given him years ago. He smiled, although he barely recognized it. We set it up so it was in full view about five feet away from Dad's bed. He was now permanently on his side, with a donut-shaped cushion under him, only turning for me to massage the redness out of the pressure site of his hip bone.

We celebrated Christmas with an uneasy tension. Valerie was talking about moving a hospital bed into the living room so he could see out the window. She was talking as though he had a disability, not a death sentence, but I felt Dad was merely days or hours away from dying.

Around the clock we played bagpipe music and Scottish ballads. I had massaged John McDermott, a visiting performer at our local theatre, because he was one of my dad's and my favorite singers. John had lost his own father a couple of months before and gave me 10 albums of his music to play for my dad. At the sound of the first musical note, the voice and passion of McDermott's music brought a peace to the household!

Over the next few days, Dad grew increasingly itchy—itchy all over, so that I had to put socks on his hands to keep him from scratching himself raw as he slept. His skin was reacting to the toxicity of his kidneys slowing down. The lack of urinary output meant that his life-giving systems were turning off. Itchiness, like bluing, is a classic end-stage symptom. I knew that. What I wasn't familiar with was the symbiotic relationship between my dad's skin reactions and my own. When he itched, I itched.

When a rash started on my stomach. I used the same Chinese ointments that I was using on my dad, but nothing seemed to help. I resorted to oatmeal baths and slathering calamine over my entire abdomen. But despite my efforts, the rash spread and I still itched. Valerie placed cold tea compresses on my tummy as I lay beside my dad.

It was 7 a.m. on New Year's Eve when, after massaging my dad, I turned back the cover to reveal his legs. His toes were turning blue. Midnight was gently coming towards us—my dad's favorite time to celebrate. He used to get into trouble with the police wherever he lived for ringing—or, rather, piping—in the New Year on his bagpipes at midnight and celebrating Hogmanay.

As the day wore on, my dad's color continued to change. The blueness traveled up from his feet to his legs, from his hands up his arms. We kept massaging him and keeping him warm with hot-water bottles and heating pads.

After supper Valerie and I both massaged him. His extremities were blue all the way up to his trunk. By 10 o'clock that evening, the only place that was warm was right around his heart. His cheeks were cool and he looked very relaxed. Valerie and I were on either side, listening to CBC radio announcing midnight around the world. Dad tried to talk.

We turned down the radio. I heard him say "M'am."

"Valerie," I said, "Dad said 'M'am.'"

"That's the pet word he used for his mother," she told me.

I hadn't known this, but Valerie told me that it was the secret code that my dad and his mom shared. He had always called her "M'am" as an endearment when he spoke to her directly.

Now, on his deathbed, my dad was being greeted by his mother; she was with us, she was with him. *M'am*: what a comforting word.

Valerie and I talked about Dad's family. I called his sister, Flo, and told her that my dad was dying. I told her about "M'am," and she, too, was comforted.

His breathing became uneven, ragged, just before midnight. Valerie told my dad she loved him. He was her one and only husband. We heard him say, "And I you."

And with those final words, he left us.

He died at the stroke of midnight. With his last breath, my itching stopped, a gentle but firm disconnect. He brought in the new year with John McDermott singing and bagpipes playing in the background, passing over the threshold on Hogmanay with perfect timing. I left Valerie curled up around my dad and covered them both with a quilt.

I felt the largeness of time, how our lives are part of a vast undertaking—the human species, with all its divisions and subdivisions and challenges and errors and accomplishments. My dad's deep Scottish roots in the comfort of continuity of the Sutherland clan bestowed the clan motto *sans peur*, meaning "without fear," upon this fitting finale.

Bill with my daughter, Crystal, on his knee.

# 5

# Respiratory Massage

This chapter is dedicated to Brian Carpendale and Mary Coletti, whose indomitable spirits and inspiring lives will make a difference in the world of palliative care for ALS patients.

Of all the impending symptoms of death, the gradual slowing and final shutting down of the respiration system is the most important. We can live without our digestive system functioning or without eating. It won't kill us—at least not right away. We can live quite a while, too, with our circulatory system a mess, or with pressure sores or skin breakdown. But we cannot live without breathing. Without breath, we are dead.

This chapter will show how respiratory massage is integral to the care of the dying. I will explore a variety of massage techniques to deliver the best respiratory massages to your patients and loved ones. I will also show you how to clear a person's lungs using massage, how to perform postural drainage and chest compressions, as well as how to encourage productive coughing.

## Why Do Respiratory Massage?

Palliative respiratory massage has one primary purpose: to help those who are dying breathe comfortably right to their last breath.

Everyone has different symptoms with terminal respiratory illnesses. Some have shortness of breath; others have severe spasms of the upper or lower respiratory muscles; still others have atrophy of the muscles and no muscle tone to allow respiratory functioning. These symptoms all respond well to massages that keep the lungs clear and the breathing comfortable.

As a dying person slows down physically, their breathing is compromised because it is no longer being stimulated by gravity and activity. When someone is standing, gravitational forces work to excite the lungs and diaphragm. When someone is active—especially when they move their arms above their head—their chest gets the pumping action it needs to maintain its health. Swimmers have great lung capacity because they put their shoulders into rotations, flexions, and full extensions. Gymnasts and runners develop their breathing capacity with exercise that pumps the heart fast enough to speed up their breathing. Deeper breaths make healthier lungs.

But deep, oxygen-rich breathing is not the breath of the dying, whose breaths become shallower. When someone lies down, their respiratory system also automatically quiets, slowing down the action of the diaphragm so it does not have to work as hard. Horizontal living compromises our breathing, just as vertical living challenges our heart to pump faster.

### Clearing lungs

Chronic smokers have a morning smoker's cough simply because, when they stand up, their diaphragm muscle wakes up and tries to get exudate buildup out of the lungs. The sticky stuff in a smoker's lungs is an irritant that the body is always trying to clear. A healthy body's natural reflexes do a great job of clearing the lungs. Just the act of standing and moving around is enough to activate the lungs' natural clearing action.

But when the body slows down, the diaphragm muscle gets lazy. It does not use the same strong action to kick the junk out. The diaphragm may also be affected by the medications the patient takes to be more comfortable: it may be artificially relaxed and not acting in its usual, lifesaving way, instead letting fluid accumulate in the lungs.

When people are dying, we can massage to help the lungs and diaphragm do their work. We can massage and move the shoulders, and we can mobilize the diaphragm to get the lungs working to lose their congestion. Most dying people are prone to lung congestion and pneumonia. By keeping the lungs clear and pneumonia at bay, the dying person can have better oxygen levels and greater gaseous exchange.

Preventing pneumonia is one of the most important goals of respiratory massage; this will help the dying person's family avoid panicking over respiratory distress, and can help people who want to die at home stay at home, rather than being moved to the hospital. Mary Coletti, an ALS patient, used oxygen at home for the last weeks of her life, spending only the final 48 hours in the hospital. Her family, best friend, and massage team gave her continual respiratory massages, both at home and in the hospital, right up until her last breath. She breathed easier, without panic, because of this hands-on care.

Respiratory massage also helps increase the ciliary action of the lung walls. Tiny hairs called cilia line our respiratory system, helping to roll congestion up and out of our lungs. When we are immobile, weak, and debilitated, these walls dry up and the hairs do not wave as easily. Massage brings blood to the area, which helps the hairs become more flexible as they are fed a diet of rich blood. Mechanically working the chest also stimulates the ciliary action that will move loosened exudate up and into the mouth to be spit out.

Massage helps dying patients avoid the added discomfort of ineffective coughing in which they strain their diaphragm and pull at their ribs to fight to clear their lungs. Massage helps loosen the exudate from the lung wall. The muscles recover instead of spasming from all the continuous, ineffective coughing. The prevention of muscle spasticity (continuous contraction) and the increase of lung elasticity is critical when dealing with the growing respiratory challenges of the dying.

### Preventing panic

Anyone who has ever choked on food or had anaphylactic response, an asthma attack, whooping cough, a respiratory impairment from chemical poisoning, an anxiety attack, a broken nose, or a punctured lung knows first-hand the panic of not being able to breathe. Those dying of ALS, lung cancer, upper respiratory obstructions, or head-and-neck tumors can experience breathing problems that make this panic an everyday reality. The body fights for oxygen until the end, employing the muscles of respiration to help. As the patient's lungs struggle, the nostrils flare and try to gather air into the lungs in a primal reflex.

But simply being touched physically changes things in the body. The nervous system is interrupted as the brain tries to sense the new information that the touch is bringing. Relaxation replaces panic and contracted muscles. And relaxation helps you to breathe more easily. A comforting hand on the shoulder lifts the human spirit; a comforting massage to the shoulders can help lift and ease difficult breathing.

### Helping the caregiver

There is another benefit to being hands-on for breathing difficulties: it calms the caregiver. The helplessness a caregiver feels when a loved one is having difficulty breathing can also lead to anxiety and panic.

It is natural to feel fear when someone cannot breathe: it means, after all, that they might die. Having our hands on the person with breathing difficulties can ease their discomfort as well as our own natural fears about losing our friends, patients, or loved ones. The opportunity to help with a person's end-of-life breathing is a gift. It helps dissolve our own fears by putting the other person's fear in the foreground. It is often easier for us to be brave for others, and this can help us access that bravery for ourselves at the same time.

## When to Do Respiratory Massage

Respiratory massage can be done at both critical moments and more relaxed ones. Adapt to your patient's daily ups and downs. Some days, people can tolerate a lot of respiratory work—some people even sleep through the treatment. Other days, their tolerance may be lower, even when they can barely breathe.

Those with terminal lung diseases such as cancer, other terminal cancers, or more systemic illnesses such as ALS or MS will all benefit from respiratory massage in the early stages of their disease. This type of massage will help them preserve their health and keep them from dying prematurely of pneumonia. These people can get respiratory massage every day as part of their full-body massage routine.

In the more acute and critical end stage of their illness, people can get respiratory massage more often—up to 10 times a day, if it makes each breath more breathable!

### Massage for sleep

If a patient is still following a normal pattern of sleeping more at night than during the day, doing a massage in the evening that emphasizes the respiratory system is a good way to induce the best sleep. In these cases, I am particularly picky with my students about not talking or chatting with the patient and instead letting them sink into slumber.

Help the patient clear their lungs and relax before a long period of rest. The more you can promote the natural sleeping pattern through massage, the more restorative the sleep will be.

Often, friends and family will be sleeping in the same room as their dying loved one. In these close quarters, the sound of the dying person's breaths becomes a natural alert to changes in the person's respiration. Sometimes, as tumors grow, they push on the lungs, throat, or upper sinuses, causing additional upper respiratory problems to appear. It is therefore always helpful to be aware of changes in the person's breathing and respond with massage to whatever part of their respiratory system needs attention. For example, I massaged my patient Cec's diaphragm in the middle of the night while he slept to sooth his constant hiccups, allowing him a more restful sleep.

### Massage in the morning

Respiratory massage first thing in the morning helps mobilize the lungs and aids with an early-morning clearing cough (like the smoker's cough). Animals stretch when they are waking, mobilizing the body and rousing all of the systems. Think of your morning respiratory massage as that cat-like stretch. Stretching out the shoulders and getting a large breath helps get the ciliary action of the lung walls started. Morning massage often gets the most expectoration out of the lungs because the patient has been quiet during the night.

## Treatment Approach

I use a five-part combination of respiratory massage techniques to help palliative or paralyzed patients breathe more comfortably:

1. Postural drainage
2. Shoulder movements
3. Massage (primarily to the diaphragm and the intercostal muscles)
4. Chest compressions
5. Productive coughing

These five parts are meant to be adapted to the strengths or weaknesses of the patient and the progression of their condition. Self-massage, especially in the early stages, when the patient still has strength, can also be an important component of treatment.

We'll look first at techniques for postural drainage and shoulder movements. Then we'll move to the types of massage strokes best suited for respiration, and finally to chest compressions and productive coughing.

## Postural Drainage

Postural drainage is using body positioning and gravity to passively drain the lungs of fluid buildup. Understanding the anatomy of the lungs can help you decide which positions and techniques to use.

Anatomically, the lungs are divided into three lobes: the upper, middle, and lower lobes. The upper lobes are right behind the top ribs and clavicle. The middle lobe is around mid-chest, and the lower lobes are above the waist. The diaphragm is a muscle that contracts when you breathe in, creating a vacuum in the lungs that allows them to take in air. When you breathe out, the diaphragm relaxes, pushing air out of the lungs.

The place where we have the most trouble with congestion is where gravity has the most effect: in the lower lobes. This is because the opening to the lungs is in the middle lobe, between the upper and lower. We pretty much have to be tipped upside down to get stuff out of our lower lungs, where congestion collects and infections can most easily start.

Lying on one's side, turning every few hours, sitting up in different angles, lying down, standing when possible—all of these positions and changes help the lungs get rid of congestion. In addition, the postural drainage positions I describe here can be used both during your respiratory massage routines and during rest periods. If the person has a weak cough with little diaphragm strength, postural drainage is particularly important.

The postural drainage positions should be held for at least a half hour, but longer is better. Use pillows or tilt the bed to support the various postures. Using postural drainage in concert with massage and productive coughing techniques (discussed later in this chapter) is an effective way to help your patient breathe better.

### Upper lobe drainage postures

Have the patient sit upright, with pillows in front or behind.

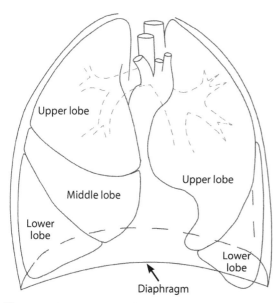

**Figure 5.1.** Basic structure of the lungs.

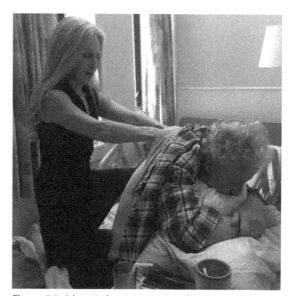

**Figure 5.2.** A hospital patient can lean forward on their eating table to help drain the back of the upper lobes.

- Leaning the patient forward helps drain the back, posterior aspect of the upper lobes.
- Leaning the patient backward helps drain the front, anterior aspect of the upper lobes.

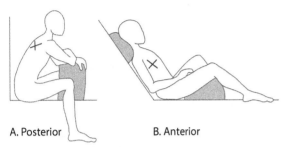

A. Posterior          B. Anterior

**Figure 5.3.** Upper lobe drainage.

### Middle lobe drainage postures

Have the patient lie down and use pillows to support one of the following postures:

- Patient rolled slightly forward.
- Patient rolled slightly backward.

A. Posterior

B. Anterior

**Figure 5.4.** Middle lobe drainage positions.

### Lower lobe drainage posture

Elevate the hips with pillows or jackknife the hospital bed for passive drainage.

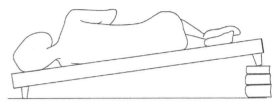

**Figure 5.5.** Use passive postural drainage of the lower lobes during rest or sleep.

- **Prone:** Facedown, head turned to the side, hips higher than head
- **Supine:** Faceup, hips higher than head
- **Side-lying:** Hips arched over pillows, head lower than hips, change side halfway through

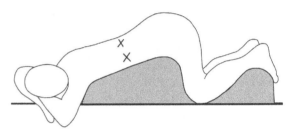

**Figure 5.6.** Prone lower lobe drainage position.

**Figure 5.7.** Supine lower lobe drainage position.

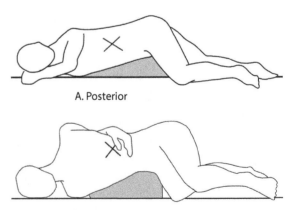

A. Posterior

B. Anterior

**Figure 5.8.** Side-lying lower lobe drainage. Lean patient forward to drain the posterior and back to drain the anterior.

## Shoulder Movements

Simply getting the body vertical is exciting to the lungs. But if your patient cannot get vertical, you can get the lungs working using upper body movements. Even if the patient is passive, the action of pumping the arms in turn pumps the lungs and increases lung capacity. Rotate the arms in both directions starting with just the shoulders, then the elbow, then the whole arm. This will pump oxygen into the system and mechanically help the muscles rid the lungs of sludge by stirring it up.

People who can sit up in bed can do arm rotations with or without help. This is a good warm-up to productive coughing, often eliciting a cough reflex right away. Moving the arms as if doing a swimmer's backstroke is an especially effective shoulder rotation. In general, replicating any swimming movements on dry land will help mobilize the lungs and get things moving.

Mobilizing the person's shoulders first thing in the morning is a good addition to a morning massage. The shoulders should be massaged first to loosen the muscles. Then mobilize and rotate the arms and shoulders.

## Key Respiratory Massage Treatments

Respiratory massage can be tailored to your patient's needs. The strokes below are divided into three regions of the body: the upper respiratory system (head and neck), the lower respiratory system (thorax, the part of the body between the neck and the abdomen), and the abdomen. Incorporate these strokes into your full-body massage as needed.

### Upper respiratory (head and neck)

Patients with impaired respiration are usually best massaged in an upright position. Seat them in an upper-lobe drainage position with the head of the bed tilted up. You can also seat them in a wheelchair or recliner.

### FACE, SCALP, AND SINUS MASSAGE

Massage the face and scalp to open up your patient's breathing and increase their general relaxation. Do a general face and scalp massage from the full-body massage routine described in Chapter 3, with particular attention to the following strokes:

- Ear rotations and pressure points
- Ear attachment kneading
- Fingertip kneading on the jaw and temples
- Claw-like fingertip kneading to the entire scalp

> **See a full description of the face and scalp massage on pages 83 to 87.**

Add in the following strokes to further ease upper respiratory congestion:

1. **Orbital ridge and sinus thumb stroking.** Start with the thumbs on the inner aspect of the eyebrows nearest the nose. With slow, steady pressure on each upper orbital ridge, move along the eyebrows from the nose toward

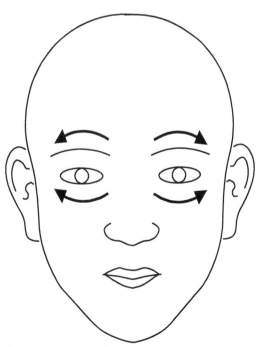

**Figure 5.9.** With your thumbs, stroke slowly and steadily along the orbital ridges above and below the eyes.

the temples—midline to lateral. Repeat three times. Do the same to the lower orbital ridge below the eyes.

2. **Working pressure points.** To work a pressure point, just press on the spot and have the patient breathe deeply. A pressure point will usually feel tender for the patient. Deep breathing will increase the patient's oxygen level until the tenderness dissipates and, presto, breathing will open up too. There are respiration-related pressure points on the face under the cheekbones and at the side of the nose where it attaches to the face. There are also a series of pressure points around the orbit of the eye, with the most sensitive being the supraorbital foramen and the infraorbital foramen. Figure 5.10 shows a map of these pressure points.

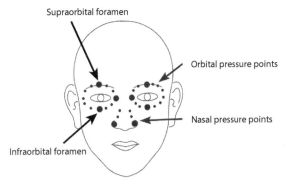

Figure 5.10. Sinus pressure points.

3. **Nasal root shaking and laryngeal shaking.** For nasal root shaking, use the thumb and pointer finger along the base of the nose where it attaches to the face. Laryngeal shaking is done with a gentle cupping grip on the front of the neck. With a gentle grip, shake your hand back and forth. See Figure 5.11 for the hand position of each.

4. **Kneading to neck.** Massage the front and back of the neck with single-handed thumb kneading, alternate thumb kneading, alternate digital thumb compression, and whole-handed scooping to the entire back of the neck, alternating between hands.

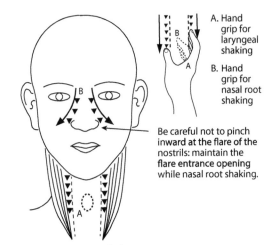

A. Hand grip for laryngeal shaking

B. Hand grip for nasal root shaking

Be careful not to pinch inward at the flare of the nostrils: maintain the flare entrance opening while nasal root shaking.

Figure 5.11. Respiratory shaking.

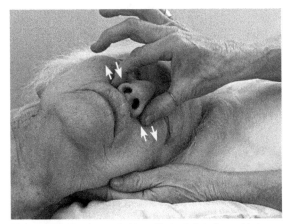

Figure 5.12. Nasal root shaking. Shake lightly from side to side while pressing into the face. Run the shaking up and down the nose from the eyes back to the flare of the nostrils.

Figure 5.13. If the person is seated, support their head with one hand on their forehead while you massage the back of their neck.

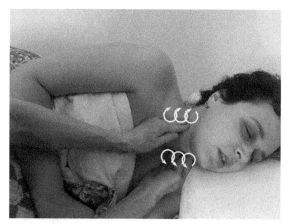

**Figure 5.14.** Bilateral fingertip kneading will help reduce tension in the throat, especially if someone is coughing a lot.

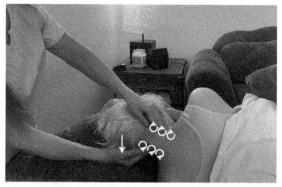

**Figure 5.15.** In side-lying position, support the head with one hand and use the other to knead the neck with your fingertips.

## Lower respiratory (thoracic)

For respiratory problems, there are three key parts of the thorax to target with massage: the chest, the diaphragm, and the intercostal rib muscles. You can supplement the massage for the back and shoulder girdle (front and back) described in the full-body massage routine in Chapter 3 with some of the strokes that follow. The nerve supply for the lungs and diaphragm comes from the thoracic spine, so be thorough when alternate thumb kneading, working close to the spine on the erector spinae. The lower back is also an important place for stimulating the diaphragm; the nerves that influence the diaphragm are located directly behind the muscle itself, around the mid to lower back.

See a full description of the shoulder girdle massage on page 63 and the back massage on pages 76 to 82.

CHEST AND UPPER BACK

1. **Stretching and kneading to chest.** Do the basic full-body massage to the front and back shoulder girdle, but add in extra stretching strokes to open the chest, as shown in the images that follow.

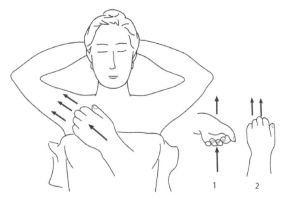

**Figure 5.16.** Stretch the pectoral muscles with the backs of your fingers by rolling your fingers across the muscles.

**Figure 5.17.** Do some overhanded palmar stretching, pushing away from the pectoral attachment at the sternum (chest bone) toward the shoulder. Alternate hands.

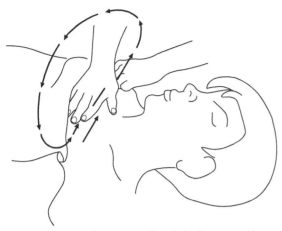

**Figure 5.18.** Now do some overhanded palmar stretching, pulling toward yourself from the patient's sternum to the shoulder.

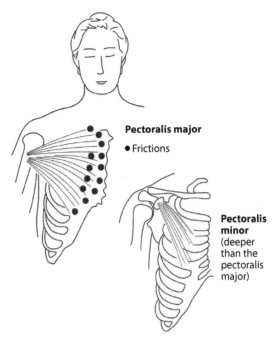

**Figure 5.20.** Pressure points along the pectoral muscles.

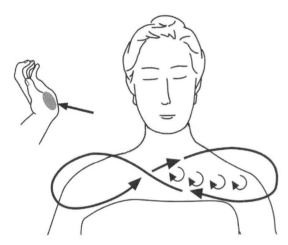

**Figure 5.19.** To finish, use your palms to do a figure eight across the chest. Use the thenar eminence at the base of the thumb to knead circles around this path. This can also be used as the first stretch of this routine.

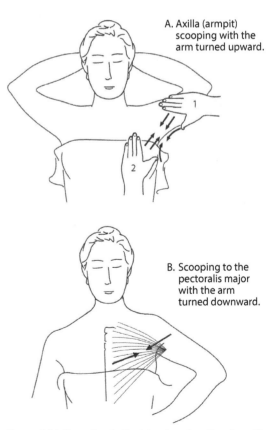

**Figure 5.21.** Scooping to the lateral pectoral border with alternating hands.

2. **Frictioning to pressure points.** Use your thumbs, fingertips, or palms to apply friction to pressure points along the pectorals. (Figure 5.20)

3. **Stretching and kneading to the chest.** Repeat the palmar stretching and kneading done in step 1.

4. **Scooping to the pectoral muscles.** (Figure 5.21)

Remember to ask for feedback about the pressure of your touch and about your patient's position and general comfort. Establish a cooperative approach for the best results.

5. **Gentle pressure points on the back.** After warming up the shoulders with some kneading or trapezius scooping, do some gentle pressure release to points on the back.

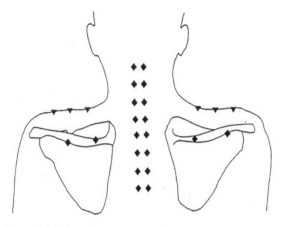

**Figure 5.22.** Seated or prone gentle pressure release points on the back.

6. **Bilateral lifting and palmar kneading.**

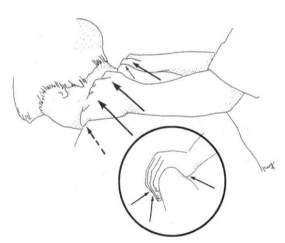

**Figure 5.23.** Lifting bilaterally and then palmar kneading bilaterally, prone, seated or side lying (with deep breathing).

DIAPHRAGM

The big, dome-shaped diaphragm muscle is the pump for respiratory functioning. This is important to massage as this muscle tends to go into spasm with a patient's constant coughing. It needs massage directly from the front of the body along the angle of the bottom of the ribs and then around to the attachments at the mid- to lower back. This muscle is a focus for our respiratory work in all palliative massage, whether the person is seated, or side-lying, supine, or prone.

Diaphragm massage is easiest when the patient is lying faceup with pillows under the knees to make the abdomen soft. If the patient has drainage tubes for the liver and lungs, move these out of the way of your work.

1. **Thumb stroking to the costal angle.** Place your thumbs at the center of the diaphragm where it attaches at the base of the breastbone (at the xiphoid process).

   With steady pressure around the bottom curve of the ribs, move your thumbs slowly down the costal angle, stretching the diaphragm muscle along the lower edge of the rib cage from the front of the body around to the sides. Move all the way to the attachments of the ribs at the back.

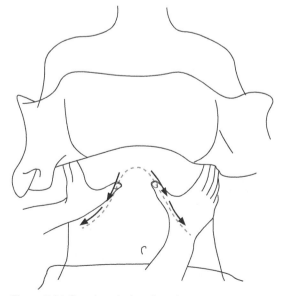

**Figure 5.24.** Costal angle thumb stroking.

2. **Fingertip kneading to the costal angle.** Knead all along the angle of the ribs with your fingertips. Knead up one side and down the other and then reverse. This loosens the diaphragm attachments at the costal angle.

**Figure 5.25.** Fingertip kneading along the edge of the costal border. Your fingers should roll over the edge of the costal angle (bottom rib) to get the diaphragm attachments.

3. **Single-handed thumb stroking.** This is a good stroke to do after the fingertip kneading; try alternating between the two strokes. Keep your thumbs up and under the ribs to stretch and relieve the diaphragm. Stroke, knead, stroke, knead, and repeat!

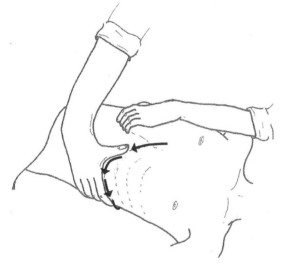

**Figure 5.26.** Costal angle thumb st    retching.

## "RIB RAKING" THE INTERCOSTAL RIB MUSCLES

The intercostal rib muscles are another important focus of respiratory massage: breathing occurs with the action of these tight little muscles. Each rib has two sets of intercostal muscles designed to help lift and depress the ribs with each breath. One set lifts for the breath into the lungs, and the other set depresses to push air out. These intercostal muscles work with the diaphragm and heart to keep us breathing. To massage the intercostals on some parts of the body, you will need to massage through other layers of muscles, such as the pectoralis minor and serratus anterior muscles.

Rib raking is the most effective respiratory massage stroke. Your fingers groove in between the ribs to stretch the tiny, tough intercostal muscles, making them more elastic and helping them cope with their coughing job. Rib raking can ease a patient's breathing in a minute (or less)!

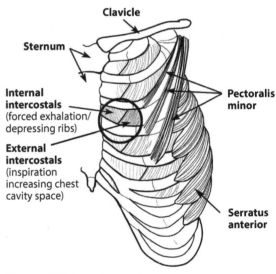

**Figure 5.27.** Intercostal muscles.

### INTERCOSTAL RIB RAKING MASSAGE ROUTINE

Standing at the side of the bed, reach across to the far side of the patient at the mid to lower lobe level. Try to reach as far as you can, if possible to the patient's spine where the ribs attach.

With fingertips in a claw-like position, pull your hand towards the center of the patient's body, grooving your fingers into the gaps between the ribs as you do. The stroke ends at the spot where the ribs disappear into the sternum or the attaching costal angle of the rib cage.

As soon as your hand is free from the back and sliding around front, slip your other hand into the starting position, once again reaching as far as you can around the back.

Alternate pulling each hand towards yourself, hand over hand. Work up and down one side, then switch to the other.

If the patient is female, move around the breasts, lifting the breast out of the way of rib-raking

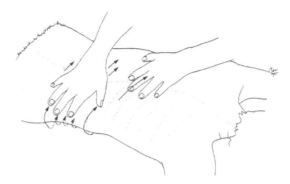

**Figure 5.30.** Overhanded rib raking. One hand follows the other repeatedly.

**Figure 5.31.** Reinforced rib raking.

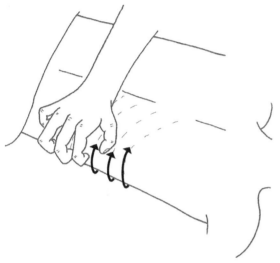

**Figure 5.28.** For all styles of rib-raking, use a claw-like hand, fit your fingers between the ribs, and pull to help stretch the intercostal muscles.

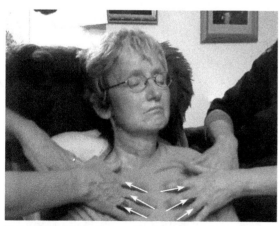

**Figure 5.29.** Bilateral upper rib raking. Press down at the start with your fingertips and move out firmly across the upper chest, grooving your fingers in between the upper ribs.

strokes if necessary. I wedge myself up against the bed or wheelchair when rib raking to get a good grip.

If your patient is seated, you can also rib rake from the back. Instead of pulling up from the sides to the front of the body, push away from the spine out to the edges of the back and around as far as you can reach towards the front of the body. You can also work both sides from the front by stretching your arms around the back and pulling up towards the center. Use the figures on this page to guide you to the three different styles of rib raking (overhanded, bilateral, and reinforced).

Making someone's last breath as comfortable as possible is a marriage of working the diaphragm and the intercostals together. I massage the diaphragm, then the intercostals, then the diaphragm, then the intercostals. I will throw in some other strokes to make the introduction and finale different, but the main entrée of this respiratory work is the diaphragm and intercostal massages.

## TAPOTEMENT

The percussive tapotement strokes of cupping, loose fingertip hacking, stiff fingertip hacking, beating, and pounding on both the front and back of the thorax are all appropriate in the early stages of respiratory impairment, but cupping is the golden boy of all the percussive strokes. It gets more excitement into the lungs than its counterparts. All of these strokes can be done in all three postural drainage positions: sitting, side-lying, and inverted. See pages 53 to 56 for a complete description of tapotement techniques, including adaptive cupping and pounding for palliative massage.

> **Before applying tapotement strokes to the ribs of patients who are thin from extreme weight loss, place a folded towel over the patients' ribs as a cushion.**

## Chest Compressions

Chest compressions are an important component of respiratory massage. Include them after a warm-up massage and before your patient's productive coughing. You don't want to perform chest compressions first because you have not created the elasticity needed to make the compressions most effective.

Applying pressure to a chest that is already feeling full seems unnatural. However, chest compressions use a different kind of pressure—a relieving pressure. Getting the junk out of the lungs is important; it means that the person will not feel like they are drowning in their own fluids. With chest compressions, we can dislodge sticky stuff from the side of the lungs so it can be spit out during productive coughing.

In the section that follows, I first describe three postures for chest compressions, then two techniques that can be used in each posture, and finally I provide a step-by-step routine for chest compressions.

> **Be firm but gentle when doing chest compressions as the person might be prone to bone fractures in their weakened state.**

### Three chest compression postures with a supine patient

1. **Reinforced palmar compressions.** With your patient lying supine, stand at their head (either beside or behind them at the head of the bed) and place both hands, one palm on top of the other, on the sternum or breastbone. Lean forward with your body weight transferred onto your hands to compress the chest three or four times as the patient breathes out.

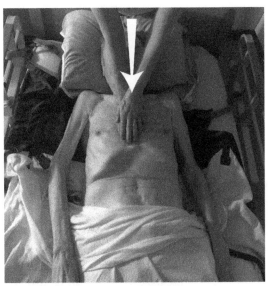

**Figure 5.32.** Reinforced palmer pumping on the sternum (standing at the head of the patient).

2. **Bilateral palmar compressions.** Standing at the head of the person, place both hands on the upper chest, one on either side of the sternum, hands about six inches apart.

3. **Thoracic compressions.** Stand at the patient's side in a lunge position. Do compressions along the side of the patient's body along the mid and lower lobe regions. If your patient has a bony rib cage, place a soft towel between their body and your hands so that you do not bruise or damage their ribs during the pumping.

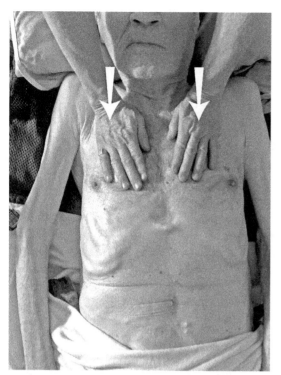

**Figure 5.33.** Bilateral palmer pumping (standing at the patient's head). Pump the chest three times.

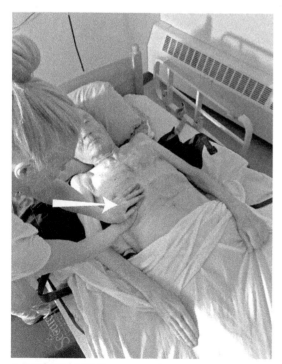

A. Reinforced midlobe compression.

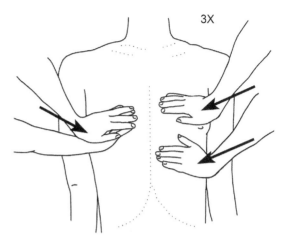

B. Reinforced and bilateral midlobe compression.

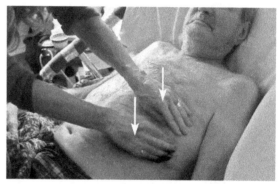

C. Thoracic compressions from the far side.

**Figure 5.34.** Stand at the side of the patient in a stride position leaning onto your hands and pump three times. Have the patient breathe slowly and deeply; compress on the out breath.

If your patient is able to lie prone, this is also an excellent posture for thoracic chest compression to clear the lungs.

### Two chest compression methods

1. **The pumping method.** Standing in one of the postures described above, place your hands on the patient's chest. Hands can be one on top of the other (reinforced palmar) or bilateral, with one hand on each side of the sternum. Lean your body weight onto your hands and press

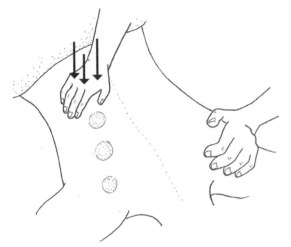

**Figure 5.35.** Prone thoracic chest compressions. Support the patient's body with one hand while the other moves down the back, pumping three times in each position. Then do the other side.

down with a pumping action three or four times each time the patient exhales.

2. **The popping method.** Stand in one of the postures described above and place your hands as described in the pumping method. Press down, leaning your body weight into your hands, on the breath out. At the end of the breath, as your patient start to breathe in, continue to hold the downward pressure. Then let go suddenly, about a fifth of the way into the breath in.

Holding down the compression longer than the end of the out breath means that when the patient tries to take a deep breath, their lungs meet resistance. As the patient begins to fill their lungs against the pressure, you "pop" your hands off the chest. The effect of this popping technique is profound—the patient automatically gets a deep surge of new air. It reminds me of a toilet plunger, keeping the suction going and pulling the stuck material up and out of the lungs. It also reminds me of how we strengthen a muscle. When you are training against resistance, the work feels hard—but when the resistance is removed, you get a stronger reaction than you did before.

I had always done traditional chest compressions (the pumping method) until one of our local physiotherapists, Janice Morrison, showed me this "popping method." In my classes we experiment with both and "popping" wins every time!

### Chest compressions routine

Massage your patient before doing the chest compressions to loosen things up. Massaging after compressions helps the body recover. During compressions, I encourage the patient to take big, deep breaths. I usually say, "Take a deep breath, as deep as possible, and then focus on breathing out as empty as possible before breathing in again. Slow your breathing down, making each breath a little bigger than the breath before." Although the routine here uses the pumping method, you can substitute the popping method.

During chest compressions, the patient may want to clear their lungs by spitting and coughing. I pause for bouts of productive coughing and then start again with the compressions.

Another technique, thoracic shaking, can be added as you perform the compression. Thoracic shaking is a rolling motion, rocking the patient's body as you perform the compression. You can apply thoracic shaking throughout your entire respiratory massage—beginning, middle, and end.

1. **Reinforced palmar pumping to the sternum.** Standing at the head of the bed or table, do some reinforced palmar pumping to the sternum.

2. **Bilateral palmar pumping to the sternum.** Move to bilateral palmar pumping to the upper chest and clavicular area.

3. **Thoracic pumping.** Move to the side of the table or bed and stand in a stride position. Do some bilateral thoracic pumping around the breast.

4. **Reinforced palmar pumping on the side of the chest.** Perform reinforced palmar pumping all over the side of the chest closest to you.

5. **Pumping on the opposite side.** Repeat steps 1 through 4 on the opposite side.

6. **Running vibrations.** Use running vibrations from the bottom up—the direction that the lungs would like to clear. Adding vibrations to chest compressions increases the mobilization of the lungs. I move in different angles over the chest with running, shaking vibrations that combine compression with movement.

> **Turn to pages 56 to 57 for how to do vibrations.**

7. **Rib raking.** Try rib raking combined with a shaking, vibrating compression.
8. **Costal angle pumping.** Try some single-sided or tandem costal angle pumping.

The motions of chest compression are controlled and performed while the patient's body is still. The patient's breathing is connected to the compression. Compressions can be a short pumping action during the out breath. On the inward breath we can start again with fresh compression.

## Abdomen Massage

If you've ever had whooping cough or a serious chest infection where coughing is constant, your tummy gets sore from the exertions of the whole front of the trunk of the body. That is why coughing folks are given a pillow to hold to their abdomen when they are coughing. The pillow can help prevent muscle strain or even herniations from persistent coughing.

Abdominal massage helps to relieve upper abdominal tension associated with diaphragm stress. Patients often enjoy abdominal massage both before and after the tapotement or chest compressions, as this helps to encourage positive muscle memory after the massage. The patient's breathing will work better as abdominal tension subsides. Most singers can attest that relaxing the abdomen helps produce a better voice—and a better voice is a function of better breathing.

> **The full abdominal massage routine is covered, starting on page 153.**

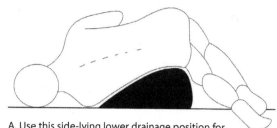

A. Use this side-lying lower drainage position for costal angle pumping, running vibrations, and shaking.

B. Costal angle pumping.

Thoracic pumping on exhalation

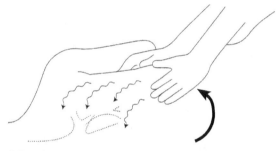

C. Running coarse vibrations towards the bronchia

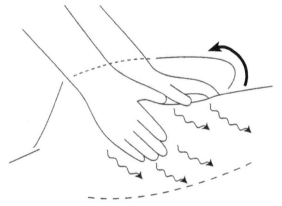

D. Thoracic shaking.

**Figure 5.36.** Both chest compressions and thoracic shaking loosen the expectorant in the lungs, leading to productive coughing.

## Productive Coughing

The patient should be in a sitting or standing position to do the productive coughing routine. Early on in their palliative massages, the person might be strong enough to stand up, but usually sitting is best.

This is an exercise in expectoration. The goal is to have the patient cough a lot of congestion or sputum up out of the lungs. (The secondary goal is to have the person survive the coughing and want to cough again!)

In order to produce a good, strong cough, the diaphragm should be ready to react to the deep breathing and postural shifting. Since it cannot be counted on to help in palliative cases, we need to start up the lungs' action artificially.

### Productive coughing routine

Massage helps people with respiratory trouble cough more easily and safely by mobilizing the thorax. This can help them avoid pulling or straining their rib or abdominal muscles, or having their diaphragm become spastic.

For this routine, begin with a respiratory massage, including cupping to the thoracic region, diaphragm massage, compressions, and deep breathing. Have tissues, a bowl for sputum, and a pillow handy. If the patient is able, have them run on the spot before pressing a pillow against their abdomen and proceeding with step 3. (If they are able to do this at all, it will usually only be in the early stages of palliative care.)

1. **Prepare support for the patient's abdomen.** With the patient standing or in a seated position, provide a pillow to hold up against their front so the breathing muscle has support. When patients are very weak and cannot be seated on the edge of their hospital bed, pile some pillows up on their tray table, crank the hospital bed into an upright position, and tilt the person forward onto the pillow pile.

2. **Rotate the arms in both directions.**

3. **Get the patient coughing.** Have the patient take deep breaths and throw themselves forward onto the pillow or pillows while coughing. If they are standing, have them bend at the waist. When patients are standing, they should be held by a massage volunteer so they don't collapse. Have the patient cough as much as possible during the full exhale, right to the very end of their breath.

4. **Assist the coughing with cupping.** Cup around the thoracic region. Throughout the coughing, the patient should continue holding the pillow firmly into the abdomen. If the patient can't do this, help them.

5. **Have the patient spit out.** After a bout of coughing, patient stays leaning down or forward for a breath or two, spitting out dislodged expectoration.

6. **Do some more cupping.**

7. **Have the patient slowly rise up with an inward breath.**

8. **Repeat three or more times.** Continue the process until the patient's lungs are cleared.

9. **Massage the entire back.**

10. **Rest.**

---

Breathing better to the end is not always possible. But with hands-on help, whatever discomfort

**Figure 5.37.** Steam inhalations can help loosen expectorant and can be done before or after massage. Add a drop of carminative oil (e.g., peppermint, eucalyptus) to the steaming water. Have the patient breathe slowly and deeply while tenting the head with a towel. Make sure the towel is tight to the bowl to trap the steam.

around breathing exists can be lessened. Try also adding warmth and steam inhalations to your massage, productive coughing, and tapotement routines. All of these can make a dying person feel confident that they will not suffer.

### After productive coughing or mechanical suctioning

After any respiratory procedure like productive coughing or mechanical suctioning is always a good time to massage the entire respiratory system—from the abdomen to the nose. This helps restore the optimum quality of the patient's breathing. Neck massage is particularly helpful to open up the breathing at the nose and mouth (see pages 128 and 129). Massage removes the painful reminders of those useful, yet awkward and sometimes painful, therapeutic events.

## Respiratory Self-Massage

Self-massage gives patients some control over their breathing and can help with the feelings of helplessness and panic when their breathing is compromised. It is, however, only workable at the beginning of palliative care, when the patient is strong enough and can handle giving themselves a little massage. Self-massage can be done to the face and sinuses, throat, and upper chest.

### For headache or sinus congestion

It is easy for patients to massage the pressure points of their own face. Pressing these pressure points with their thumbs or pointer fingers for a couple of deep breaths will help clear the sinuses, relieve a headache, and generally open up breathing. See Figure 5.10 for a map of the pressure points in the sinuses of the face.

### For sinus congestion and dry throat or mouth

With tiny kneading strokes, have the patient work their fingertips all along the jawline and under in the soft palate of the lower mouth. This will help them produce more saliva for a dry mouth and lubricate the throat and nose.

Nasal root shaking / laryngeal shaking is also good for a dry mouth and throat. Have the patient grasp the nose with the thumb and forefinger and shake it side to side. Similarly, throat (laryngeal) shaking will make the throat more lubricated and make it easier to swallow or spit up. Have the patient clasp one hand around the throat and move the larynx from side to side, then run their hands up and down the neck to give more ease and flexibility. See Figure 5.11 for a diagram of respiratory shaking.

### For a stiff neck

Have the patient use their fingertips to knead up and down the length of the sternocleidomastoid muscles from the base of the skull to their attachment at the breast bone. This will give the patient a better voice and greater ease of movement. As the patient moves less and less, the neck tends to stiffen; this self-massage can help when no one else is around to give a massage. If possible, have the patient apply hot packs to the neck before and after self-massage to keep the circulatory system stimulated.

### For general lower respiratory impairment

1. **Pressure points on the chest.** The upper chest is full of pressure points that are easy to access for a self-massage. Have the patient use the tips of their thumbs to push down on the pressure points along the sternum and below the clavicle (the breast bone and collar bone). There are 10 to 12 points that the patient can press and breathe into; instruct them to go looking for the most tender spots with their thumbs.

2. **Rib raking and diaphragm massage.** With their fingertips in a claw-like grip, have the patient run them along the ribs, alternating between pulling and pushing in a whole-handed raking motion.

   To access the diaphragm, have the patient sit or lie down and grip underneath the costal angle. Instruct them to pull up and along the angle of the bottom rib, curving their fingers around the ribs into the abdomen. Make sure

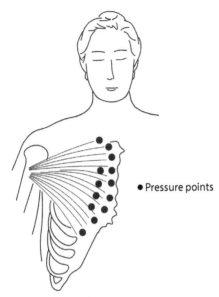

• Pressure points

**Figure 5.38.** Pressure points accessible for self-massage.

that they breathe deeply into the tension and take it slowly.

3. **Cupping.** Instruct the patient to make a hollow cup with their fingers curved and pressed tightly together, then thump their cupped hand across the upper chest—around the breasts if the patient is female and on top of the breasts if they are male. If they are large-breasted, they should lift each breast out of the way and continue the cupping underneath the breast on the ribs. The sound of the hand should be hollow, not slapping. Have the patient continue along as if giving themselves a pat on the back over the shoulder and around the side, lifting their arm to get to the upper back.

A vigorous cupping massage may produce therapeutic coughing and productive expectoration. Instruct the patient to be ready to cough up the congestion that is loosened with this massage. Steam inhalation is also helpful to loosen expectorant.

Self-massage is useful when no other hands are available. Usually, self-massage takes about five minutes to take effect. When we massage ourselves, we do not have the instant, dramatic relaxation reflex that we get when someone else touches

us. We are already in full contact with ourselves, so we do not feel the strong change when we start a self-massage. However, I have been surprised to find that I can get myself from severe pain to tolerable discomfort with self-massage alone. The nervous system responds whether you, another person, or a machine is touching you, and it will start to shift the focus and unwind the pain cycle.

## Online Classroom
Visit brusheducation.ca/dying-in-good-hands to watch these videos:

Postural drainage

Shoulder movements

Face, scalp, and sinus massage

Kneading to neck

Thoracic massage

Diaphragm massage and rib raking

Rib raking 1

Rib raking 2

Rib raking 3

Tapotement 1

Tapotement 2

Abdomen massage

Chest compression – popping method

Running, shaking chest compressions

Productive coughing

Steam inhalations

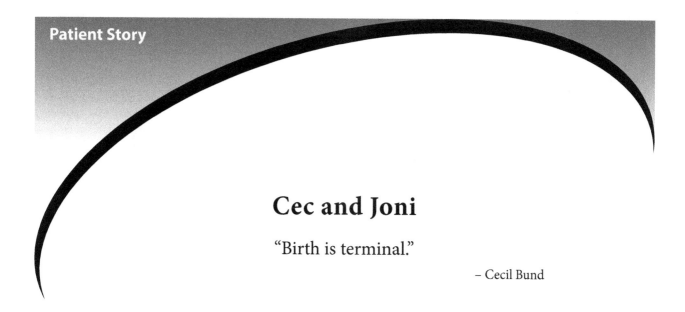

# Cec and Joni

"Birth is terminal."

– Cecil Bund

Twenty years before I met him, Cec had overcome cancer. After that, his wife, Joni, had had two heart attacks, but had made a great recovery with Cec learning to massage her. Everyone had assumed that Cec and Joni were great candidates to live to one hundred—but, what with Joni's heart attacks, that Joni would be the first to go when the time came.

In the end, though, it was Cec who would be the first one to head to heaven, though they knew they would be together again. Their religious belief in the afterlife was working its way into real life, and they talked openly about this to everyone who visited. I found the frankness of the talk about Cec's dying to be helpful. I was relieved every time I heard them speak about their beliefs, understanding that Joni wouldn't suffer as badly when he wasn't there because they saw themselves as eternally together.

Joni had a nightly routine of sending out an email to report on Cec's progress. She reported on the activities of the day and the people involved, and she included photos to illustrate her stories. Her computer was at the end of their bed and she would sit on her huge exercise ball in front of her monitor and compose her updates. She posted her pictures while wearing her nightie and communicated with her clan every night. Every morning she would open their responses and read them to Cec.

Late one night, after returning home from their place, I checked my email to discover that the world according to Joni and Cec had already seen me; there I was, in the update from Joni. I began to receive emails from the family. One night there was an email from a relative thanking me for being "her hands": She wanted to be there for Cec, and seeing the photos of him being massaged by those around him helped to relieve her anxiety. Another person asked me to give Cec a massage from her, and yet another simply thanked me for being hands-on. She could see that he was dying in good hands.

Joni and her family are doers. Within 10 minutes of me suggesting we get Cec out of his lounge chair and into a bed so he and Joni could lie close to each other, their son had moved a bed for Cec from the other part of the house and into the bedroom. Cec had a side that he preferred to lie on, and I soon realized that Joni's bed was on the wrong side—she was looking at his back. This time we moved the bodies instead of the beds: we slid Cec easily over to the far side of Joni's so she was able to be nose-to-nose with him. Incidentally, this also put Joni on the side that was the best resting position for her sore hip. Most importantly, though, it put her in the best position to keep her hands on Cec. She could lie there all day long if she wanted to.

Joni continued to take my suggestions seriously; she was adaptable, open-minded, and willing to try everything. She sang to Cec as she lay beside him. She talked with him about all the memories of their prairie life, homesteading in the Kootenays, and the move to Vancouver, British Columbia.

Cec was failing quickly and we concentrated on his breathing, massaging his ribs and diaphragm. Joni learned all my massage techniques for keeping his skin intact, his breathing steady, and his extremities warm.

Cec had gut wrenching hiccupping, a disconcerting and painful symptom of diaphragmatic pressure resulting from the growth of his cancerous liver. The constant hiccups kept him from resting, so I taught everyone on his team to massage his diaphragm. We eased up the pressure by massaging around his liver and worked his entire respiratory system, past his throat and up to his mouth and jaw as he lay gasping, hour after hour. His diaphragmatic spasms were rhythmic and noisy. We worked for hours around his diaphragm and digestive system and got results, helping Cec sleep for four hour stretches.

### FEBRUARY 7

Cec's tumor was growing and interfering with his respiration. I worked to stretch him out, to find more room for him to breathe comfortably. Cec and Joni's son Bob came before and after work to massage his dad. Catherine, a close friend, massaged Cec during the day. Joni learned all the advanced massages for helping Cec breathe better, including massages for loosening up the accumulating exudate in Cec's lungs. She worked between his ribs with intercostal rib raking and learned to massage his tummy to help move his bowels. She was precise in copying my movements, but at the same time she always added a little something extra. She was an expert at lying beside him and simply stroking his arm or face or chest as she talked or sang to him.

### FEBRUARY 10

I arrived at Joni and Cec's place at 10 a.m. to meet their daughter Roxy and her two kids. They were leaving for their home in Alberta that morning.

Roxy was attending to some of Joni's needs, so her two kids—teenagers—joined me to give their grandpa a massage before they left. The three of us cheerfully worked Cec's extremities. His hiccups had subsided, and he was able to speak. He told them, "That's nice," and, "Thank you, that feels so good." Positive feedback for them. Then their mom joined our massage while Joni took pictures to send out on her email loop. Roxie took her position on the bed, behind Cec, and the kids showed their mom what to do. As I listened to them pass on their massage instruction to her, I felt deeply satisfied. The kids massaged Cec's feet, and I massaged Joni.

### FEBRUARY 12

I was massaging Joni to sleep late on the night of the 11th. I had always done home calls for Joni since it was difficult for her to climb the stairs to my clinic. I had convinced her to let me massage Cec while she slept after her massage. Joni always rested as I left her house, but now it was difficult for her to rest deeply with the sound of Cec's spastic hiccups right beside her.

At the same time, it was the best place for Joni to be sleeping, right up close to Cec. When I finished his massage, he was on his side, breathing better, and facing her.

It happened organically. There was room for me to lie down along the edge of the bed, so I clung to the edge of the bed as Joni slept soundly and, now, so did Cec. I stayed the night, waking up in the early morning, still acting as the human guardrail on the far side of their combined beds. Joni was surprised to see me, but, at the same time, not surprised. I massaged Joni's back, and then I massaged Cec and left for my office. I knew that Cec would die any day now. I knew that it could be during the night as easily as during the day.

His diaphragmatic spasms weren't going away, but the massages were making a difference in his comfort level and breathing. Even though we were letting him stay wherever he was comfortable, he still didn't have any pressure sores. He had graciously acclimatized to the diapers and bowel care. Still, frail as he was, he would, now and again, fling himself nearly out of bed in a strong effort to get up: the pattern of getting up to go somewhere, that urgency to get going, to move out and up.

We'd been telling Cec that we knew where he was going and he could leave without getting up. I was, however, concerned about Joni and her heart condition. It was so common for couples like these two to go together, dying one after the other. In the meantime, it seemed important to massage Joni where Cec could see from his horizontal position. I knew that his greatest worry was her well-being. He loved watching her get massaged. In his dying, he was more concerned about her future without him than losing his own life.

### FEBRUARY 14

I spent the day with Joni, fully expecting Cec to leave anytime, as it was Valentine's Day, the love day. I had made a bet with Bob that Valentine's Day would be Cec's big parting day. Cec continued to fade, and was starting to breathe without hiccupping.

### FEBRUARY 15

Once in a while during the night, Cec had had a delayed breathing rhythm: two breaths, then no breath. But in the morning, he was still there. Bob said that he knew his dad would not have wanted to be remembered for dying on Valentine's Day. I had lost the bet.

Joni was waiting for the bus to come into Castlegar with Van, who was, for all intents and purposes, their son. As soon as Van arrived, I put him to work. He took one of Cec's arms and I took the other. Together we massaged Cec, who now lay semi comatose. Van learned the massage techniques for Cec's respiratory congestion and compression to help ease the hiccupping. Cec's breathing deepened and quieted, and Van, having said his goodbyes, left by bus to Calgary, Alberta.

### FEBRUARY 16

When I was in town that morning, Joni phoned me and said that Cec's breathing was changing. I asked her to mimic it. She took two breaths and then a long pause with no breath. I put a sign on the clinic door—*Death in the family*—and raced to the house. Driving the edge of the speed limit, then abandoning my car in the snowbank, I ran down the rutted driveway, my elderly dog Bert running in front of me.

Reaching the bedroom, I removed the blankets from Cec's legs and saw the answer to the question that had been on my mind. He was blue from his feet to his knees, and his legs were cool to his hips. Cec's heart was pounding away, but his feet looked like he was dead already. Apparently, his heart had not yet gotten the "finished and it's time to die now" message.

In fact, the heart is often the last organ to get this message. The brain can close down most functioning, the kidneys can quit entirely, the other internal organs figure out that they have nothing more to do, and the lungs don't give the same gaseous exchange. But what makes the heart know when it's time to quit?

With continuous massaging, Cec inched his way towards the heavenly gates. I massaged his legs and we worked over his entire body. Due to the rib-raking massage along his intercostal muscles, his breathing changed again and became quieter.

When we turned him, Cec's face was showing— for the first time—a pooling of blood. There was a red outline along his cheekbone, which had been resting on the soft velour pillow. His hip, on the other hand, was blue where the head of the femur contacted the bed.

I finished massaging Cec and walked around to massage Joni's shoulders as she sang a favorite song, completing it with her own ending: "You are my sunshine, my only sunshine / You make me happy, when skies are gray / You'll never know dear, how much I love you / So please keep my sunshine safe."

Van had reached Alberta and was on the phone. As we spoke, Joni touched my hand and pointed to Cec. I put the phone on speaker mode and told Van that Cec was stopping breathing. I moved around Joni and took up my position, facing Cec across from Joni. I asked Van if he wanted to stay with us. He said, "Please let me stay."

I gave Van the play-by-play of Cec's last moments:

"Cec is starting to completely stop breathing now.

"He is having one more breath, unlike the rest.

"His shoulders are starting to rise like he is shrugging. Now he's contracting everywhere.

"His face is starting to move like he's surprised.

"His eyebrows are lifting now and his mouth is tightening up.

"He's shrugging his shoulders forward and now they are dropping.

"His face is relaxing.

"He is pulling in a breath that is not a breath.

"He breathes the absence of breath out.

"He lets go.

"He is completely still now.

"All his tension and sounds are gone.

"He has passed on.

"He looks very peaceful and serene."

I had never heard anyone, much less myself, speak about these bodily reactions. It was as though I was delivering the details from all the deaths that I had attended.

Joni stroked Cec's arm and then his face. On the phone, Van was telling Cec that he loved him. Joni was telling Cec that she loved him. They were a choir of love. As it turned out, Cec did leave us on a love day, after all.

And we had launched an angel.

Cec and Joni.

# 6

# Digestive Massage

In palliative massage, the tummy is a very important place. When someone is dying, massage can relieve a large range of digestive complaints, including constipation, abdominal cramping, diarrhea, thrush, salivary insufficiency, throat constriction, localized pain, discomfort due to tumor invasion, irritated bowels, pain from surgery, associated headaches, and dehydration.

This chapter will give you remedies I have found effective for promoting better digestive function. The aim of palliative massage is to increase the absorption of nutrients, produce digestive enzymes, and move the contents of the digestive tract along the system. Relieving abdominal discomfort of any kind can be accomplished through a practical application of hands in digestive massage; leg pumping; hydrotherapy; and, importantly, a good sense of humor. We want people to happily toot, burp, urinate, and move their bowels comfortably and without embarrassment until the day they die.

Normal abdominal massage routines can become complicated by biliary drains, ileostomy and urinary bags, stoma sites, surgery scars, and wounds. But dying with a comfortable tummy is possible for everyone who is terminally ill. In this chapter, I give you a road map to keep your patient or loved one's digestion going the right way.

## Typical Palliative Digestive Symptoms

Many people feel like they are dying of constipation rather than the terminal disease with which

they are diagnosed. Medications are sometimes to blame. Heavy-duty drugs like morphine and codeine relieve pain, but the related overall body relaxation brings with it the slowing down of our digestion. The colon can become impacted and life becomes a series of stool softeners and enemas.

Those who escape constipation may encounter the opposite problem: diarrhea. When I treat my AIDS patients, they often have a bowel that will not stop! They are exhausted from the overactivity of their colons and do not want to eat or excite the bowel in any way.

Inactivity, infection, or the mechanical rearranging of an abdomen with growing tumors can also create digestive challenges. Whether things are moving through the digestive system too fast or not fast enough, massage can help normalize digestive function.

## Palliative Massage for Digestion

In palliative conditions, the entire digestive system is affected—from the mouth to the rear end. We must include the face, throat, neck, diaphragm, and abdominal area in our digestive treatment. Massage will reduce tension in the jaw and improve chewing. Massage also helps increase secretions in the mouth, throat, stomach, liver, spleen, kidneys, and colon by increasing blood flow to these areas. Increased saliva production eases swallowing, and increased gastric juices result in a more comfortable digestion process without spasms. Greater lubrication of the digestive tract is truly a lifesaver!

## Professional Politics of Touch

Professional massage therapists cannot perform any massage directly to the urogenital systems of any patients. But friends and families of the patients can be called in to massage around the rectum to stimulate or soothe. Family members and medical professionals, excluding massage therapists, can also manually excavate impacted fecal matter. My experience in the barnyards of palliative animal care taught me these same techniques. My neighbors sometimes saved their livestock by being able to "uncork" the suffering animal with manual manipulation of the colon.

## Gut Reactions

The stress dying people experience often shows up as the classic "nervous" stomach, producing uncomfortable acidity and abdominal pain. Too many visitors, too much activity, and too many tearful partings can resonate in the gut. Just as we have "gut" feelings, our guts have feelings all their own, as well.

I am a long-time sufferer of tummy tension. During my second week in massage school, I landed in the emergency ward with terrible pain in my stomach. I thought that the source of the problem had to be something physical because I was tied up in knots and the pain was so extreme that I couldn't stand. As it turned out, it was a bad case of homesickness. I'd had this level of pain a couple of times in my teens, and it still happens today, 50 years later. I am amazed now, as I was then, at how touch can take away a huge amount of pain and undo a tummy tangle!

## Letting Go

At the end of life, people may begin going through their memories. Memories often unleash a flood of feelings, some of which are sad or unresolved. My patient Mary found herself crying at the thought of things both happy and sad. Her husband, Lou, commented, "Mary always cries, not to worry!" I got used to Mary's tears. Often, I would cry with her.

Massage—particularly massage to the abdomen, which can house a lot of this pain—sometimes brings spontaneous release of these emotions. People often cry when they are massaged because the touch elicits a letting-go reflex in the body, stimulating a release of oxytocin, the "love hormone."

What should we do when people cry during our massages? Keep in contact with the person who is releasing their emotions. I adapt some of my massage strokes, maybe adding more long, comforting effleurage strokes and more palmar kneading, instead of tapotement or fingertip kneading. I also slow the speed of my strokes. My aim with any type of spontaneous emotional release is to stay with my patient and facilitate the release of these strong reactions—often weeping about loss of family, future, hopes, and dreams. I always feel like it is a compliment when someone shares on this level. I learned early in my career that people usually let go only when and where they feel safe enough to do so.

This abdominal massage, in particular, takes on both physical and emotional dimensions for palliative patients. The front of our body is the place we protect instinctively. We curl up naturally in a fetal position as we die—a protective posture. This closed posture can also close us off emotionally. But massage helps us stay available and stretched out, relaxing the naturally contracting flexors of the front of the body, exposing the vulnerable and sensitive abdomen, and opening the person being massaged both physically and emotionally.

My aim is to facilitate the patient's ability to let go. Some people are ready to go, and they let everyone know it. Other patients are in denial until their last breath. Massage works for both the leapers and the foot draggers.

Most massage therapists do not include the abdomen in their everyday full-body massages, but in palliative massage, this area is important to always include in your massage routine. As I write this, I'm thinking of a patient I had this evening. Even as he lay, extremely relaxed and gently snoozing, I still included his abdominal massage.

## The Awkwardness of Diapers

Changing diapers can become a natural part of abdominal massage. The dying person can avoid embarrassment about diaper-associated smells if you are able change their diapers and freshen them up before, during, or after your massage with confidence. Sometimes—especially with abdominal massage—a full diaper when you're done is the biggest compliment!

When my stepmom was dying, we shared many intimate moments as I massaged her rear end while she sat in her commode chair. This chair gave me wonderful access to rub those hard-to-get-at parts with the greatest of ease. We joked every night for the last week of her life about me massaging her on her throne!

Her humor was her saving grace, as she was a very reserved woman. I frequently found myself under the toilet chair taking care of her personal hygiene. This wasn't the kind of intimacy I had envisioned in our relationship, and yet there I was, helping her digestion work its way along. She was very grateful for the hands-on help, and it was one of our most touching experiences together in those last days of her life.

## Tubes and Drains

Sometimes a patient's surgically implanted tubes and drains can give them additional adhesions and discomfort. Careful massage around these stoma sites in the abdominal wall can give the patient relief and soften the scar tissue.

I taught my patient Bev to massage around her newly acquired colostomy bag and to include ice in her postsurgical massages. She used ice to massage along the surgical incision line, which helped stimulate the circulation, minimize adhesions, and numb the uncomfortable area.

My father acquired an artificial bladder that affected his digestion in ways that were not explained by the textbooks. Yet his abdominal massages, including around his stoma site, helped his digestion immensely. Massaging around stomas also helps those openings in the abdominal cavity stay healthy and free of infection.

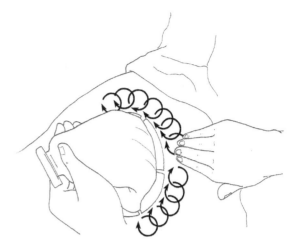

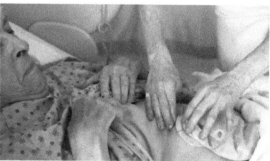

**Figure 6.1.** Many palliative patients have various sites of abdominal interventions. Get used to single-handed kneading around the abdomen with one hand while holding the pouch or bag with the other.

## When to Massage the Abdomen

There is never a bad time to massage the abdomen. It can be done during the day or in the middle of the night when people are restless and making unconscious motions to leave their bed.

Abdominal massage can be done through a patient's clothing, through their hospital gown, or skin on skin. The massage can be done with or without oil. It can be delivered when the person is seated or lying on their back. A mini-massage lasting only a few minutes will still have a positive effect.

There are times during an abdominal massage when it is not necessary to move in "massage-like" ways. Just putting your hands on the person's tummy and breathing with them can help decrease feelings of panic and increase feelings of relaxation, which, in turn, will help digestion.

Coaching someone who is terminally ill through a tough digestive episode is like being with someone in childbirth. Ask the person to take deep breaths, to focus on your hands, to bring their breath down into their abdomen and to continue breathing through the pain. Stay in that position until the spasms subside, all the while giving breathing instructions.

Massaging the lower back and abdomen before a bowel movement, after a bowel movement, and even during a bowel movement can be helpful. When people do not have any strength to push, your massage can sometimes give them extra resources.

### Massage and meals

Before a meal, massaging the face and jaw area with fingertip kneading eases the upper digestive system and prepares the muscles for chewing and the glands for lubrication. During meals, massage can help patients swallow and keep food down. Stroke directly down the front of the throat with an open, C-shaped hand until the food has completely passed the point of coming back up. Sometimes this means stroking during a swallow so the patient doesn't choke on or spit up food. Other times, it means stroking after the swallow to keep the food going down and preventing a reflex upchuck!

A gentle massage after a meal can help patients tolerate any uncomfortable abdominal activity and aid in their digestion. The postmeal massage will also soothe any discomfort when the large intestine gets into action.

Everyone is different in the timing of the touch they require. My mom needed stroking to make swallowing easier only in the last days of her life when she was simply swallowing juice nectars; others may need it much sooner. I have had patients who can only eat if they are rubbed before, during, and after ingesting their food.

## Mobilizing the Hips with Leg Pumping

Leg pumping is a specialized sequence used primarily on palliative or immobile patients. Because the majority of palliative patients are unable to walk or exercise their legs, one of the ways to assist the circulatory and digestive process is to pump the patient's legs. It is also ideal for loosening up the entire lower torso. I usually perform the leg pumping sequence before and after a leg or abdominal massage, but I also try to incorporate the movements as many times as possible throughout the entire massage.

Leg pumping is excellent for both constipation and achy, immobilized hips. It is a direct route to better bowel activity, like letting the horse out of the barn. (After standing immobile all night, a horse lifts its tail to release built-up gas the minute it leaves the barn.) There is rarely a time when leg pumping in palliative patients isn't appropriate or enjoyed.

There are three basic leg pumping movements, each explained below:

1. Alternate leg pumping
2. Simultaneous leg pumping
3. Rotational leg pumping

For each, one hand does the moving and the other hand supports the leg. Make sure to adequately drape the patient before you begin, covering their genitals so that they can fully relax. Working in teams of two, each person moving one leg, can be ideal. Tandem massaging for the legs both before and after the leg-pumping movements brings even greater success.

### Alternate leg pumping

Stand in a stride position or half-kneel on the bed. Hold the leg at the heel and at the back or top of the knee. Bend the leg at the knee and flex the leg at the hip toward the patient's chest, pressing gently into the abdomen once, then lower the leg back down until straight. Bend the patient's knee and hip only as far as is comfortable for them. Use the heel to steer. Do each leg at least three times and up to 10 times before switching to the other leg.

Tandem leg pumping is done with two people—one on each side of the patient pumping the legs one after the other.

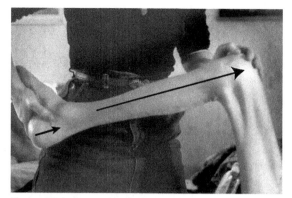

**Figure 6.2.** Leg pumping flexion.

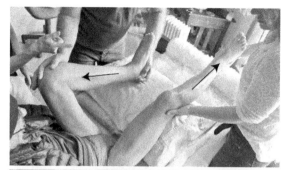

**Figure 6.4.** Tandem leg pumping. Support the ascending leg under the heel to push upward. Support the descending leg under the knee.

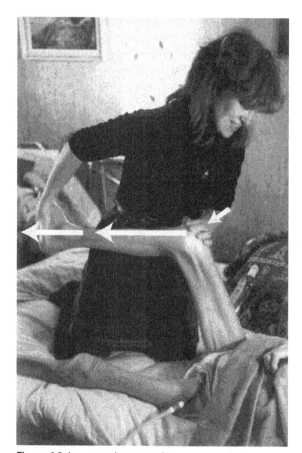

**Figure 6.3.** Leg pumping extension.

### Simultaneous leg pumping

This can be done with one or two people. Flex both legs to the chest and press the knees into the abdomen by slipping your hand onto the front of the knees and gently pressing them down towards the

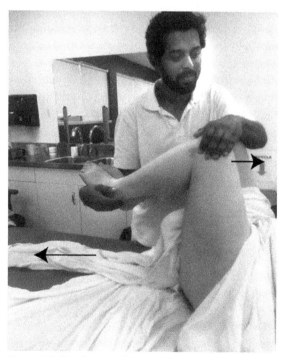

**Figure 6.5.** Simultaneous leg pumping.

chest. Then extend both legs at the same time. If you're working alone, use one hand to hold both the patients ankles together and use the other hand or your forearms to guide the knees to the chest. In tandem, each person works one leg. Repeat three to 10 times.

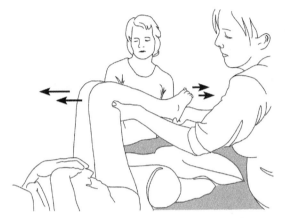

**Figure 6.6.** Tandem simultaneous leg pumping, with one person on each side of the patient.

### Rotational leg pumping

With both knees fully bent towards the chest, move the bent legs in slow, broad circles, pressing down on them to create gentle pressure on the sacrum. This pressure can stimulate the peristaltic action of the digestive system because the innervation for this part of the digestive system comes from the lumbar spine (see Figure 6.7). Back massage stimulates the nerves to release the muscles affecting the digestive system. That is why we pat or rub a baby's back after feeding. We can "burp" an adult by simply rubbing their whole back, paying specific attention to the part of the lower back (thoracic 12 to lumbar 3) that houses the nerve supply for the digestive system: the liver, stomach, intestines, and colon.

Moving the legs three to 10 times in one direction, then repeat in the opposite direction.

### Leg stretches

Stretching can also be a beneficial part of your leg pumping routine.

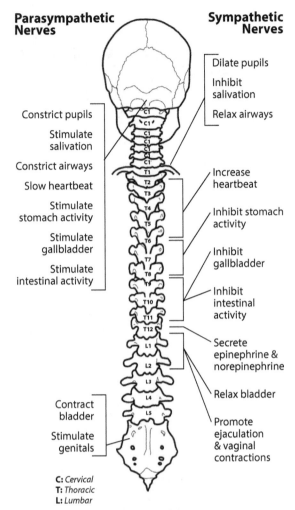

**Parasympathetic Nerves**

Constrict pupils
Stimulate salivation
Constrict airways
Slow heartbeat
Stimulate stomach activity
Stimulate gallbladder
Stimulate intestinal activity

Contract bladder
Stimulate genitals

**Sympathetic Nerves**

Dilate pupils
Inhibit salivation
Relax airways

Increase heartbeat
Inhibit stomach activity
Inhibit gallbladder
Inhibit intestinal activity
Secrete epinephrine & norepinephrine
Relax bladder
Promote ejaculation & vaginal contractions

**C:** *Cervical*
**T:** *Thoracic*
**L:** *Lumbar*

**Figure 6.7.** Nervous system. The sympathetic nervous system helps the body respond to danger, while the parasympathetic nervous system helps restore calm to the body.

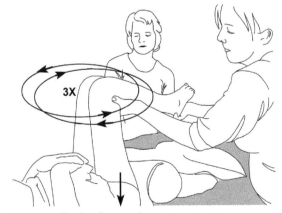

**Figure 6.8.** Tandem leg rotations.

- **Traction:** Apply traction to the entire leg by holding on at the ankle and foot while leaning back and slowly pulling away from the person.
- **Hamstring stretch:** Place your hand beneath the knee to provide adequate support, then stretch the leg straight up so the person can see their toes. Ask them, if they can, to bend their toes in both directions at the height of the stretch.

Always ask the person if they are comfortable with the movements so you will know how far to go. If the patient is unable to communicate, you can still do these movements gently to the point of resistance to keep the digestive momentum moving forward.

## My Digestive Massage Formula

My formula for treating digestive complaints is "massage, mobilize, massage." Whether the problem is local abdominal pain, tumor invasion, constipation, diarrhea, or respiratory abdominal soreness due to coughing, the timing is the same. Massage the abdomen, move the hips, then massage the abdomen again. It's a good idea to repeat this cycle a number of times in your abdominal massage routine.

Because massage brings blood to the area, which the patient needs for helping with their digestion, you rarely run into a problem of too much abdominal massage. The one exception may be when a patient is already experiencing overactive bowels. Still, make sure you check in with your patients: with the rampant diarrhea in AIDS patients that I worked with 30 years ago, I thought I would have to be careful and moderate my abdominal massage, but these patients taught me that the massages helped both their pain levels and their digestive systems. Their feedback also changed my teaching about contraindications, such as not massaging right after eating. I learned that massaging before, during, and after eating could have beneficial effects. For my mother in her last two weeks, any food was too much stimulation, and no

functioning digestion was left in her to process liquid meal supplements. The massages to her abdomen were very important when inexperienced helpers tried to feed her and agony resulted. The massages to her tummy were the only relief from acute abdominal pain until everything had passed through and her system was empty of food except for the odd sip of water or juice.

### Upper digestive massage

For the elderly or ill, the throat muscles can weaken and make coughing and choking a problem. The ease of movement for all food begins at the oral cavity. Efficient functioning in the mouth provides a good start to effective digestion farther down the line.

Massaging the temporal mandibular joint where the jaw and skull meet is a great way to help palliative patients keep chewing so they can continue to enjoy the taste and texture of their food instead of only blenderized roast beef and mashed potatoes. Massaging the jaw before and after a meal promotes the flow of salivary juices that help the mastication and digestive process.

When massaging the face, always use upward strokes from the center of the face to the outer edges. Perform the upper digestive massage before and after a meal, no matter how little the patient is eating.

1. **Fingertip kneading to the temporal mandibular joint.** Stand behind the patient and lean forward, resting your elbows on the hospital bed, reclining chair or back of the wheelchair. Place your fingertips on the jaw joint in front of the ear; there is a notch here that your fingertips should fit into. At this point, I often go from three fingertips to just one in order to be more accurate as I massage the ligaments and the parotid glands, which are located behind the ear. Extend your fingertip massage all around the ear where it attaches to the side of the head (this is an important part of the face and scalp massage routine). Two other salivary glands, the sublingual and the submandibular, also live in the same neighborhood and are an important part of the digestive system.

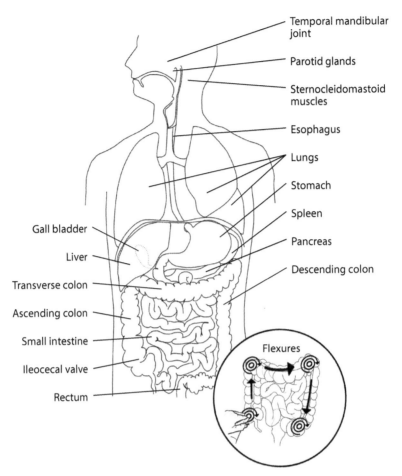

**Figure 6.9.** Digestive anatomy.

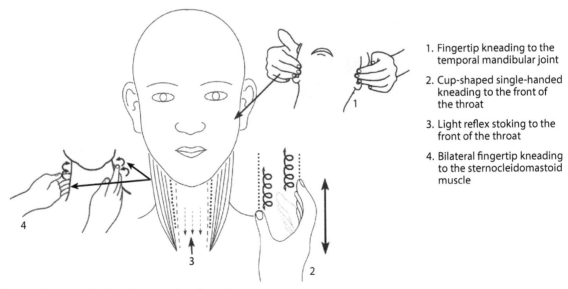

1. Fingertip kneading to the temporal mandibular joint

2. Cup-shaped single-handed kneading to the front of the throat

3. Light reflex stoking to the front of the throat

4. Bilateral fingertip kneading to the sternocleidomastoid muscle

**Figure 6.10.** Four strokes for the upper digestive system.

2. **Cup-shaped, single-handed kneading to the front of the throat.** This makes the act of swallowing easier. This can be especially helpful for people with ALS.

3. **Light reflex stroking down the front of the throat.** This helps your patient swallow.

4. **Bilateral fingertip kneading to the sterno-cleidomastoid muscles.** Massage up and down these ropey throat muscles from the sternum to the point under the ears where they attach.

5. **Finish.** I finish this routine by reaching around to the back of the neck and kneading with my fingertips. You can massage with both hands at the same time or do one side at a time. After I've done my fingertip kneading massage to the back of the neck, I place a hot pack around the neck for the finishing touch.

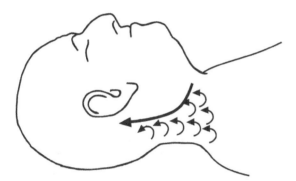

**Figure 6.11.** Single-handed and bilateral fingertip kneading to the back of the neck.

### Transition

Bridge your upper and lower digestive massages by simply rubbing the chest (sternum) and breastbone with the palm of your hand. This also seems to help people breathe easier after the exertion of eating, swallowing, and chewing.

### Lower digestive massage

The main goal of the lower digestive massage routine is to stimulate the colon. Our aim is to keep the digestive system working as best we can, to encourage nutritional uptake in the patient's stomach and small intestine, and to move waste products out of the body.

As you can see in the inset drawing in Figure 6.9, the colon has corners, called flexures, where food can slow down. We can help move food around these corners with massage from the beginning of the colon, where it meets the small intestine in the lower right of the abdomen, to the other side of the abdomen, where it turns down from the transverse colon to the descending colon on its way to the exit through the rectum.

To ensure that food doesn't get stuck in the flexures of the colon, I spend extra time in these areas, using reinforced fingertip kneading interspersed with over-handed palmar kneading. This combination helps release tension in the colon.

If the digestive system is hyperactive, I use more palmar kneading and light reflex stroking. If it is sluggish, I use more reinforced fingertip kneading.

#### BEGINNING STROKES FOR THE LOWER DIGESTIVE SYSTEM

1. **Over-handed palmar kneading.** Place one hand on the abdomen and slowly circle with firm, steady pressure around clockwise, which is the direction of peristaltic action in the intestines. Chase that hand with the other, one after the other, so that the motion is never interrupted. This continuous stroke helps the patient get accustomed to your touch.

   Do this at least three times slowly and firmly, getting feedback from the person about your pressure. Most people are too light with this stroke. It needs to be firm to help alleviate constipation.

2. **Abdominal effleurage.** Position yourself so both hands are side by side, palms down, on the abdomen, with the heels of your hands at the pubic bone. The fingertips should point upwards towards the patient's head. Press down with flat hands and push up to the center of the ribs where the costal angle meets at the apex: the xiphoid process. Then spread your hands out to the edges of the patient's body, wrap your hands around the back above the waistline, and come down the sides. This stroke will cover all the skin of the abdomen as

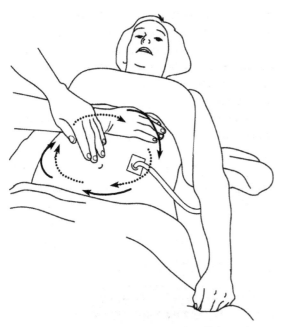

**Figure 6.12.** Overhanded palmar kneading. If the patient has a stoma or tube site, just hop over it and continue with your circles.

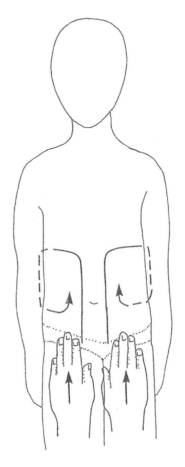

your hands move up and then back down in a square of stroking. Check in with your patient about your hand pressure as you apply the stroke. (Figure 6.13)

3. **Abdominal wringing**. Stand at the patient's side at the level of the abdomen. Start in the center of the abdomen with your hands side by side. As one hand pushes away from you, the other hand comes towards you; they pass by each other in the middle of the stroke, on the abdomen.

Wring back and forth across the abdomen slowly and with a good grip, keeping all of your fingers together so there's a smooth palmar sensation, not a fingertip grip. Slowly work your way up and down across the entire abdomen. Reach far around the sides of the patient so your hands wrap right around their body.

If you can, move from one side of the bed to the other and repeat the stroke. Usually, it is easy to walk around a hospital or hospice bed, but at home sometimes the bed is up against the wall and you might have to climb over the patient to sit on the other side of the bed. This

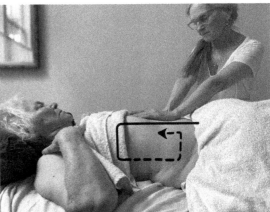

**Figure 6.13.** Abdominal effleurage.

is well worth the effort, however, as wringing is a favorite, yet underutilized massage stroke.

4. **Alternate thumb kneading.** Move your thumbs in overlapping circles across the entire abdomen. The direction of the strokes is always

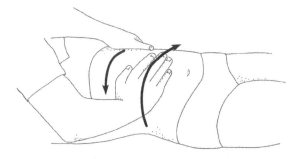

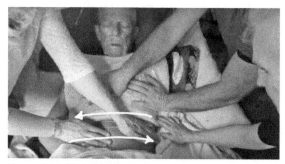

**Figure 6.14.** Abdominal wringing.

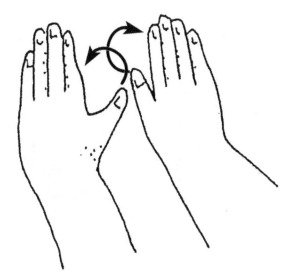

**Figure 6.15.** Alternate thumb kneading.

from feet to head, making circles that move up and out. Each thumb travels in the opposite direction. Do not take any shortcuts or lift your thumbs off the skin. The thumbs stay down on the skin surface for the entire stroke.

These starting strokes are very good for getting things moving and for navigating around any tubes, drains, bags, or stomas. The focused strokes that follow will not feel as penetrating or invasive for the patient once you have established the intensity of contact with your introductory strokes.

### FOCUSED STROKES FOR THE LOWER DIGESTIVE SYSTEM

To effectively assist the colon (large intestine) in its function, it is first important to understand its anatomy and the path the massage will take. Once this is established, I'll describe the strokes to use in detail.

The colon begins on the patient's lower right-hand side, where it hooks up to the small intestine through the ileocecal valve. To help this valve open

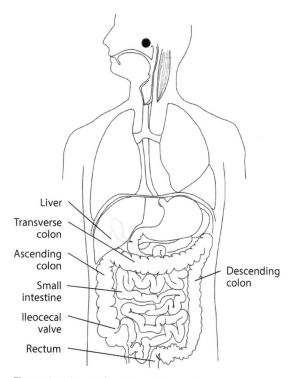

**Figure 6.16.** Lower digestive system anatomy.

and relax, our massage will begin here, working slowly with reinforced or single-handed fingertip kneading.

After that, we will slide up the ascending colon with fingertip kneading and then slow down at the colon's first corner, which is underneath the ribs by the liver. Linger here. The transverse colon, running from the right side of the person to the next corner on the left side, gets the same slow massage. Now massage down the final stretch of the colon, lingering in the last, lower corner underneath the stomach and ribs. Don't worry too much about direction—even if you massage the colon backwards, the body will still move the contents forward towards the back door.

During the massage, you can feel the spots where the colon is impacted. This can be anywhere up to the first corner over by the liver, or in extreme cases of constipation, the colon may be impacted right up to the ileocecal valve.

The difference between treating an impacted and nonimpacted area is not so much that you treat it differently but that you treat it more extensively with a longer massage or firmer strokes. The colon can be manipulated firmly in some unusual situations where the intestines are entangled. To be effective, however, massage to release colonic tangles and spasms has to be very strong and can be very uncomfortable.

**Figure 6.17.** Reinforced fingertip kneading to the ascending colon. Dominique, Gaston's daughter, massages his digestive system as part of her daily lunchtime massage visits.

---

The three strokes described next can be used over the path of the colon described above.

1. **Reinforced fingertip kneading.** Place the fingertips from one hand on top of the fingertips of the other, holding the fingers close together so they act as one unit and do not spread out in a fan shape. Your fingers should be straight, not bent, so they have some structural strength. This is important to avoid straining your hand or fingers. Keep the posture of your hand stiff so just the tips of the fingers make contact with each other (the thumbs should not touch). With this pose, your patient will experience the strokes as small and specific.

   The colon can be very tender, so it's important to divide up the massage into tiny, tolerable applications. Create small, focused circles with your wrist held high and your hand pivoting

from the wrist. Perform this fingertip kneading all along the length of the large colon.

Make tiny, circular kneading strokes as you move along the length of the straight stretches of the colon. Pause to spend extra time in the corners. (This pivoting action comes naturally to some folks and is awkward for others.) Be sure to switch hands and stack them up in reverse, with the one that was on top going to the bottom and vice versa. Most right-handed people feel that their right hand on the bottom is a natural fit, but I encourage people to practice both ways of stacking their hands. (It's good for the brain!)

2. **Single-handed fingertip kneading.** This is an excellent stroke if you have site restrictions on the abdominal surface. I used this stroke a lot with my dad when he had an artificial bladder. I could work around the stoma site where the plastic bladder bag was hooked up while still being very careful and focused. In order to do single-handed fingertip kneading, use one hand in the same shape as the previous stroke—straight fingers all together, with the palm arching up so only the fingertips make contact with the skin. The other hand can simply rest somewhere, usually on the patient's arm or shoulder. Trace the abdominal square with your strokes and follow the colon from beginning to end.

I usually start with reinforced fingertip kneading and then switch to single-handed fingertip kneading, doing about three circles of the large intestine with each variety.

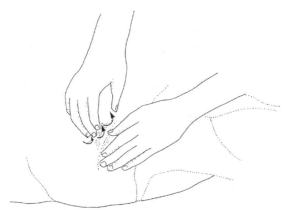

**Figure 6.18.** Single-handed fingertip kneading to the abdomen.

3. **Vibrations**. Use both fine and coarse vibrations along the path of the colon. On the last descent of the colon, where you turn the corner below the heart and below the diagonal edge of the ribs, vibrate up and down on the left-hand side of the body. I use a lot of running vibrations, moving my fingertips along the entire area.

I also use static vibrations to linger in the corners of the large intestine, especially at the bottom of the descending colon where it moves to the back. This bottom section is the most important part of the colon to work on. Removing impactions from this section will help everything else move along the digestive system. Massage will help to reclaim normalcy, even with a digestive system that is shutting down.

I like to keep up the palmer vibrations for about three minutes so it has a penetrating effect. This is very important for pain management. The longer you keep up this stroke, the more effective and far reaching it is for reducing pain. It overrides the painful contracting of the abdominal muscles.

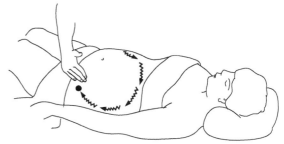

**Figure 6.19.** Vibrations and fingertip kneading along the large intestine are effective treatments for constipation and gas.

### FINISHING STROKES FOR THE LOWER DIGESTIVE SYSTEM

1. **Scooping.**
2. **Reinforced palmar kneading.**
3. **Effleurage and light reflex stroking.** Finish your abdominal massage with three repetitions of effleurage and 10 of light reflex stroking.

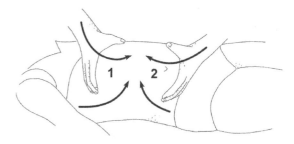

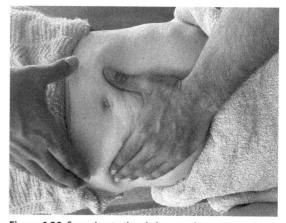

**Figure 6.20.** Scooping to the abdomen, alternating right and left hands.

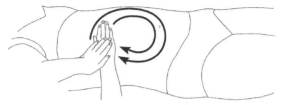

**Figure 6.21.** Reinforced palmar kneading.

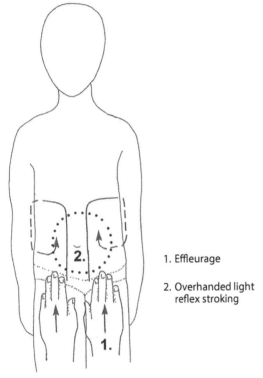

1. Effleurage

2. Overhanded light
   reflex stroking

**Figure 6.22.** Effleurage and light reflex stroking to the abdomen.

Most people can feel their way along a spastic colon and work out the tension just on their own instincts and the patient's feedback. The patient often knows intuitively the benefits of someone trying to apply hands-on help, and they can coach you on touch, pressure, and most effective strokes. When I check back in with my digestively challenged patients, they often tell me what the results of the massage were after I left, what they would like to try again, and what they tried to do themselves with self-massage.

## Positions for Massaging the Digestive System

### Supine

When the person is lying supine (faceup), you have the easiest access to their digestive system. You can clearly see any drains, tubes, tumors, and surgical scars. This is also typically a comfortable position for someone with abdominal pain. However, if the patient is only comfortable in a supine position, then you must remember work underneath the hips to massage the areas here that influence the patient's digestion. I often massage with one hand under the patient's back and the other on the abdomen. This sandwich of hands works well to calm a spasming digestive system or create quicker relaxation.

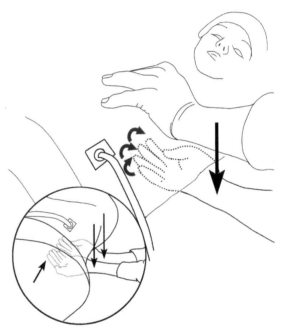

**Figure 6.23.** Supine digestive massage with levered fingertip kneading.

### Side-lying

Some palliative patients curl into the fetal position and stay that way for days on end. This is the body's natural position when it is conserving heat and keeping our vital organs warm for survival. It is a palliative reflex that we can work with because it can also have advantages for a patient's digestive functioning. This side-lying position helps the digestive system use gravity by tipping the person so digestive material can be encouraged to travel along its route. Again, put one hand on the abdomen and one hand on the lower back to make a massage sandwich of energetic contact that encourages peristaltic action with the pressure of the strokes along the pathway of digestion.

In the side-lying position, the lower back, which supplies the nerves for the digestive system, can get a massage at the same time as the abdomen. To begin a side-lying massage, make big alternating circles around the patient's stomach and lower back with your palms. Cover the entire surface of the abdomen with the surface of your hands (remember that the palmar kneading is not only the palm of the hand but the entire palmar surface of the hand from the wrist to the fingertips).

The other stroke I use when the patient is side-lying is single-handed palmar kneading, keeping the hand that is not massaging the abdomen bracing the lower back. This supports the person on their side so they do not roll backwards with the pressure of the abdominal stroke. Brace yourself to get more force in the stroke and to protect your own lower back. Remember to always use the stride posture, putting one leg forward, whether you are working alongside the patient, facing them, or behind them.

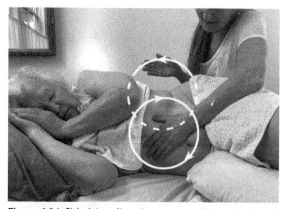
**Figure 6.24.** Side-lying digestive massage. Rotate the hand on the abdomen in one direction and the hand on the back in the other.

The side-lying position is best for abdominal massage when the patient has new post-surgical abdominal incisions. When bandages, tubes, and drains have been newly inserted on the front of the body, sometimes the abdominal area cannot be directly massaged. Instead, work reflexively through the nervous system, massaging the lower back. Indirectly, we can calm the digestive system by influencing the nerve supply for the abdominal organs.

### Prone

If your patient can tolerate lying prone for any amount of time, this can be an effective posture for digestive enhancement. The pressure on the abdomen when in a facedown position is therapeutic, helping to displace gas and unwind the tension of the abdomen. Support the patient comfortably (see pages 21 to 22) and be sure to frequently check in to see if a position change is needed.

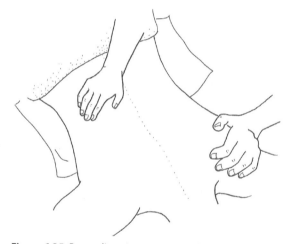
**Figure 6.25.** Prone digestive massage with pillow support.

### Seated

Often a seated position is the best option for the patient's breathing and swallowing. When my ALS patient, Mary, was in the last month of her life, she could only tolerate a seated position—she would choke in any other position. Her seated posture gave me good access to massage her upper digestive tract. Even though she was not eating orally, but through a gastric tube, massage to the front of

Mary's throat made it easier for her to swallow the saliva that collected in her mouth and threatened to choke her.

Some people get spasms around mealtimes, so it is important to massage them and relieve the spasticity when they are eating, no matter where they might be. You can massage their lower back and abdomen through their clothing while they are seated in a chair or wheelchair. Although it can be cramped, you can do the entire abdominal massage routine on a seated patient.

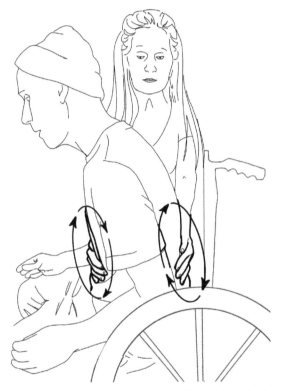

**Figure 6.26.** Seated digestive massage. Sandwich the body between your hands as you would do with a side-lying digestive massage. Move your palms in alternating circles.

These four positions for digestive massage will give you more options than you might have imagined for massaging the abdomen. If the patient is able, you can also try putting them on all fours as you go through the massage. It's helpful to try a variety of postures so you have options as the person's health

declines. It also allows the patient to experience the difference of these varied techniques.

## Abdominal Self-Massage

Teaching someone to massage their own abdomen requires that they are strong enough to perform the strokes. If they can lift their arms, they can usually perform the self-massage routine. I have learned the most effective self-massage techniques from my dying patients themselves.

Gaston, the patient you met earlier in the book, was able to massage his own digestive system. He showed me what he did to himself three times a day. Although he could not feel much sensation in his lower body, he massaged his abdomen and around his tumor site, which distended to his side. He used fingertip kneading to make his colon move, and he showed his daughters how to help.

The strokes used in self-massage are all used in the digestive massage routine described above; it's just the person who delivers them that changes!

*STEPS IN SELF MASSAGE*

1. Overhanded palmar kneading
2. Fingertip kneading to the entire abdomen
3. Scooping into the center of the abdomen
4. Running vibrations to the descending colon
5. Repeat scooping
6. Overhanded palmar kneading to finish

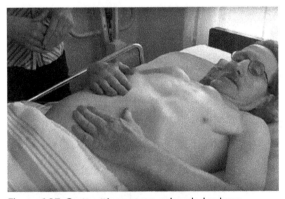

**Figure 6.27.** Gaston tries some overhanded palmar kneading as part of his self-massage routine.

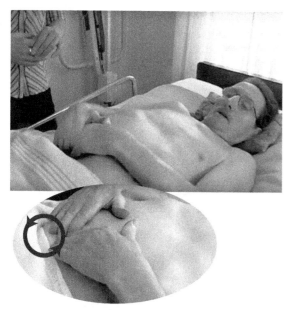

**Figure 6.28.** Reinforced and single-handed fingertip kneading is also a useful part of the self-massage routine.

## Food for Thought

Food, like touch, is one of the lasting pleasures of life. Smelling food, like smelling flowers, helps the digestive system start to function by encouraging it to release its enzymes and juices. Even after a dying person can no longer eat, pleasant food smells will still have an effect. By using coconut and vanilla oils in your abdominal massages, you can link the body's experience of massage to the positive aroma of your patient's favorite foods. When I am dying, I hope someone will use digestive massage to help me enjoy my food while I can still taste it. I know massage and touch will help ease the loss of my appetite. I also hope to be massaged with coconut and orange oils to give me that sensory memory of some of my favorite foods.

Even though my friend Brian was living on a ventilator and could not eat, he did taste his sixtieth birthday cake. He chewed a tiny bit of cake and got a good taste of the treat before he had to spit it out. Brian was a great inspiration in the healthy food department. Back in the early seventies, before the onset of his ALS, he was quite creative with food. We learned to make goat yogurt together using a light bulb as a heat source. Though I never picked

up his British love of marmite, I followed his recipes for dehydrating foods, making fresh apple juice, freezing garden vegetables, and making as many products from our goat milk as our imaginations would allow.

It seems natural, then, that this engineer and inventor would continue to teach me new ways of

**Figure 6.29.** Brian ingested a variety of nutritious foods strained through various sieves until the concoction reached the right consistency for Brian's feed line.

cooking during his illness. When he was no longer able to chew, Brian and Joan, his partner, invented Green Slime, a healthy, fresh alternative to store-bought concentrates. Their concoction was easily digested and packed full of nutrients.

Making Brian's feed was a weekly production. It took days to cook the veggies and beans and grains. Then everything—fruit, vitamins, oils, vegetables, and grains—were pureed and strained through three graduated sizes of sieve until they reached the proper consistency to be injected straight into Brian's stomach through his stomach tube. We used an IV bag hung high for gravity feeding. Once a three-day supply had been made and refrigerated, the whole process would start over again.

I thought that this concoction of Green Slime was gold. I wish that all my patients using commercial brands of concentrated nutrition could benefit from this kind of culinary creativity. Though it's a lot of work, you too can create some nonconstipating liquid foods for your loved ones, which will eliminate the pain of sluggish colons.

### To eat or not to eat?

When someone is dying, certain foods can cause reactions. Even if they can physically eat, people often stop being able to tolerate their favorite foods due to changes in their sense of taste related to their medications or their disease. I have found that my patients sometimes get a metallic taste when they eat any food. Disappointingly, everything starts to taste toxic. Some people even lose their ability to taste altogether.

Valerie, my stepmother, lost her sense of taste, and yet she enjoyed the Christmas dinner she ate just a couple of days before she died. I had to massage her in every position to get the food moving along.

My mother had a slower departure than Valerie, so we could see her appetite change and her interest in food diminish. She still had a sweet tooth; tiny pieces of chocolate would melt on her tongue and cause her to smile. Chocolate flavoring was the magic ingredient for feeding her liquid formula in her last weeks. But the only time my mom

was in pain in the last weeks and days of her life was directly related to her digestive system.

If we fed her meal supplements, she would restlessly move her legs in discomfort and her sleep would be disturbed. Her stomach couldn't take it any longer. In her last week, I realized that we were responsible for her discomfort. We were the ones feeding her. After a final mess and the abdominal pain that ensued, I never wanted her to feel that again.

I was torn about what to do. How could I stop feeding her? But at the same time, how could we continue to feed her if it made her so uncomfortable? Most families eventually find themselves in this predicament. They still want to feed the person who is dying, even when it might be increasing their discomfort.

Our physician settled the issue: he told me to stop feeding her; give her water, but no food or formula. My brother and I were both relieved to follow his directive.

For the last two weeks of my mom's life, I gave her sips of nectar juice and tea from a tiny teacup with a fluted edge that perfectly fit her lips. She was comfortable. I still massaged her tummy as part of her full-body daily massages. She never had another bowel movement again, and she continued to sip her nectar juice and peppermint tea. She had her last sip just an hour before she died, having a final afternoon tea on the balcony in the August sunshine.

## Digestive Tips

Drinking lots of water is the main prevention for constipation problems. Vegetable or fruit juice can be added in as supplements to water, but should not be used to replace water. If the patient does not want to drink water, you can try giving them ice chips instead.

I found that "easy-to-chew" food are not guaranteed to be easy on the digestive system. In fact, things that are easy to eat often lead to constipation. Bananas, for example, are bad for those with constipation or for codeine users; conversely, they are great for those with diarrhea. Adding flax oil and ground flax to a patient's favorite fruit smoothie, on the other hand, can keep things moving forward.

Often patients enjoy the coolness of ice cream to soothe their throats. However, dairy products can cause increased mucus production, which can be difficult for a patient who is, for example, having trouble swallowing. Using frozen fruit puree is an excellent way to get the same soothing and cooling effect on the upper digestive tract without using ice cream.

Teas can also aid digestion. I encourage people to drink pain-relieving valerian root tea, as well as chamomile, peppermint, or ginger teas, which can all aid in relaxation.

### Hydrotherapy help for digestion

When I was working at my first job in a physiotherapy clinic in Toronto, I had a patient who, unbeknownst to me, was constipated. During an appointment with her, I used hot clay packs on her lower back during the massage treatment. She later reported that her persistent constipation was relieved later that day. I had not studied constipation treatments in school, and I was fascinated to learn about the effect of the massage. Her treatment plan emerged: massage, hot packs to the lower back and abdomen, and walking every night for 15 minutes. Today I apply this patient's constipation relief system to people who are dying, teaching families and hospice volunteers to use heat treatments such as hot clay packs, and to mobilize the hips through massage and leg motion in place of walking.

There is a scientific basis for the old wives tale that a hot-water bottle relieves abdominal pain such as stomach aches, colic, or cramps. In a *Science Daily* article, Dr. Brian King, from University College London, explains that abdominal pain is often caused by a "reduction of blood flow or distention of your hollow organs—such as the bowel or uterus." When you apply heat, "it switches on your heat receptors, which in turn block the pain messengers." It isn't a placebo effect. In fact, it blocks your pain receptors in the same way pharmaceutical pain relievers do: in essence, your heat receptors block your pain receptors.[21]

Several types of hydrotherapy techniques can help digestive problems:

1. **Hot-water bottles.** Hot-water bottles and hot packs put positive pressure on the abdomen to help with gas discomfort. Applying hot-water bottles to the lower back or directly on the abdomen will help soothe a patient's digestion. This localized heat will positively affect the intestines right down to the rear end.

2. **Hot clay packs.** These packs are available in hospitals from hydrocollator units. They are another great pre- and postmassage application in all the same areas as hot-water bottles.

3. **Castor oil packs.** With my palliative patients, castor oil packs are applied around the abdomen as a warmth wrap, creating better circulation in the abdominal area. To make a castor oil pack, soak heavy cloth (such as flannel) in castor oil, wrap in more layers of cloth as insulation, and apply along with a warm or hot heating pad or hot-water bottle. I use plastic to insulate and protect any blanket or towel covering from the oil.

4. **Cold water abdominal wash or wrap.** Cold-water washes to the abdominals after massaging are an excellent stimulus to digestion. The same is true of wrapping the abdominals in a cold wrap. Simply take a facecloth and rinse it in cold water, then wring it out so it is wet, but not dripping. Quickly (before the cloth warms up) wrap your hand in the facecloth and apply palmar circles to the abdomen. Do not warm the area up by rubbing it afterwards, but rather let the body respond by warming back up on its own. This is a good way to cool down an inflamed or highly irritated bowel. You can repeat the cold washing a number of times throughout the day or night.

5. **Epsom salt bath.** Epsom salt baths are a good way to encourage sweating and stimulate the natural cooling action of an overheated body. Give your patients lots of water while they are soaking to flush their system and help them tolerate the heat.

**6. Sitz baths.** When a person has extreme digestive problems, sitz baths (a shallow bath with water up to the hips) are excellent for soothing. Bathing the floor of the pelvis and rear end can help relieve hemorrhoids, diarrhea, wounds, or an inflamed anus. The temperature can be anywhere from warm or tepid to cool or cold. I always use warm temperatures and add Epsom salts to the water to speed up the healing of surgery sites and hemorrhoids and to dry up weeping wounds.

Massaging around the stoma site
Leg pumping
Alternate leg pumping
Lower digestive massage 1
Lower digestive massage 2
Digestive massage – supine
Digestive massage – side-lying
Digestive massage – seated
Abdominal self-massage

Feedback from your patient will give you the information you need to make your abdominal massage the perfect fit. Questions to ask are: How much pressure? How long? Where is the discomfort? How did the last tummy rub go? What do you want me to do again?

You might hear the results of your abdominal massage, especially if your patient is constipated and the colon starts to respond with the gurgling, murmuring, and sometimes spasms of a digestive system waking up. The sounds are a compliment to the therapist—I always return the compliment to the patient, thanking them for the chorus of sounds.

If your patient is comatose, then you must use your intuition and listen with your hands to the body's feedback. You can use the same massage techniques (including leg pumping) that you would in a full-body massage, moving your patient into a side-lying position and working the tummy and lower back together, or massaging the nerve supply to the digestive tract. Even if the comatose person is being fed by tube, your efforts are still necessary to help nourish their dying body.

## Online Classroom
Visit brusheducation.ca/dying-in-good-hands to watch these videos:

Moving the biliary pouch
Massaging around the ileostomy site

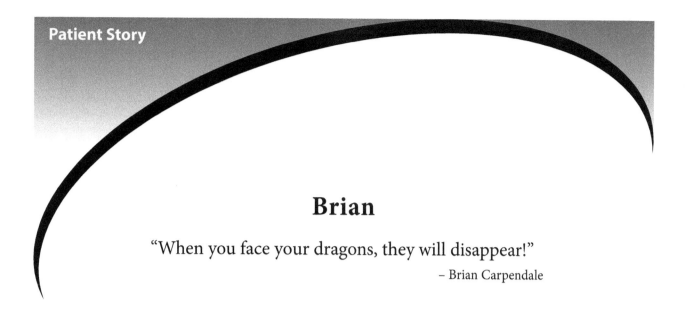

# Brian

## "When you face your dragons, they will disappear!"

– Brian Carpendale

I had an in-depth experience in palliative care with my friend Brian Carpendale, who died of ALS, a fatal neurological disease with extreme muscle wasting.

Brian, 20 years my senior, had been my mentor, showing me the fundamentals of massage. He encouraged me to continue with my interest in massage and train in Toronto. Under his tutelage, I learned to massage horses, cattle, and the occasional dog. When I was a massage student studying for my board exams, he gave me his air force motto, *per ardua ad astra*, which means, "Through hard work to the stars."

Brian had led an extraordinary life. Among other things, he was a Gestalt therapy student and had trained directly under Fritz Perls. Brian had been in the engineering faculty at the University of Toronto and then in the communications department at Simon Fraser University. He moved to the Slocan Valley during a "back to the land" movement with his family.

Brian was living with his girlfriend, Joan, when he was diagnosed with ALS. I became an enthusiastic student of hands-on home-care possibilities with him. He lived with a ventilator and breathing machine for more than four years and continued to enrich the lives of everyone that came in contact with him.

Joan had been my best friend for years and now taught me the intricacies of daily living with someone with ALS. I massaged the two of them every day and was grateful that I had something to contribute to their lives. My basic principles of palliative massage originated from those days back in the early eighties with Brian.

Brian's symptoms of ALS started shortly after he suffered an injury to his head. He had been riding his bicycle down a country road and went over the handlebars. He suffered impact injuries to his head and started to experience changes in his gait, tripping over things. When Joan sent me photos of Brian's injuries, he looked like he had been in a fight. I gave her instructions over the phone for helping him. Massage would relieve the whiplash to his neck and back, and ice massage would help the facial wounds heal faster.

Brian was never the same after that injury. His symptoms of staggering and tripping increased. Within months of his crash, his speech began to fail. The following year, Brian's symptoms worsened, and his reliance on massage increased. I spent that summer in Nelson and taught Joan to massage Brian's legs and arms to relieve his increasing spasticity (muscles becoming so tight that they go into contraction). Brian was now using a wheelchair. He was unable to speak and communicated using an alphabet board and hand signals. I missed our talks.

Then a crisis came. Brian was in the emergency ward in Nelson, struggling to breathe. In all the bedlam and fear, Brian made a decision not to die. He chose to live with the aid of a respirator.

A respirator is a machine that breathes for a person. It is a lifeline, but it requires electricity. For people living in the country, where there are frequent power outages, it's a dangerous way to live. Brian's family built a wheelchair ramp to his front door to help Brian navigate his new wheelchair-bound life, but it became painfully clear that Brian needed to be closer to a constant, dependable power supply. Joan decided to move with Brian to her father's home near Vancouver. There, they were in the care of a team of volunteers and medical experts, but they were far from much of Brian's significant family back in the interior of BC.

Joan's paintings hung from the walls of her father's home, bringing their Kootenay life with them. From Brian's bed, he could see all his favorite places from back home. When I visited, I massaged him on his side while looking at a painting of the Slocan River that ran past their front door. Massaging on his other side brought a view of the beautiful birch trees that grew along that same river. As he lay on his back, he could contemplate the paintings on the ceiling of the bedroom, which showed the views from his attic desk window in the Kootenays.

During the day, Brian was moved into the living room where he could see the world around him, people coming and going, the animals, both dogs and cats, and kitchen activities. In the early days, he stayed in his wheelchair at the computer, which the local service club had donated so Brian could write and communicate.

In 1985, Brian made his last posting from his antiquated computer. It took him two hours to get the following words onto the screen:

The most important thing is Love.
Strength comes from Love,
Individuality comes from Love.
And Generosity also comes from Love.

Today, I use this quote in all my work and display the screen of Brian's computer in my educational slideshows.

During Brian's last year, I moved into Joan's dad's guest house for months at a time so that I could help out, while my mother looked after my two-year-old daughter. Working with them was a truly satisfying experience. I massaged Joan every night after getting Brian to bed, and every morning when she got up.

Joan had become an expert in wheelchair transfers. Joan described her transfer as her daily hug, as she never had contact with Brian standing up anymore. Brian would wrap his arms around Joan's neck, and she would encompass his frail body with her arms, gathering him up close to her body.

Moving Brian had a special complication because he had to be disconnected from his breathing machine for the procedure. Transfers had to be quick and efficient so Brian didn't go long without air. She had Brian's transfers down to a fine art. She had a transfer board designed with smooth edges for board transfers. She had made belts of all kinds to wrap around Brian's waist for belt transfers. Joan was also an intuitive teacher. Although I am a tiny person, she was able to teach even me to transfer Brian effortlessly.

As Brian became weaker, she began using the transfer belts. She placed Brian's arms over her shoulders to balance the two of them together as they stood up straight. She then shuffled the two of them around, keeping his feet between her feet, to aim him at the landing site. Whether it was the bed at night or the couch for the day, Brian would land softly and gently with Joan's transfer technique.

When Joan taught me to transfer Brian, I was too slow at first. By the time I landed Brian into his new location, his nostrils would be flaring. This is the body's natural signal that it is fighting to get oxygen into the lungs. I became better with practice, and Brian lost the big-eyed look of panic.

One day Joan leaned over too far when moving Brian. She had the classic workup for a back injury: she had been under the weather at the time and not thinking clearly. That day, she moved

Brian a bit differently than the hundreds of times she had done it before, now she had strained her back muscles. The miscalculation was costly. The muscle spasms in her back were so severe that she could not get out of bed afterwards. Now she was in pain right beside Brian, nose to nose.

I flew out from Toronto to help. This was to be my steepest learning curve. Now I had to learn to do the dressing changes for Brian's stoma site. Brian's tube feed outlet on his stomach allowed him to be well-fed, even as his disease ravaged his muscle bulk.

Once, after I'd hooked up his bag of Green Slime, the food mix that Joan and others prepared for him (see page 162), I got busy reading Brian's book to him. He kept on interrupting the reading, and I wondered why. He peered at me and repeatedly rang his bell, obviously trying to convey something. Joan called out to me from the other room, reminding me to undo the clip and start the flow—a typical thing for a newbie to forget!

Through my many visits to Brian, I had learned all his exercises from his physiotherapist, Wendy. I included massages before and especially after these stretching exercises. The massages before the physiotherapy enhanced the elasticity of Brian's muscles, and the massages after the treatments provided relief from any discomfort that occurred during the workout. With Joan down for the count, I was happy to add the physiotherapy workout to Brian's massage routine. I learned to troubleshoot and problem solve with Joan coaching me and Brian supervising and nodding his approval.

The story of changing Brian's condom catheter was not a coached exercise, however. I had seen Joan do it before, and I had documented the step-by-step process on camera. I thought I knew it all.

I gracefully got through the procedure and was feeling very proud of myself when Joan decided to check my work. She commented that Brian was giving her one of those looks, so she looked at the condom and asked Brian if it was too tight. Evidently, I had his penis in a bit of a vice grip. After administering this tourniquet, I was definitely not graduating from condom cathetering with honors!

Fortunately, Brian gave my genital hygiene and diaper changing skills his approval, and my ratings started to pull out of the ditch.

Next was the breathing cuff. Brian had a hole in his throat where the ventilator was inserted. This opening had a pressure cuff around it designed to keep the tubing carrying the oxygen mixture to the right place. The cuff fitted around the tubing, and the tubing fitted into Brian's throat. I learned to measure the pressure in the cuff in order to keep a tight fit with the surrounding tissue.

I also learned to suck Brian's throat clear of any congestion. This was a delicate job. The suction machine was easy to run, but when I inserted the wand into Brian's throat and turned on the suction, he would involuntarily grimace. The choking motions and noisy suctioning sounds were alarming, and while Joan reassured me that I was doing a good job, Brian's gagging left me unconvinced. This was a terrible chore. Disturbing Brian's peace like this was right up there with shooting deer as one of the hardest things I had done in my life. Still, Brian gave me full marks for getting the most buildup of expectorate out of his throat. He really did feel better, and I noticed a difference in his raspy breathing sounds. I checked with the stethoscope and found that, yes, I had made a difference.

Those recovery days of Joan's back injury were like a honeymoon for our friendship. The three of us spent long, happy times hanging out, massaging and chatting, plotting and planning. Joan encouraged me to document my work, and we started taking pictures of everything we did. By the time Joan recovered, we had a slideshow of every detail of ALS homecare. We were excited to show it to people who needed support in keeping their loved ones at home when it looked like institutional care was their only option.

Brian had always felt confident that he could be looked after at home, but Joan's injury and convalescence was a strong reminder to all of us that the caregiver is central to the options available to the patient. By massaging Joan through her back injury—caring for Brian's caregiver—I became committed to teaching "care for the caregivers" as one of the central themes of my palliative massage training. After Joan's recovery, she continued to get massages and chiropractic treatments from others—but it was time for me to go home.

The day I flew back to Toronto, I tiptoed in to say goodbye to Brian. It was 6:00 a.m. and Joan was sleeping. Brian's eyes were open, and he motioned me to come nearer. I kneeled beside their bed. I told him that I loved him, that he had changed my life, and that I didn't want to leave him. I was up close to Brian, nose to nose, whispering. Suddenly his hand smashed into my face.

I burst into tears while Joan slept on. "Brian, that hurt!"

I couldn't see him very clearly through my tears, but I could see he was crying. He had tried to touch me, and the action had elicited a spastic response. The gentle touch was instead a big hit and a big hurt. We both cried. I whispered my goodbyes as Brian talked to me with his eyes. He knew something I did not yet know.

I had a bruise on my face for weeks that told the story of my last, dramatic goodbye with Brian.

I checked in with Joan by phone over the fall. In December, I got a call from her. This would be the third time in the whole course of our relationship that she had called me. The first time was to ask me about neutering my cat when I was at massage school as they were heading to the vet. The next time, five years later, was to ask me to be the executor of their estate.

This morning, she just needed to talk.

Brian had left. He no longer communicated. He did not make eye contact or reach out to touch her. She said that he had drifted into this state overnight. He was now gnashing on his tongue, cutting it with his teeth and leaving it mangled. His eyes moved around in his head, not focusing on anything.

We talked about ways to protect Brian's mouth and tongue and came up with an idea to use some of the extra ventilator tubing as a sort of mouth guard, wedging the tubing into his mouth so he could not bite down on his tongue. Our idea worked.

But this solution created another problem. His lips needed protection from the pressure of the tubing itself. Moleskin was the solution. Joan adhered the soft patch to his lower lip and rested the tubing on it. Brian did not register any discomfort. His eyes continued to wander, his tongue continued to wander, but his spirit never wavered from its course.

Brian was visited on Christmas Day by one of his care workers, a nurse from England called Debbie. She brought along her visiting niece and nephew. Brian was bedridden, so the kids visited him at his bedside. Brian seemed to respond to them and stirred. The older boy, who was about 10 years old, sat with Brian after the others had left to have Christmas tea in the living room.

Joan looked into their bedroom at one point to see if the nephew would like some tea and found him stroking Brian's face. She tiptoed out and got her camera. In the photo, the clock beside the bed reads 5:00 p.m., the time when a young boy from England gave Brian his final benediction, his loving touch.

Brian died at 10 o'clock that night.

At Brian's memorial, Joan played a meditation and relaxation tape that Brian had once made for me, teaching me self-hypnosis. There were people at the funeral who had never heard Brian speak. For them, hearing his voice was a glimpse into his other life, before his illness: his life as a helper, an educator, a therapist, and a philosopher. He sounded well-educated and very British. His voice was strong, confident, and caring.

I had not heard Brian's voice in three years; it was instantly intimate. I heard him speak my name.

Brian had taught me self-reliance. He taught me how to overhaul and sharpen my chainsaw, generate methane from our chicken manure, build pyramids, design rural technologies, and change my karma. He taught me to leave the past behind. He put me in touch with myself. Brian gave me the confidence that I did not possess on my own. He coached me and showed me courage.

It still amazes me that one person can have such impact. One person can make such a difference, not just to me, but to many people. It was his courage and his generosity. At the last, it his willingness to grow in spite of his illness—or, rather, to grow because of it. This was how he conducted his life, and this is his legacy.

*Per ardua ad astra*
Through adversity, to the stars!

Brian at work.

# 7

# The Last Breath

Breathing: it's what living is all about. I wonder what it will be like to breathe my last breath.

In this chapter, I discuss the kinds of last breaths that dying patients experience and how massage can help induce a peaceful passing. Sometimes there are final breaths that last for days. Others are much quicker: a patient talking to you one minute and gone the next.

The final breath can be unnerving, but there are massage techniques that can make the body's last attempts to breathe more comfortable. One of these is the end-stage upper-respiratory massage, which is taught in this chapter. Through discussion of techniques and explaining how individuals die differently, we can learn to see when the last breath is coming and be better prepared for the final moment.

## Stories of Last Breaths

Margaret Beveridge was a documentary pioneer at the National Film Board of Canada and helped establish film schools and boards in the United States and India. Margaret's daughter Nina asked me to show her how to massage her mother in the last weeks and days of her life.

The last time I massaged Margaret with Nina was a late afternoon session. I was on my way home and checked in with Nina about Margaret's progress. I always looked forward to massaging Margaret; I felt like I owed her something for all her work in the Canadian documentary film world.

Margaret was very quiet and did not speak much. Nina and I massaged her together. Nina asked me about Margaret's eyes, which were glazing over. I told Nina that people's eyes often get that look when the body is finally shutting down: she had the look of approaching death. Even as I told her, Nina seemed to already know; she saw that her mother's eyes didn't see her anymore.

I left to catch the ferry home and called back to the hospital an hour later to find out that Margaret had died.

Nina told me the story of her mom's last breath. She had decided to go and get some dinner. She leaned over and told her mom that she was going. "Goodbye," she said. Her mom responded, "Goodbye," and then breathed her last breath. She took her cue and moved forward.

As I write this, I'm reminded that, just yesterday, the daughter of one of my patients had a similar experience of her mom's last moment. This patient, Joan, had been my one-visit wonder. She had invited my palliative massage summer class to her place so her husband could learn to massage her. She was diagnosed with inoperable cancer and was hoping to live until the fall. When I asked her how long she thought she would live, she said October.

Two weeks later, at her funeral, I thought back to her daughter's description of the last moments of her mom's life. The family was gathered in the bedroom, but decided that their mom would be better off with just one person instead of the family mob.

They all filed out into the living room, leaving Joan with her husband. He read a prayer to her twice and, as he finished reading, she died. They all believed that the strong hunch to change their location was a God-given urge, and they were thankful that they had acted on that powerful instinct.

The day my mother died, I called her doctor to come by the house to check on her condition. She had been breathing in a "last breath" pattern for a day or two, taking minute-long pauses between breaths. The doctor arrived about an hour later, concluding that her heart was strong, and she wasn't dying today. However, the surprise of death prevailed. About 10 minutes later, my mother breathed her last.

My dad's departure was gentle. On New Year's Eve, he called his mother's name between eleven and midnight, then breathed his final breaths as the new year began. He did not labor or struggle with his breathing; he just softly drifted away.

When my stepmom, Valerie, died, her breathing did not change. One minute she was alive, and the next minute she was dead. At one point, she completely stopped breathing, and we thought she'd passed—but she came back one or two minutes later, fully alive and speaking! Soon after, though, she stopped breathing again and was finally gone.

With Sylvan, there were no surprises. I was right beside him when he passed away. I had been massaging him for about an hour while his friends rested downstairs when I suddenly realized that he was slipping fast, first skipping breaths and then stopping breathing entirely.

I didn't want to leave Sylvan's side, so I called down to his friends from his room. They arrived after he stopped breathing and was quiet. Although I had wished for him a death with the others present, I was glad I was there to help him breathe his last gurgled breaths.

Old friends and intimate new friends are often the pilots of the final transition. When Lynnie died, I was massaging her, with her friends Christine and Sabine beside her. Lynnie had been last-breath breathing for days. Two days before, her mother and sister had come to say goodbye. They knew that she would die soon—they thought probably that same day. Two days later, she was still breathing, but for the first time her neck was contracted and extremely difficult to straighten out. That morning, I was turning Lynnie to massage her back when she suddenly stopped breathing.

I asked her friends to get into my position and wrap their arms around her. They both replaced me. We gently put her on her back, stretching her out to give her a comfortable pose, and then we phoned her husband, Bob. She looked so peaceful and smooth. It was so quiet. Up until then, her breathing had been rhythmical and noisy. We had gotten used to the sounds of her departing life; when she left, it was so quiet.

## Signs of Departure

Although we can take cues from various signs of departure—bluing in the extremities, kidneys quitting, interrupted breathing, missing breaths, or a comatose body with no one home—the breathing is, typically, the last thing to really go, the final sign that living is over. The body has quit.

Sometimes, the breathing just stops, and people die before any physical breakdown in their lungs occurs. Usually, however, the lungs get weakened in their efforts to keep oxygen exchange working, which often results in them filling with fluid, then heart failure or lack of oxygen to the body when the lungs can't do their job anymore.

Many palliative patients are on pain medications with side effects that compromise their breathing. These medications slow down the body's reflexes and alertness. It's a difficult decision: more comfortable and less alert, or less comfortable and more alert? Most families would like to see their loved one more comfortable, even if they become unable to communicate. I, for one, hope most people become comfortably comatose before they die so they will not have any panic about not being able to catch their breath. I hope, too, that we will find more ways to help them be comfortable as their lungs fill up.

Often, people get frisky and energetic just before they die. Even if they have been nearly comatose for days, they may open their eyes, talk, and move around. If this happens, keep your hands on them; they might be so active that they think they can leave by getting up out of bed and heading out. Following this burst of energy, a palliative person will tend to settle again, then quickly die. The flurry of activity and excitement is often hard on caregivers; it "de-prepares" them for the fast exit that can follow such normal-looking behavior. Massage can be very soothing for both parties in these exciting, yet unpredictable times.

## Reach Out and Touch

In my ideal world of last breaths, the family and friends of those dying would be hands-on, actually touching the person. Whether we are formally massaging them or not, touching has a tremendous effect on a person's pain threshold. Just one resting hand can change their breathing and pain, and perhaps lessen their need for medications.

One of my most painful experiences was dulled with the hand of an ambulance driver. She took away the pain that had plagued me for hours, just with an absentminded touch while she wrote her report with her other hand. Her reassuring touch eased my pain and let me sleep.

With my dying patients, I encourage the family to keep a hand on the person while they are reading to them or reading to themselves. The contact makes a difference in the world of practicalities, and it can also make a big difference to the family, giving them an opportunity to stay connected during these last breaths.

## End-Stage Upper Respiratory Massage

Rib raking brings immediate relief to a dying person. Making a claw-like shape with your hand will get your fingertips in between the ribs to stretch the contracting intercostal muscles that are becoming fixed as the person breathes less and more shallowly. This rib raking is the most effective relief, so make sure to practice it in the last weeks and days of the person's life so you can hear their positive

feedback about how it helps them breathe more easily.

Next, continue to stroke the diaphragm along the edge of the ribs with some long, sweeping strokes. The side farthest away from you is easy to stroke using an open hand with the thumb tracing the edge of the ribcage. Take the hand along the side closest to you with the same angle in an open-handed gesture using the edge of your hand so it fits along the costal angle up underneath the ribs, not down into the abdomen.

You can also use small fingertip-kneading motions along the costal angle, both on and off the edge, to ease up the action of the diaphragm. Fingertip kneading is done with the fingertips held together so they feel like one contact point and then making tiny circles to the lower aspect of the collarbone and the sternum, then moving out to the armpit (axilla) attachments of the pectoral muscles. Then move to the pectorals themselves; massaging this large frontal muscle of the chest helps to relax a struggling breathing pattern.

Lastly, smooth and soothe the overall chest with large general strokes of effleurage. These can be used at the start or end of the massage, or in between the other strokes. A steady, continuous general stroking done with the palm of your hand will ease the tension in the thorax and help the person to relax and rest. This gentle stroking is excellent for guiding a dying person to the edge. You can follow your instincts on this with side-to-side movements and continuous chest strokes up and down the breastbone. The most important thing is the steadiness of the moves.

### Last breath team

Not many people get a practice run at death. We usually witness death in the movies or at someone else's bedside. We will never know how our last breath will be, but we can plan ahead for our departure by asking the people in our lives to sign up for our bedside hand-holding.

In the early part of my life, I used to promise my friends that I would be there for their baby deliveries. I also promised them that I would help them with the deaths and departures of their parents.

Now that I'm older, I promise to be there for my friends' deaths if they die before me. It is lovely to hear my friends (and sometimes my patients and students) wish for me to be on their team when they are dying.

For your last breath, think about the people you would like to have around you. Who would be good at being hands-on to ease your breathing? As you read this, you're probably already thinking about your "last breath" team, quickly adding those who have already helped to soothe, comfort, or just simply be with you.

We know who eases our discomfort and who adds to our discomfort. It isn't any different in dying. Some people have great instincts for comforting and soothing us. They literally take away our pain.

## Calm Words

At the height of my labor, I wanted my mom. I cried out loud, "I want my mom, I want my mom, I want my mom." My husband, Willie, called my mom for me. When she told me that I was going to be okay, that I was in good hands, and that nothing bad was going to happen to me, the discomfort changed. I was more comfortable in the contractions. Willie repeated my mother's words and they continued to calm me.

Calming words have their place at deaths as much as at births. The combination of loving words and touch is the best formula for last breaths.

When Valerie, my stepmom, was breathing her last breaths, I instinctively told her that I loved her, that my dad (who was already dead) loved her, and that she could go to him; he was waiting for her. I held her and talked to her, telling her how much I loved her in the same departure scenario we had shared months before when my dad died.

That process of aiding someone's movement from life to death with caring caress and talk is like the midwifery of dying. We can make a difference in how people take their last breaths. With words and touch we are able to lift them out of their pain, ease their breathing, and give ourselves everlasting comfort.

Just as our bodies respond automatically and reflexively to a lover or family member's familiar touch, so we can be "sensed" by those we love when they are dying. People might think that someone who is comatose or barely there will not know the difference between being touched and not being touched, but research has shown that there are somatic responses in pain reduction, even in comatose patients, and a deeper and more restful sleep when touch is applied. In 2012, a research team in Tehran, Iran, conducted a clinical trial on 45 patients in ICU to assess the impact of massage therapy by family members by measuring the patients' vital signs and Glasgow Coma Scale (GSC) scores before and after the massage. The study demonstrated that "full body massage by family members increases the level of consciousness of patients." They summed up the study by saying that there was a significant difference in patients massaged by family members, and that massage should therefore "be recognized as one of the most important clinical considerations in hospitalized patients."[22]

We as human beings are responsive to touch up until and including our last breath. We can help our friends, relatives, and patients prepare to let go with our relaxing massages, reassure them with our caring touch, and coach them with our words and acquired intuition. Remember, our last breaths can take many forms—they might be quick, at the side of the road in an accident scene; they could be lingering, labored breaths at home or in a hospice; or our breath be here one breath and gone the next without any dramatic finale. For the best death and the best last breath, nothing is better than the touch of another caring human being.

## Online Classroom

Visit brusheducation.ca/dying-in-good-hands to watch this video:

End-stage respiratory massage

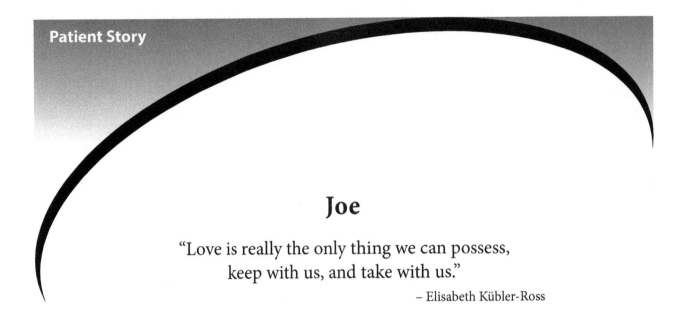

# Joe

"Love is really the only thing we can possess,
keep with us, and take with us."

– Elisabeth Kübler-Ross

It is 8:30 on Sunday morning.

I walk into Joe's hospital room, sweaty and energized from my morning run, and head straight to the bed. I look into Joe's eyes. They are glazing over with the veil of approaching death. They are eyes not seeing, looking beyond the horizon of the festive, balloon-filled room. I touch his hand and say, "Joe, it's Christine. I'm here to give you a massage."

I'm aware of the extreme labor of his breathing. He is gasping for air. His lips are opening and closing, a reflex beyond his control. The muscles around his mouth are rhythmically pulsing, helping him to gather the air into himself.

As his nostrils flare, I ask his wife, Carol, how long he's been breathing this way.

"All night," she says. She's sitting curled in a hospital chair jammed up to the bed. Carol is a slim, attractive woman. She has dark brown, shiny, shoulder-length hair. She has a well-loved look.

I have seen this breathing many times before, just before death. I have watched this panting and these lip-gathering movements bring small bits of air into dying lungs. Most of the time, this type of breathing continues for two hours at the most. It is an effort that seems to use up all the reserve of life force, gathering it up from the legs and arms into the very center of the person. I have seen this phenomenon last for as little as five minutes before

a gentle departure, but I had never witnessed 12 hours of Olympic strength like Joe's. As I start to massage Joe's temples, he involuntarily wrinkles his brow. His body is extraordinarily strong.

Carol uncurls from her nest in the chair by his side and straightens up. "Joe hasn't drunk anything since yesterday," she murmurs. My fingers travel over Joe's neck muscles. They are fixed and rigid. "He hasn't turned his head from that position since last night." I rub the back of his head with tiny massage strokes along the bony ridges. I am increasingly aware of the urgency of our situation.

I glance up at Carol's face and see behind her the faces of family and friends embroidering the hospital wall. In the darkness of the previous evenings' visits, I hadn't noticed the colorful collage papering the length of his room. Joe looks young in the pictures. He looks like his 48-year-old self. I have never seen Joe standing, as he is in all of these pictures: walking, skiing, and boating. There are scenes from beach campfires, birthdays, and family celebrations of every kind. All these faces look down on his bed. In the photos, Joe looks very healthy, sandy-bearded with sparkling eyes. He exudes charisma and life. There are images of him on the beach with Carol. The way he holds her, the tenderness of his touch, shows all the love he has for her.

I lift the sheets from Joe's legs and show Carol his mottled blue, translucent skin. He's draped in graduated shades of dark blue and light purple from his toes to his hips. This is an accurate indication of imminent death. I know that Carol's midwifery background won't give her the same message I see clearly, and I wonder what I should say. As I massage his cooling extremities, I am reminded of the warmth and radiant heat of Joe's normal circulation; his feet and hands were always toasty.

Carol circles around to Joe's head, climbs onto the bed and lies down, nose to nose. I don't want to disturb them, but I have to speak up.

"I don't think Joe is going to be here for much longer," I say. "He might be here this afternoon, but he won't be here tonight or tomorrow.

"You're the one to coach him. You're the one to help him along. Be sure to tell him you'll be fine, that he doesn't have to worry about you or the kids. He's given you everything you'll need. And he can let go."

She looks at him and touches his shoulder.

I say, "Are the kids able to come right now?" I'm aware of the directness of my question. What if he isn't dying right this minute? What if it is tomorrow or the next day? I have seen these miracles in reverse. What if I'm the fire caller of false hunches?

But what's the worst that can happen? Some might think I was too quick to judge the situation—but I remember similar situations where I didn't speak up and still regret it. "Maybe the kids should bring things to do here so they could spend the day or night?"

Carol gets it. "Should I call the kids—now?"

I nod. "Tell Joe what you're going to do."

She places her hands around his head. She speaks distinctly. "Joe, I'm going to call the kids."

"Tell him their names," I whisper.

"Joe, I'm going to call Michael and Hudi and Katrina and Olivia and Jessica and Grandma. They're going to come and say goodbye to you. I love you."

"Tell him you'll be right back."

She doesn't miss a beat and continues in the same steady voice, "I'll be right back, honey; I'm just going out in the hall to call home." Carol collects her phone and leaves the room.

I wrap Joe's legs in warm blankets and start to arrange the pillows and sheets to massage his back. He's still warm and pink all along his back. I use long, smooth effleurage strokes to cover the full length of his back from his lower pelvis up to his wide shoulders, out to his upper arms, looping around down his sides to start again.

Carol slips quietly into the room and quickly climbs onto her spot at the head of the bed. She curls into a cocoon and strokes his face, says that the kids are coming, and tells him in great detail how much she loves him.

Then, as though summoned, Joe lets go. My hands are still slowly moving over his back in sweeping, comforting movements. The rhythm of the massage slows to match the pace of his body shutting down. Gradually my hands come to rest on his shoulders, gently massaging the tension of his neck. His firmly contracted throat swallows to close itself. My heart leaps at the motion of his throat. I know we are there. We are at the gates and they are swinging open.

"He's going now," I murmur.

Carol calls to him. She keeps caressing his face through his last movements and beyond, until the sounds of his breathing, the regular rhythm of life, are gone. Gone is the ebb and flow of his physical struggle. The quiet sets in.

Joe.

# 8

# Where to Die

I ask my writing partner Wendy where she would like to die, and she is quick with her answer: "At home, of course!" I explain that many people want to die in the hospital. They are afraid of pain. They want to be where drugs are easily available and hospital staff are all around them. They fear they wouldn't be comfortable at home; they would be on edge. And then there are those who do not have anyone at home, so they want to be in the hospital where there are people to help them die.

She is unconvinced: "My dad wanted to die at home. He was really keen on being in his own home when he died." Wendy had a lineage of home departures and had a clear idea of her death in her own familiar surroundings. I could see it. I told her that if she dies before me, I would be there, and if I die before her, then we will have to do a pretaped video to show her how to massage her husband and how he could massage her, so I could be there in spirit and practicalities.

Most of us have limited exposure to people dying, and we might not know what we want for ourselves. The same goes for childbirth. And yet, less than a hundred years ago, things were different. All babies were born at home. Most people died at home. And most people had exposure to the processes of birthing and dying because they happened in their homes and everyone helped. Births and deaths happened within community. In recent decades, however, we entered a hospital-only phase for deliveries and departures; but now, things are shifting back again. I have attended numerous home births and hospital births in

about a fifty–fifty split. The same is true for death and departures.

The world of palliative care has become more humane, thoughtful, and smart. It has begun to give people choices about how they want to manage their care and how they want to die. People have options today; they can die at home with lots of medical support or in the hospital with lots of friends and family support. Hospices are now state-of-the-art in Canada. Now we have many small hospices in the most beautiful settings, such as Cottage Hospice in the heart of Vancouver, and Moog and Friends Hospice House in the Okanagan Valley in Penticton. At these places, you can be in a tranquil environment with expert medical care. But whether we choose to die at home or in a hospice or hospital, family members can easily offer palliative massage as part of the care.

As physician assisted dying is becoming legal in more and more jurisdictions, assisted deaths are becoming more common in palliative scenarios in which people have long-term or terminal disabilities or illnesses. Whenever I listen to a story about assisted dying, I wonder if the person had massage written into their departure plan. Providing comfort and relaxation are as important in elected deaths as in natural deaths.

## Hospitals

Hospitals have entire floors dedicated to palliative and hospice care. Hospitals are familiar with deaths and the process of dying. They are equipped to handle the medical issues that come up with drugs and oxygen, drips and drains, and lots of practical and emotional help.

Families get used to learning about the ins and outs of the different palliative possibilities in hospitals. These institutions usually have procedures for family members to take the dying person out in the sunshine, or on an outing to the gardens or a movie, or simply on a stroll through the neighborhood. These rules and regulations are normally easy to work with—and with budgetary cutbacks to hospitals, hands-on help from families is usually welcomed. It used to be that home was the only place a person could personalize their death, but now things have changed. Dying patients in my local hospital, for example, can have their dog or cat in the room. Family members can stay the night on the couch, in a bed in the hallway, and even in bed with the dying person.

When my next-door neighbor Norma was dying, we didn't know where she should die. She was single, in her eighties, and soft hearted with a soft touch. We didn't know how long she could stay at home or if this was reasonable. Although her friends came frequently to massage her and the summer-school palliative massage students loved her, without someone who could be with her 24 hours a day, she opted to go to the hospital in her final days. I had taught her entire church congregation to massage her. When they saw the prominent "Massage me" cards at the head of her bed, they all took turns giving her more massages in the hospital than she had been receiving at home. Norma's story is the best example of the easy accessibility that hospitals can create. She was doing great at home with lots of helpful visitors and a great massage team, but the hospital gave her security about her death, and it also gave the larger community an opportunity to wish her well.

## Chronic Care Facilities

Chronic care facilities are another place to die comfortably. Often there is a room close to the nursing station, as in our local hospital, so the dying person can be closely monitored. My palliative massage teams have been welcomed in every chronic care facility we have visited. I've found the same is true in other countries. When I visited chronic care facilities in Africa, staff wanted to hear all the massage possibilities in palliative care, particularly for patients with AIDS and tuberculosis. In Guatemala, they wanted to learn massage for spinal cord injuries and too many other conditions to count.

## Hospices

Hospitals are designed to have a revolving door of palliative patients, taking them in for a few days, then sending them back out—and repeating this rotation a few times. At hospices, however, you usually are admitted until death.

The palliative care movement helped to create separate medical facilities for those who are dying, resulting in beautiful hospices around the world. Every hospice is different—it's own little community. In this section, I describe some of the hospices I have visited and worked with in my life.

When I taught in South Africa for the Stephen Lewis Foundation in Durban, the hospice was a community project with vegetable gardens and artwork that they used to raise funds to cover the cost of palliative care. In the Cayman Islands, as in Guatemala and South Africa, traveling palliative nurses have created a strong outreach network for home hospice care. In my hometown of Nelson, our hospice outreach network is strong, and is an ideal option for those who want to die at home with the help of hospice volunteers.

In Canada, I have taught many hospice groups to massage their dying clients in the most perfect facilities. Our Rotary organization and other service groups help to fund these buildings and hospice societies. With this help, no one needs to die alone or isolated these days.

In the 1980s, I worked to help build Casey House, an AIDS hospice in Toronto. I was on the multidisciplinary committee to establish the systems for massage delivery, to design the massage facilities, and to supervise the programs and installation of the rooms. We built a magnificent facility in a stately turn-of-the-century house in downtown Toronto. Architecture companies from the city sponsored the design and decor of each room. It was a state-of-the-art design, complete with a hydrotherapy room, a whirlpool, and family rooms for folks sleeping over. Casey House had the first hospice massage program in Canada.

Although I didn't know it at the time, I soon discovered that the massage facilities at Casey House were not practical. Palliative massages are best delivered in the patient's room, as they are rarely very mobile by the time they enter into hospice care. As beautiful as the Casey House facilities were, I never used the massage room or the equipment situated on the main floor of the hospice. Instead, I went to the patients' own rooms, keeping my hot packs and cold eye bags in the nearby nursing station, and heating up my oil in the microwave—sometimes exploding the bottle and spraying the precious oils all over the machine! (It was messy, but it smelled great.)

However, the fancy hydrotherapy whirlpool unit was worth its weight in gold. So many patients had hard-to-handle skin lesions, skin breakdowns, and other skin afflictions, so the sling that we used to move patients into the pool was invaluable. Using the whirlpool with its underwater jets was yet another way people could get a full-body massage.

Casey House expanded into a second facility in 2013. The massage services there are still well-used today. AIDS is a changing disease, but the Casey House massage team stays strong, giving relief and pain management for bedridden residents.

On the other side of Canada, in the rolling hills of British Columbia's interior, is the most beautiful setting I've ever seen for a hospice. A view of the desert valley served as a breathtaking panoramic backdrop for a palliative massage class I gave at the Marjorie Snowden Willoughby Hospice Home in Kamloops. In addition to the standard hospice design elements, this hospice lends itself to the possibilities of outdoor massage with expansive and fully wheelchair-accessible gardens.

**Figure 8.2.** Marjorie Snowden Willoughby Hospice Home, Kamloops, British Columbia.

The Moog and Friends Hospice House, in Penticton, was named after Andy Moog, the NHL hockey player who helped to build it. It is a wonderful, cottage-style facility that housed the first Canadian volunteer massage team. When I visited the facility, the support for massage was in full swing. One of the volunteer coordinators was especially enthusiastic about her volunteer team. She had expanded the hospice's massage services to take the team out into the community in order to help palliative patients who wanted to receive massage at home.

I was thrilled to help here, where the commitment was so high. I watched the families in this hospice respond to the massage team with their appreciation and welcome. They called them angels. The team worked around the facility while I followed them with my camera, capturing their

**Figure 8.1.** Casey House, Toronto, Ontario.

**Figure 8.3.** Moog and Friends Hospice House, Penticton, British Columbia.

stories. First thing in the morning, they met as a group, starting with a session about the patients and then dividing into teams to cover all the massages for that morning. They used surgical gloves to administer their massages, slipping gloves onto the hands of family and friends as they included them into the massage routines.

I filmed Arlene, a new massage volunteer, teaching the elderly sister of a palliative patient how to give a massage. The visiting little sister was now able to give comfort in the last day of her big sister's life.

Next, I watched a big, tough trucker being massaged by his high school buddy. They had done their newspaper delivery routes together when they were 10 and 12 years old. We showed the high school buddy, still wearing his baseball cap, how to massage his dying friend's swollen legs. He learned quickly and said he was glad he had something useful to do. Without the team's encouragement to join in and help, those two men would not have considered making massage part of their final visits. If I hadn't already been a convert to the atmosphere of love and affection that can be generated by massaging people in these dying moments, the sight of these two friends would have sold me.

The Moog Hospice Massage Team also makes good use of tandem massages, massaging in teams of two to five volunteers. Sometimes both volunteers massage the patient, each taking an arm or leg. Or, for patients with visitors, one team member massages the patient, while the second person massages the family or friends in the room. The massage team would naturally divide every time they entered a patient's room, with some massaging the family and others massaging the dying person.

A strong aspect of the Moog program is its focus on teaching family and friends to massage. The volunteers are the day team that teaches families how to be the night team. Now that the massage team has moved out into the community, they continue to keep this family focus central to their work, massaging patients' families alongside their dying loved ones.

**Figure 8.4.** Cottage Hospice in Vancouver became my most intimate hospice experience. I lived here for nearly three months with my dear friend, Don Grayston. Although I'd taught at Cottage Hospice years before, living there was an extraordinary learning experience.

## Home

When I ask people, from teenagers to seniors to dying people, where they want to die, dying at home is usually the clear winner. Medical professionals tell me that dying at home is best, as long as people have adequate support. They say this because most people are comfortable at home, with the memories of their life around them. The community that builds up around the home of the dying is magical. The neighbors have an outlet for their care and concern, helping with the garden, the food, the chores, and the massages. As Gail Potter, Selkirk College's Director of Nursing Studies (Online Geriatric Care) puts it, "When patients are put in facilities, they get more and more caregivers. There are more and more people coming and going; they also have a lot fewer choices, so it is not always conducive to a peaceful death."

When my mom was dying, we moved her lovely brocade-covered couch into her facility so I could sleep overnight in her room. But after a week, I bundled her up and let her doctor know that I was kidnapping her. I got it into my head that I was going to take her home, and I was going to look after her. I was very fortunate that her doctor made house calls.

My mother lay on the daybed in the living room when friends and family came for tea. I didn't go out to work; my patients came to me. I wheeled my mom into the den where I had set up my table and massaged my patients while I kept an eye on her. It reminded me of the times I took my daughter, then a baby, to work at the massage school. She was always in the corner of the office in her crib. Now my mom was in the same situation. I took her everywhere I went.

We looked after her at home for a month. She died in the afternoon sun, lying between me, my brother, and my best friend on the deck of my condo in an old, reclining wheelchair. We could have done it all at the facility, but bringing her out of the institutional setting (as beautiful as it was) and home to die just felt like the right thing to do.

The traditional approaches to home deaths can be enhanced with modern technology. Medical backups such as oxygen tanks, new types of medications, and visiting teams of professionals can all be a part of home palliative care.

## Deciding Where to Die

Beyond just knowing the options available, there are a number of factors to consider when deciding where to die.

### Restrictions to touch

Since you're reading this book, I can assume you would prefer dying in a location that is open to touch. Just keep in mind that not all palliative massage programs are as progressive as, for example, the Moog and Friends Hospice House. Not all hospitals and hospices are proactive in their beliefs and systems of care. Indeed, some are careful to the point of exclusivity about when, where, and by whom residents can be massaged. Usually, family members do not need to abide by hands-off policies—no one can override a family member or next of kin's wishes about massaging a dying person—but massage volunteers who are not related to the dying person may be restricted.

### Pets

For pet owners, dying with beloved animals that they have slept with for years may be a key wish. Pets are the favorite home-setting advantage. Having your cat or dog sleep with you is easier at home than in institutions, but pets adapt quickly in order to be where you are. I have massaged in many hospital and hospice settings with the person's dogs and cats right beside them.

**Figure 8.5.** Friends to the end.

### Co-sleeping

Another ingredient you might want to consider is where you would most comfortably sleep with your loved one. Some people, even at home, worry that they could hurt the palliative person if they try to sleep beside them. Just remember that most pets find a way to fit in without any problem, so you should be able to as well!

My friend Sydnee climbed into bed with her dying mom all the time during the day and especially in the evenings. The environment of this home death was extremely loving due to the physicality of the family. When my lifelong friend, Don Grayston, died at Cottage Hospice in Vancouver, I had first-hand experience as the partner at the end. We curled up together every night and watched every episode of *Call the Midwife*. The comfort of holding hands for hours at a time and feeling his body up against mine was not only comforting for him, but also for me long after he died.

I encourage people to rediscover the comforting quality of full-body contact, and to climb in and lie up against the dying person so they are literally surrounded with their family. That soothing caress and the instinctive stroking that we do in these horizontal positions for the dying person seem so right!

### After death

Another important consideration when it comes to deciding where to die is what will happen after the last breath. While many wishes can be facilitated in institutional settings, some people may feel more comfortable carrying them out at home.

In accordance with Buddhist tradition, for example, the body of one of my patients lay in her home for three days after she passed on. She was kept cool with all the windows of the room open to the winter air, making it easy for people to spend time (warmly dressed) with her, saying prayers for her and saying their goodbyes.

After our Rotary president, David, died at home, his wife kept him in the same position in bed for people to come and say prayers and goodbyes. He was there for more than 24 hours. After my dad died at midnight, my stepmom slept with him through the night until 8 a.m., when the doctor arrived to pronounce him officially dead.

With David and my dad, their partners were probably more comfortable sleeping with their deceased husbands at home than they would have been at the hospital, but don't assume the hospital is out of the question. Opportunities to stay with the dying or dead person are sometimes as easy to facilitate in hospitals as it is in hospices and homes.

Sometimes hospitals are under certain protocols and timelines, but if you ask for an exception, it is often granted. In writing this book, I have checked with my local hospital about the rules postmortem and was happy to be reminded that they have no rules; as long as the room is not needed, it is very much the family that decides the timing about when to move the body. Rules may, of course, be different at the facilities near you, so be sure to check.

## One Size Doesn't Fit All

Gail Stinson, one of the faculty of our local nursing program, told me that extroverts and introverts need different settings for comfort. Although each person and each circumstance is different, the introvert may prefer a quieter and calmer setting than an extrovert—no music, few people, less stimulation, and less interaction. The extrovert may prefer having many people around, and in many circumstances will thrive on stimulation. I take this into consideration and translate this theory into my own world of massage. For instance, the introverted person might just want one person to handle them, massage them, and care for them, whereas an extrovert welcomes many people. Always check in with your patient about their specific preferences.

I once had a massage patient who was a loner—a classic introvert. She was also feisty and a bit grumpy. The person who massaged her was a male hospice volunteer. He was a handsome, tall nurse who was looking after his dying dad. He "adopted" this woman in her chronic care facility and cared for her till her death. Another female hospice volunteer joined him, and together they took the woman everywhere and kept her happier than she had ever been in her life. She passed away under the watchful eyes and loving touch of her two loyal caregiver volunteers. More than that, in her final days she crossed over from massive introvert to mini-extrovert.

## Connecting with Technology

Ultimately, one of the factors that makes a great difference in the quality of dying is the ability to be connected with friends and family. In my mind, this is the most important factor. We can do that with the traditions of touch and massage. Any location for dying, whether it be a backyard garden, ICU ward, hospice, hospital, bedroom, living room, or favorite mountain top, can be facilitated and enhanced with massage.

Being physically in touch isn't always possible for far-flung family and friends, and we don't always have a choice about our final days. With social media, the decision about where to die doesn't always have to be based on who to include or exclude from the end. Friends and family who are not able to be at the bedside, to touch and massage their loved one, are now able to be close by using various forms of technology. We have the ability to be in touch with each other in challenging times through texting, emailing, blogging, Zooming, and Skyping, among other options.

A young pregnant friend of mine discovered that her partner was not able to be in Canada for the birth of their baby. Being used to Skyping every day already, the couple was able to use this technology to bring the partner into the room throughout my friend's labor and delivery. He was able to watch his son being born, hear his first cry, and share the joy, moment to moment. The same is possible with deaths; no one needs to be left out if they want to be included. I am reminded of Rob Hall, a guide who died on Everest in 1996 with his wife talking to him on his cell phone. They were able to share his last moments with technology.

A digital camera or smartphone that takes stills and short movie clips is an asset in these palliative locations as a way of documenting the palliative journey. And while using technology may be difficult for some, don't forget about 88-year-old Joni sending out emails with photos and videos each night before bed during her husband Cec's final weeks!

Communication technologies don't need to be invasive. Cameras are tiny and laptop computers are very lightweight—but these little gadgets can transport both family members to the dying person, and the dying person to them. Like parents who watch their baby sleep on monitors, people who are dying can find great comfort in watching the household activities and the daily life around them. Even dying people can feel the love of their family and friends through communication technologies. Get your patient on Skype, Zoom or any other meeting app and let them "join" you for dinner.

These technologies can also facilitate the dying person's participation in the planning of their death. I've gotten used to massaging people while their family and friends sing to them. The serenades and love messages provide a true comfort: It can feel, for the dying person, like being at their own funeral. A living eulogy. Something similar can be achieved with digital photos and videos. If you are curating your loved one's pictorial or social media history for their service, consider doing it ahead of time so they can continue remember and celebrate their life until their death. Placing a computer slideshow on the patient's tray table can let them review their favorite memories. This was done for one of my patients, Bridgit. As I massaged her, we were able to watch a screen showing images of her as vibrant wife, mother, and community organizer.

## The End of the Road, On the Road

The hospital, hospice, or home can all be great choices when it comes to choosing where to die. They are not, however, the only choices. There's no reason we can't choose to die on the road.

Although I never took my mom back to visit her old residence, I did take her on the road, fully realizing that she might die on the way to see her only granddaughter, my daughter Crystal. I checked with my brother about taking my mom to see Crystal for the last time, and together, we contemplated the worst that could happen. If she died on the trip, what would I do? My friends in the police force reassured me that it was fine to travel with my dying mother, and that if she died, it wouldn't be a legal issue. That experience taught me to keep my attitude and ideas portable. It broadened my experience about locations to die. My mom didn't die on that road trip; but I'm grateful I made that last visit between my mom and my daughter possible.

Gail Potter, an expert in palliative care, teaches about facilitating patient last wishes. She says she has often encountered people who want to die outdoors, whether it be at the ski hill, at a favorite lake, on a beach, or in the mountains. Gail and I talked about how massage can help facilitate their wishes by making them more comfortable being transported, helping them recover from the journey, and keeping them comfortable in the ideal locations where they want to die.

Transitions from home to hospital are also made easier with a massage before the patient is moved, a massage during the move (if it's a long commute), and finally a massage upon arrival to smooth aches and pains and to welcome the patient tactilely to their new and last resting place.

I filmed my first palliative teaching session in 1985 for Elizabeth, a young mother in Toronto, who was in end-stage cancer. Her husband told me that she wanted to go home to England to die, so we filmed all the massage routines that I had been doing for weeks: the respiratory treatments to keep her lungs clear, the digestive massage to help her bowels keep moving, and especially the massages for avoiding pressure sores. I knew that this video would enable her family in England to help her die more comfortably. Back then, the videos I made were on VHS. Today, I have videos online that patients and their families can access no matter where they are.

Not all journeys have to be across continents. My friend Ira Schwartz followed his wife Pauline's wishes to die in the home they had built and in which they raised their family. The greenhouses she loved were in view as we carried her outside on an old army stretcher with metal feet. We tilted her so she could see her gardens as she was massaged. Her death was well-organized and peaceful, with her best friends right beside her.

### Benefits of massage "on the go"

When a dying person wants or needs to be transported, massage is the perfect way to travel more comfortably, administered before and after the travel, creating a better experience for the dying person, a softer landing, and an outlet for anxious families and friends to show their care and concern.

Although my mom and dad died at home, my stepmom, Valerie, died on a palliative ward in a hospital near Vancouver. This was miles from Nelson, in the province's interior, where she had lived for 40 years. In her final week, we moved her from Nelson by plane in a stretcher to the hospital where she was born and the town where her family still lived. Instead of them coming to her, she went to them. I moved into the hospital, too, sleeping in a bed beside her. Her family visited her each of the five days that we were there.

I massaged her both as she left the hospital in Nelson to be transported to the airport by ambulance and as soon as she arrived in Vancouver. It was a bit like a palliative sports massage session: these pre-and postgame massages definitely enhanced Valerie's experience, giving her the comfort and tolerance to make the trip.

Valerie hated flying. When I was 16, I flew to the coast with her. She spent the whole flight vomiting. It was my first time helping an adult in distress, and I wasn't entirely successful. Forty-five years later, Valerie was flying again, and was, again in distress. This time, my comforting hands could help.

## The Final Choice

Don't assume that the choice a dying person makes about where they would like to die is their final choice. Pay attention to the wishes of the palliative patient, as they can change from day to day or, in the last days, hour to hour. If the dying person is you, allow yourself to change your mind if the change feels right.

Most people will say that they want to die at home. If, however, their symptoms get out of control, their family feels too tired, they feel like they are becoming a burden, or they need special equipment, then that choice might not be the best one in the end. They may want or need to be move to a different kind of facility.

It can be a lot like a baby delivery. When I was in labor with my daughter, I planned to have a home birth—but, after 40 hours of laboring in my house, I opted to go to the hospital. In the same way, I have had patients want to die at home and then, in the final hours, go to the hospital.

Keep this dialogue going. Let the dying person change their mind. Encourage them to consider again all the choices, depending on what their individual needs are. Keep an open mind about what is best for the individual, and what is possible, in the moment, and let them know that massage is portable. Wherever they are, they can be rubbed the right way!

### Empowering the final choice

In the Quaker community of Argenta in the Kootenays, Almo Wolfe, architect and coffin maker, was always one coffin ahead to ensure he was covered for his own death. The community had a direct delivery from the bedroom to the cemetery. The coffins they made were simple, wooden designs with a touch of satin on the smooth, sanded finish of the lids. I remember the feel of the lid on Almo's coffin.

My friend Mark also makes coffins. These coffins, which Mark makes with his family in the Doukhobor tradition, are in high demand. They ship them around the world, sometimes selling them to celebrities. Still, their coffins follow the least complicated of designs, and are perfect for those wanting to keep it simple.

These families, involved in the business of dying, taught me about the importance of discussing plans well ahead of time, planning the funerals with personal touches, and allowing the dying person to put their last wishes to work.

When my stepmom was dying, I was her coordinator, writing everything she told me about what would go where and to whom in a little book. We had daily discussions about her precious things and what would happen to them when she was gone. By the time she died, I had collected her plan about what to do, how to bury her, and what ought to be given to whom. She talked to me during her massages, and I often had to pause to record the things she remembered as she relaxed. That little book had some oily fingerprints from those mid-massage entries. It was like writing any book: once the framework was in place, the stories acquired more details as time went on.

Some people have time to layer their departures with fine-tuning, while others only get halfway through their preparations before they're called away. All we can do is our best to empower dying people and to respect their final choices. At the end of the day, the key for caregivers is just to be wherever the person we love is dying and to deliver them to the other side with as much ease as our hands can manage. The time that we can spend with our dying relatives is their legacy of love to us. We give them back our gift of touch, so wherever they are, as long as they are in our hands, it is the perfect place to die.

---

## Online Classroom

Visit brusheducation.ca/dying-in-good-hands to watch these videos:

Where to die – hospice
Where to die – home
Connecting with technology
Empowering the final choice

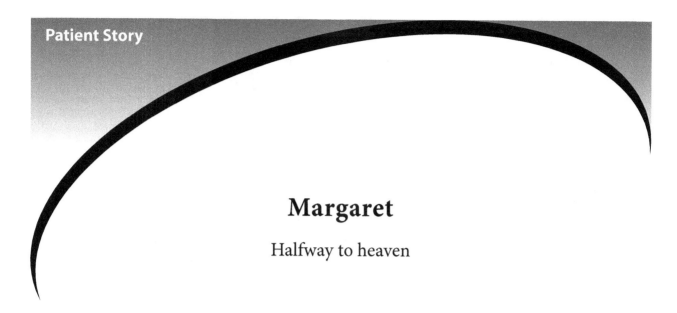

# Margaret

## Halfway to heaven

It was a hot July in Nelson, and my mom, Margaret, was dying.

Bert, my Cairn Terrier, and I had mastered the art of wheelchair walking with pets—how to keep the leash from tangling in the wheelchair levers. We became a nightly feature on Nelson's main street. The chair was easy to push and the crowds politely parted to let us through the busy summer sidewalk traffic. We would stroll along the same route every evening, past the outdoor cafés, listening to musicians and enjoying the artists and performers in the festivals and venues on our main street. We would meet my mom's hospice workers, my patients, and her friends.

I became aware that some of the bumps in the road and sidewalks caused my mom's mouth to drop open and made her look like she was taking her last breath. I would frequently check her mouth and prop it up again so she looked at rest and not at death's door.

One particular group of visitors to our city loved my dog Bert. Although it was illegal to walk dogs on our main street (no joke!), that summer I actively defied anyone to challenge our funny-looking entourage. When the tourists patted Bert and then asked about my mom, I would tell them, "She used to love to window-shop along these blocks. I think she would like to die window-shopping."

"I hope my family takes me out when I'm dying," someone said.

The next night, as I was cruising by another restaurant, I heard someone calling us and turned around. It was the same tourist group from the day before, waving at us. I waved back.

"She's still alive!" They loudly whispered and gave thumbs-up gestures.

The next night, they were on a different street, in a different restaurant, this time teasing us about how they didn't want to leave. They said that they loved seeing my mom and her different hats. They wished us good luck with her departure: "It looks like we're leaving before your mother. Thanks for the wonderful memory." My mom was still making new friends and influencing others, leaving them with ideas and provocative images to take back to their own lives.

---

On my mom's last summer, my daughter, Crystal, was working at the Easter Seals camp miles away. When I became convinced that my mom was dying, Crystal left camp to come home and say goodbye. We massaged her together and, to our surprise, she rallied. Crystal went back to camp. Two weeks later, however, there was very little question: Mom was definitely dying, and I thought it was important for her to see her granddaughter and for her granddaughter to say goodbye one last time.

I talked it over with Crystal at the camp, and with my brother, and we all agreed that if my mom died on the road, it would be perfect. She loved to travel. If she did die, we decided that I would just drive her home.

So my mom and I set off and drove through the cool night in my tiny convertible.

We slept in the car beside a beautiful lake and arrived at the camp on the hottest day of the summer, over 40°C by noon. It was so hot I felt a strong urgency to get my mom into the water. I drove to the lake and looked for a boat launch, hoping to wheel her into the lake, clothes and all. When I found a shaded boat ramp, I quickly got the wheelchair out of the car and asked a woman reading under a tree if she could help me. The wheelchair was getting stuck in the sand.

The woman turned out to be a veterinary assistant, someone not easily fazed by unusual medical emergencies. She helped me wheel my mom into the lake. I got her legs in the water nearly up to her knees when I noticed a large Canada goose heading our way. My mom was not responding and I didn't know if she would come back.

I decided then that if my mom was about to die, I'd better take a picture for my family. I tied her securely into the wheelchair so she couldn't slide out, and I ran back to the car for my camera.

The goose stopped and looked at my mom. I'd heard about nature knowing what we do not know. I thought the goose was a beacon from beyond. He stayed right in front of the submerged wheelchair, looking up at her.

As I approached the chair, careful not to scare him off, more geese headed in our direction. As I wrapped my arms around my mom, 13 more geese surrounded us. I asked her to open her eyes, to see the geese, but she didn't stir. Her pulse was weak and erratic; she was fading.

I called for the veterinary nurse and then I drove the car down to the shoreline, making a huge yacht wait for its launch while we loaded my mother back into my convertible.

I sped to the nearest gas station and bought bags of ice to pack around her. I tore the bags open and poured them down her dress, and I rested bags

A curious visitor.

on her lap and under her legs until she was packed in ice from head to toe. I drove with one hand on her pulse and the other on the wheel.

We arrived at the Easter Seals camp at the appointed time. I wheeled my unconscious mother into the open-air shelter where I was to teach the counsellors some hands-on massage skills so that they could give each other shoulder massages—a deal I'd made to secure our visit.

I parked my mom—still packed in ice—so that I could watch her while I was teaching. She was at the back, facing me. At the 50-minute mark of the one-hour session, my mother opened her eyes. She stared straight ahead as though watching me teach. I wheeled her forward for the class photo and she smiled for the camera. I didn't know how long this would last, but I was grateful that my daughter's last memory of her grandmother was going to be pleasant.

When I finished the class, my only thought was getting my mom out of there before they realized how close to the end she was, but the camp leaders wanted to thank me with a sky-high swing experience. The group ushered me into an open field that had a huge staircase parked in the middle of it. The apparatus looked like something you could bungee-jump from, with a long cable extending from it.

One of the group members climbed the staircase with me as the others chose a viewing spot on the ground below. Crystal eased my mother's chair into a reclining position so she could watch.

As I was being hooked up to the cable, I was told that I would be the one to unhook the tether and let the cable take hold and launch me into space. Taking the initiative was the therapeutic aspect of the experience: letting go.

I was in the same position as my mother, lying back looking up to heaven. I looked back at the ground—it was a long way down. Then they hoisted me higher, about twice as high into the sky. The stairs rolled away.

I looked down at my mother and daughter, who were looking up at me. Then I looked up at the clouds. I was halfway to heaven. My mother might get there before I got down to the ground, but for right now, I was closer than she was. I found the safety hook and let go. A huge, yet gentle force picked me up and swung me through the air in an enormous loop. I felt a shift, and in that moment I found peace.

---

As we prepared to leave, we opened my convertible roof and let my mom watch the clouds. "I love you, Grandma. Thanks for coming to see me." Crystal leaned forward to give her grandmother a kiss as we seat-belted her into the car. And then my mom seemed to recognize Crystal. She tried to say something; it sounded like "I love you."

Crystal caught it. "Grandma, you said 'I love you.' Thank you; I love you too. Thank you so much for being my grandma." My mom said, "And I you," which were the last words my dad had spoken—his very same last words.

I thought that this significant salutation confirmed that mother was going to die immediately, but instead, we drove out of Crystal's summer camp and all the way back to Nelson with my mom passed out in a deep, sound sleep, like a kid after a birthday party.

As I massaged my mom for the rest of that week, she rarely opened her eyes. She rarely even swallowed. She was growing tinier and tinier—skeletal to massage, but so far the massages were working. There was no reddening, no pressure sores.

I was completely preoccupied with my mom's delicate presence on the planet, thinking she might die at any moment. I massaged her a number of times every day, noticing finally, one night, that her breathing was different. It was a little delayed and she was panting slightly. We still went out for our nightly stroll, but that night I slept on a coffee table that I had pulled up close to her. I had fallen asleep holding her hand. She seemed far away and very still.

I woke up as one of Gaston's daughters, Miryam, arrived to give me an hour to go for a run. In the middle of that run, I found myself calling my best friend Jill—I asked her to come into town and spend the day with my mom and me. When she arrived, we wheeled my mom onto the balcony and positioned her between my brother and me. Jill sat facing us. Bert was asleep on Jill's lap as we reminisced together in the afternoon sun. As we spoke, my mom moved her legs involuntarily as though she was trying to get up and go for a walk. We kept covering her moving legs and continued our stories.

I was in the middle of a long tale about dissecting a roadkill fox when Bert jumped up and stood on Jill's lap. He leaned hard against Jill's restraining hands towards my mother with the same stance he took while investigating a new dog, giving her his undivided attention. He cocked his head left and right.

"What's he doing?"

Bert looked as though he was listening to something or someone. The hair on my arms started to rise.

Jill started to laugh. "Bert sees something that we can't see."

Bert was steady and intent on my mom's face, watching her as though she was talking to him. After a few minutes of this unusual behavior, Bert simply lay down again and went back to sleep on Jill's lap.

I finished my story and Jill started one of her own. It was then that I glanced at my mom and noticed she was not breathing.

"She's going."

My mom broke the silence with another breath, an unusual breath, not shallow or panting, but deep and full. Her shoulders curled and her whole body relaxed. And then she was gone.

Bert knew. He had heard her say goodbye.

We sat with my mom in the summer sun for another hour. I massaged her lovely hands with her favorite lavender fragrance. It was like a spiritual anointing, a peaceful parting, my best goodbye.

Margaret.

# 9

# Care for the Caregivers

Who are the caregivers in palliative care? They are a natural selection of friends and family. They are the homecare workers who come to clean and cook. They are the staff of any chronic care facility who look after the dying person. They are the pets that attend to the protection and comfort of their owners. The caregivers might be brand new hospice volunteers with no massage experience or old schoolmates who have come to be with their friend during the end of their life. They are right beside the bedside and they are on the other side of the world, offering care through Skype, Zoom, email, and Facebook.

Like the dying person themselves, caregivers can all be helped with massage. As they take care of those who are dying, caregivers can help each other, bond, rejuvenate, grieve, and have fun while sharing mini-massages around the room. In this chapter, I will explore the practicalities of caring for caregivers with massage.

## Self-care

There is something about witnessing someone else's pain or discomfort, or seeing someone with needs so much greater than ours, that can fuel unlimited energy resources within all of us. In labor and delivery, you often find that an attending father with a short attention span for massaging will suddenly become more hands-on. I have seen quiet husbands become more direct and hands-on than ever before when their wives are dying. I have seen caregivers in hospices go days and nights

without sleep in order to attend to those they love.

My daughter has a straightforward belief about caring. She says that you can only care for others if you can care for yourself. If the primary caregiver goes down, is laid up in bed with a bad back, or suffers other natural occurrences when caregiving, the whole caregiving system could topple.

Caregivers are a team with a duty to keep fit and healthy. This is the team that is going to come over the finish line with more fuel and rejuvenation because they have been well looked after all the way along the route towards this end. I encourage caregivers to pretend they are the ones needing care. They need to take a daily walk, breathe fresh air, eat healthy food, and keep their sense of humor.

To avoid burnout in jobs that can consume us—even jobs that we love to do, that give us great sense of purpose and satisfaction—we need to find a balance. For me, swimming in the lake every morning in the summer is a balance to my work of the day, giving me a sense of pride in myself. I feel good to have invested in my own well-being. This self-care is a must in any caregiving profession. It is important those who become caregivers not by profession, but by necessity, to follow a similar path.

I am surrounded by examples of those who excel at self-care. My friend Colleen is a popular nurse at our local hospital. She exercises every day, goes on biking, hiking, and kayaking adventures, and gives and gets massages from her friends, family, and, in quiet moments at the nursing station, her colleagues. She and her husband take real holidays from their work, and she glows with the results of her self-care.

Colleen is also a good example of how to care for caregivers both before and after the death of the person they are caring for. When her sister was dying, their large family all gathered in the Maritimes and spent quality time together. Colleen taught them all how to massage her and each other, giving them skills to be hands-on with massage in the future, after her sister had passed.

## When to Massage a Caregiver

It is always a good time to massage the shoulders of caregivers, whether they are family, friends, hospice volunteers, or nurses at the hospital. I am a favorite late-night feature at any nursing station in hospitals when my patients are in palliative care. The nurses love getting my hands-on thank-you for all their hard work.

When caregivers of a palliative patient change shifts, the person leaving and the person coming on shift can share their experience and complete their caregiver case report while giving each other a shoulder and neck rub. I encourage volunteer massage teams to massage the caregivers first when they arrive to give their massages to palliative patients. A quick shoulder rub while talking about how things are going gives the caregiver an outlet for their thoughts or worries, thus reducing their tension and encouraging an emotional relaxation. It's also such a good way to assess what to do and how to do it when it comes to massaging the patient.

## Looking After Family

Caregiver massage benefits the caregiver, but it can also benefit the dying person, who may be worried about their loved ones in the face of their approaching death. I encourage caregivers to massage each other where the patient can easily see them. In this way, it is as though the hands on their shoulders are the hands of the dying person,

saying "thank you." Your touch can represent their touch.

When I was massaging my friend Mary, we always put her husband, Lou, right at the foot of Mary's bed in a chair so she could supervise the shoulder massages we did for him. Even after Mary could no longer talk, she could still clearly communicate her enthusiasm for her family being looked after. Another patient, Lynnie, was concerned about the well-being of her husband, Bob, and their daughter, Alicia, after her death. Her daughter was only 10 and extremely close to her mother. I promised Lynnie that I would massage them every month after she died.

Years later, when Alicia was 13, she took my summer palliative massage course. I filmed her massaging an elderly Russian woman, knowing that her mother would be pleased. Watching Alicia massage Polly's hands was like watching from Lynnie's point of view. Lynnie's family had been cared for and now they were returning the kindness.

## Learning by Receiving

When I am training my summer students in palliative massage, "care for the caregiver" is the key of our outreach practicum. The families of our outreach patients receive massages, but they also learn to be our massage helpers. They massage along beside us and feel immediately useful and relaxed in response to the relaxation that their dying loved one feels. This tandem massaging passes the information along to the care team stroke by stroke and teaches them how to make other people in their family circle feel well looked after.

It only takes the right touch in good hands to convert a caregiver into a massage enthusiast. A quick exchange of shoulder rubs at the end or beginning of the volunteer bedside vigil will quickly expand the team.

## Patients Can Sometimes Massage

Sometimes, if a patient is interested and strong enough to do so, caregivers can sit in front of the patient and be on the receiving end of a massage.

Performing a neck and shoulder massage can help the dying person feel like they are still contributing and able to care for the people who care for them. The patient may need to be propped up with pillows so their massage is as effortless as possible, but I've seen patients deliver everything from thumb stroking and scooping to tapotement.

**Figure 9.1.** When teaching in Guatemala, I taught palliative orphan adults to massage their nurses.

**Figure 9.2.** Patients often like to feel like they are still contributing, still giving back to the people who are caring for them.

My most memorable experience was with a fellow who had suffered a severe stroke, which affected his ability to control one side of his body. He was eager to learn to do something as a thank-you for his wife. With my camera rolling, he got both hands onto her shoulders by placing one hand on the wrist of the other hand and lifting the paralyzed hand onto her shoulder. Then both hands in perfect balance started to massage her shoulders. I couldn't believe my eyes! That love for touching performs miracles!

## Care for the Caregiver Massage Routine

The caregivers routine is easily adapted to any setting. It can be done by the patient's bedside, at the kitchen table, on a bench in the garden, or in the hospital room. This routine is especially great for headaches, which are common for caregivers in palliative settings for a number of reasons. Lack of sleep; too much coffee (or too little!); and the stress of family emotions, outbursts, or overexposure can all lead to painful and persistent headaches. Headaches can also be caused by dietary factors. In palliative settings, people tend to bring all sorts of treats and meals that are not necessarily healthy; excess sugar is a common challenge! And then, of course, there is the constant strain of pent-up emotions within the caregivers themselves, and the people around them, simply due to the palliative situation.

Massage gives the neck a chance to loosen up; often this will cause the headache pain to disappear by freeing up the gateways of tension around the throat and neck. This simple treatment can give the person on the receiving end a chance to talk, vent, cry, or simply relax.

As always, use the feedback of the person being massaged as your guide. For example, you might spend more time around the eyes, temples, and jaws if these seem to be the areas that elicit the most relief. Remember to ask how the massage is going and what they would like for pressure. Do this from the beginning of the massage up until the last stroke.

**Remember to ask for the "F" word: Feedback!**

**Figure 9.3.** I teach the care for the caregiver massage at Camp Kerry, a bereavement camp for families. Here volunteers Natalie Bergmann Biggs and Dr. Michael Biggs practice their caregiver massage exchange.

### Make "yes" the easy answer

I tend not to use the word *massage* when asking a caregiver who has not yet become a massage convert if I can rub their shoulders, as *massage* tends to conjure up images of lying down, oil, candles, skin, naked—the whole nine yards! Instead, I ask, "Can I give your shoulders a little squeeze?" or "Can I give you a shoulder rub?" Learn to ask the question in a way that will make "yes" an automatic and easy answer.

If permission is granted, I usually start by giving caregivers mini-massage samplers. I start by saying, "Where would you like me to start: your hands or your shoulders?" It is the same question that I teach the teenagers to ask residents when massaging in chronic care facilities.

### Step-by-step caregiver massage

Stand close by the side or back of the caregiver for the following techniques, which can be done in any order. Use a stride posture to protect your back so you can lean forward with the weight of your body on your hands. Remove the caregiver's eyeglasses, if they wear them.

1. **Have the caregiver lean forward.** They can rest on the kitchen table with a pile of pillows to hug. Some people need one, and some need two or more pillows to get comfortable and feel supported.

2. **Squeeze the trapezius.** From behind the caregiver, place both hands on the big upper shoulder muscles (trapezius) and give a bilateral squeeze, lifting the big muscle and releasing it. This movement will develop a rapport and accustom the person to your touch. (Figure 9.4)

3. **Scoop the trapezius.** Develop the squeeze by giving big scoops of the trapezius with the heel of your hand. Do not dig in your fingertips; keep a flat hand with all your fingers beside each other, using the heel of your hand to lift the shoulders into your fingers.

I get the caregiver to do some deep breathing with this stroke, asking them to breathe in as I scoop up and then breathe out when I release for about three breaths. It works. Make sure you let your own shoulders drop down so they are not around your ears while you concentrate on grasping the shoulders in front of you.

You can scoop up on the trapezius close to the neck, then in the middle of the shoulders, and finally at the outer aspect of the muscle at the edge of the shoulders. (Figure 9.5)

4. **Digitally compress the rhomboids.** Move from squeezing the trapezius to working on the rhomboids with digital compression. With the thumbs of each hand, alternate pressing and releasing the rhomboids on both sides of the spine from the top of the shoulders to the bottom of the scapula. This area can be quite tight. Be sure to check with the caregiver that your pressure is accurate. Stay close to, but on either side of the spine and keep your thumbs at the same speed and rhythm. (Figure 9.6)

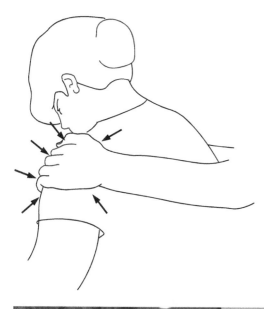

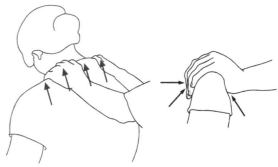

A. Scoop the trapezius muscles with the heels of your hands in a lifting action. Hold the muscle for a few breaths, and then let go.

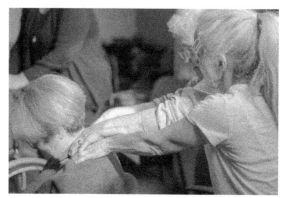

B. Here I teach scooping to the trapezius.

**Figure 9.5.** Scooping to the trapezius.

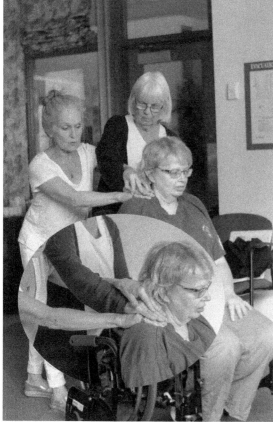

**Figure 9.4.** Here I teach a volunteer to squeeze and release the shoulder muscles as a warm-up to massage.

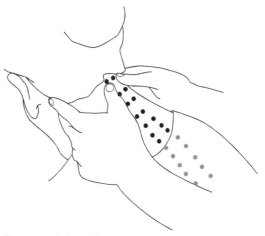

**Figure 9.6.** Poke and press. The thumbs do the work.

**5. Tilt the head.** Move to the side of the caregiver and place one hand on the forehead and one at the base of the skull in an open C-shape. Create some slight traction with the lower hand and slowly tilt the head in all four directions: forward, back, and side to side. Do this slowly.

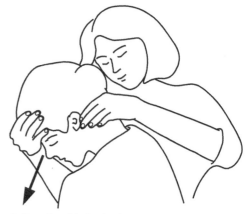

C. Drop the chin to chest.

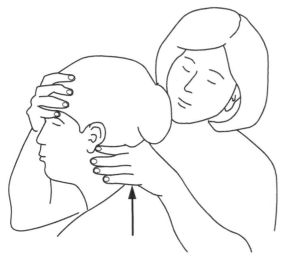

A. With a scooping action, lift at the back of the head under the occipital ridge to give traction.

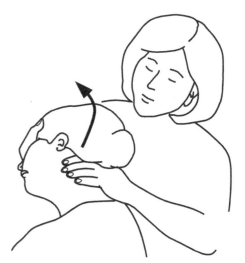

D. Gently move ear to opposite shoulder.

B. Gently move ear to shoulder.

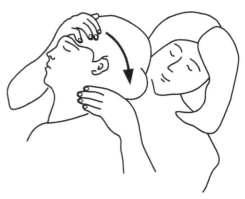

E. Tilt head backward.

**Figure 9.7.** Head tilts. Secure the head by placing one hand on the forehead. (Be careful not to cover up the eyes.)

6. **Knead jaw and temples.** Move to the back of the caregiver and place your fingertips on the temples, right at the hairline. Slowly knead all around the jaw and the temple area. Have the person release his or her jaw by opening their mouth slightly to relax it. (Figures 9.8 and 9.9)

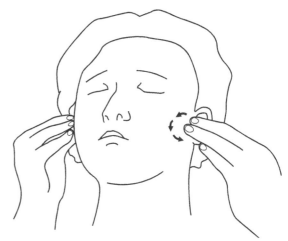

**Figure 9.9.** Temporal mandibular kneading on the chin bone below the zygomatic arch.

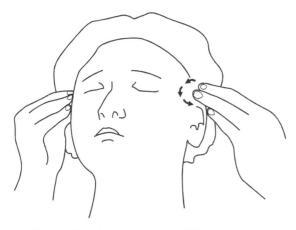

placing elbows on the knees and dropping the head down. Stand to the side and perform the same percussive strokes you used on the trapezius, deltoids, and rhomboids over the rest of the back, being careful not to thump on the spine itself.

9. **Squeeze the shoulders again.**

10. **Do the head tilts again.**

11. **Do some light reflex stroking.** Stroke the caregiver lightly with fingertips from top of the head and out the shoulders and arms.

12. **Give an optional arm and hand massage.** Face the caregiver. Start at the shoulders with palmar kneading and use alternate thumb kneading down the arm to the hand with the pressure of each stroke up towards the heart. Then massage the hand with alternate thumb kneading. Corkscrew each finger and do light reflex stroking on the entire arm to finish.

**Figure 9.8.** Temporal kneading.

7. **Perform percussive tapotement for the trapezius, deltoids, and rhomboids.** Use any of the tapotement strokes in Figure 9.10. (See pages 53 to 56 for a description of how to do these strokes.)

8. **Perform percussive tapotement for the lower back.** Have the caregiver lean forward,

If there are several caregivers present, request that they form a chain or a small circle and simultaneously massage one another. This will energize the whole room!

The time to care for the caregivers is unending. Massages from their families, friends, and

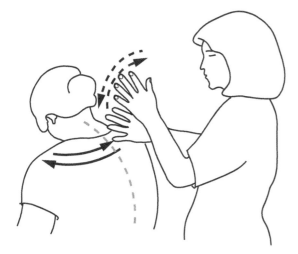

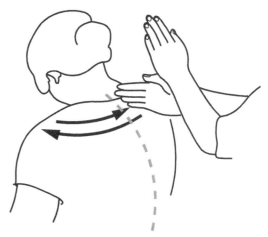

B. Stiff fingertip hacking (a.k.a. chopping).

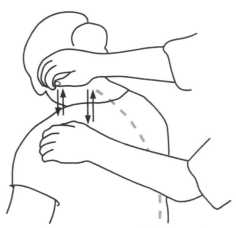

C. Cupping. Be sure you get a hollow sound, not a slapping sound.

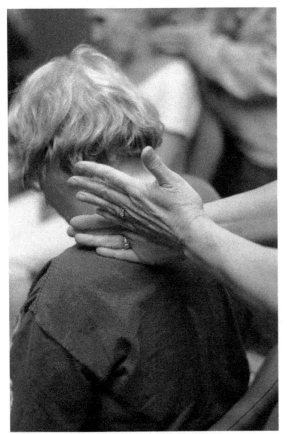

A. Loose fingertip hacking (a.k.a. flicking).

volunteers can all benefit caregivers. There are many places to deliver this hands-on help, be it outdoors or indoors, during the day, or throughout the night. There are also many times at which a massage is appropriate, not just before but also after the death of the person for whom they are caring. Serious events like the anniversary of the death of a loved one are excellent occasions for a massage. Funerals and celebrations of the loved one's life are also great settings for shoulder rubs. Other special times in months up the road, like memorial hikes with mountaintop massages, will allow you to continue caring for the caregiver left behind by the palliative person's passing. These are all times to touch and remember the caring circle of hands. Massaging through periods and moments of grief is discussed in more detail in Chapter 10.

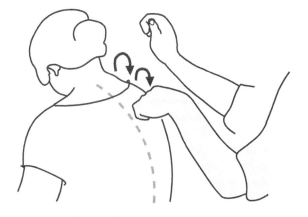

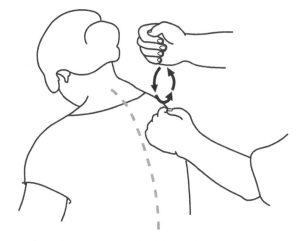

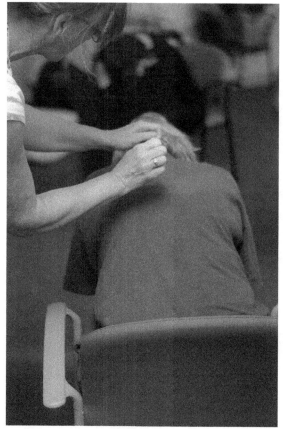

D. Beating. Use monkey paws with flip-flop wrists.

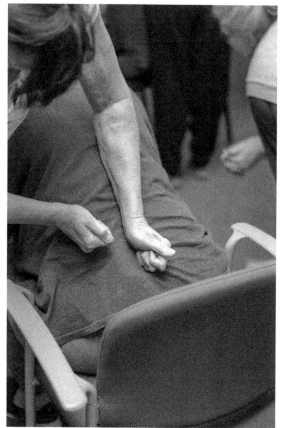

E. Pounding. Roll your fists toward your body in a continuous motion.

**Figure 9.10.** Percussive tapotement.

## Online Classroom

Visit brusheducation.ca/dying-in-good-hands
to watch these videos:

Reflecting on care for the caregivers

A tactile thank you

Looking after family – hands-on

Step-by-step caregiver massage

# Sylvan

"There is a vitality, a life force, a quickening that is translated through you into action, and because there is only one of you in all time, this expression is unique."

– Martha Graham

I can hear the melody of a Celtic harp coming from the room at the top of the stairs. The house holds a dense peacefulness. There is a sense of tranquility, a sense of anticipation or special delivery, almost like the births I have attended.

Sylvan is 55 years old, a former theatre director now in the last stages of his life, dying of AIDS. I'd met Sylvan years before while visiting with a friend in Nelson at Christmas. Sylvan was the neighbor across the hall. We always knew when Sylvan was home. His booming laughter resounded through the building. His voice was deep, rich, and luscious.

I loved his beautiful apartment, with walls covered in gourmet cooking utensils and memorabilia from theatre productions that Sylvan had been a part of. I would make up excuses to borrow things from him just to see inside. He loved my little dog Maggie, which got me into trouble with the landlady. Sylvan wanted a dog just like Maggie, and he talked to his landlady about it with great enthusiasm—which is when we all found out that there were no pets allowed in the building!

Now, Sylvan lived at Barb's house. Two years ago, Barb was one of my summer palliative massage students. It was she who brought Sylvan's illness to my attention. Now, she has brought Sylvan

to her homey retreat—a quiet part of town with a marvelous view of the Kootenay mountains—to die. This is his sanctuary, his repose.

As his health declined, Sylvan helped me in my summer program for palliative massage students. He was one of our home-visit experiences. He was a man of strong opinion and unyielding tenacity, and many of the students were intimidated by his manner of commanding the situation.

Now, on his deathbed, he is still theatrical from head to toe, although his handsome face shows the strain of his illness. His hands, graceful and expressive, dramatize every word, though his voice is thin and weak. His long legs move restlessly; his red-and-white striped flannel pajamas dance with uncomfortable motions.

As I walk into the room, I notice that Sylvan is with a friend today. Over the past month, during countless massages, I have met many of Sylvan's friends. Some I've seen in passing around downtown Nelson. Others are public people and recognizable. Some come from great distances and others live around the corner. They all have a piece of Sylvan's life and come to tend to their dying friend, offer comfort, and pay their last respects.

But this woman is new. She says her name is Gwen. I'm struck by her fresh youthfulness and her intimacy with Sylvan.

"How do you know Sylvan?" I quietly inquire.

"We worked together at the theatre," she replies. It is obvious that they have a history; they seem like tender partners. Gwen is short, about my size, and elfin-like with fair skin and freckles. She looks cheerful.

Sylvan, on the other hand, seems like the conductor of gloom. He doesn't look pleased to see me today. I imagine that my presence represents both comfort and discomfort for him. He has always looked forward to my massages and has praised and encouraged my efforts. But over the past week, he also has become increasingly fixed in a favorite posture on his left side, avoiding the discomfort of his right. His hips are very sore and his tailbone is sensitive. But by being turned, his lungs will be able to drain and hopefully stay clear, and we can try to avoid the development of bedsores. I know that my presence tells him that he will have to move—this is likely the reason for my lukewarm reception. Sylvan doesn't like to move, and I'm the person who insists that he move every two hours. It is difficult for his close friends to have the same stamina for unpopularity, so I usually get to play the taskmaster when I arrive to massage.

When I suggest to Gwen that she help me with today's massage, I am hoping to elicit some enthusiasm from Sylvan, who is still clearly miffed at my arrival.

Normally, I would massage Sylvan to get his limbs loosened and flexible before turning him; it makes him relaxed and easier to turn. But this time I realize he has already been in the same position for hours, and we need to get him turned fast, without the usual massage warm-up, to prevent a bedsore. I alert Gwen that we'll need to act quickly.

He is so lean, but he's still much longer and bigger than the two of us. It brings some humor to the process of turning him, which even Sylvan doesn't miss. As Gwen pulls his knee and shoulder towards her, I lift the draw sheet (the small, narrow second sheet under his body) at the same time, tilting him in her direction until he arrives on his right side. Protesting, Sylvan straightens his lower leg and we

bend his upper leg and support it with two soft pillows under his knee, one at his head, and another at his chest for support.

Once Sylvan has been turned, we get down to work, knowing he won't tolerate being on this side for long. Although he is locked in his thinking, as he is locked in his body, about remaining on his one comfortable side, his favorite hip is dangerously red, threatening to degrade into a pressure sore. Our touch helps him tolerate the discomfort of this new position. Sylvan responds easily and intensely to touch. More than a series of reflexes and somatic responses, touch elicits in Sylvan a sense of knowing himself. He is able to feel the love of his friends and caregivers in their touch. He is truly loved through these many hands.

As if summoned, Barb walks in to buffer Sylvan's protests about being on his least favorite side with his favorite food: boiled eggs. While Sylvan munches agreeably, Gwen and I begin to massage. The point of his hip bone is still intensely red, and it seems that my tactile coaxing of his skin to a healthier color is going unheeded. I also notice that his legs have a gray-blue tint and haven't responded as I had expected to our tandem massage.

Gwen is in front of Sylvan massaging his knee and lower leg, while I stay behind him massaging his hip. We face each other like dance partners. I can spot a truly talented pair of hands instantly, and I can see that Gwen is a natural. I watch Gwen massage Sylvan's upper back. By watching and listening to me, she has already learned all my best strokes. Sylvan loves my explanations to Gwen. He nods in a drug-veiled haze and makes clumsy gestures. Together we move through the effleurages, the palmar kneading, and the alternate thumb kneading. We use the same slow and even pace, the same sensitivity, the same song.

We massage his whole body, which, except for his bloated belly, is skin and bones. As Gwen and I complete our chest massage, we take in the difference it has made for him. His bowels have untangled, and his breathing has eased. His discomfort, although obvious, doesn't seem to hold him in the same way. I notice that he isn't interacting with us as much as he normally would. He stays with us for short periods and then drifts off into a blank stare.

He has an air of detachment, a peaceful pause from his usual way of commanding the room.

I tell him that I will be back later that night to give him another rub. His body is changing rapidly. A thick sensation stays with me throughout the rest of my day.

Around nine that evening, I walk the four blocks to Barb's house. Barb has gone to bed early, but her husband, Howard, is in his comfy chair in front of the television. Upstairs, Taylor, Sylvan's old friend and former lover of years gone by, is keeping vigil. I slide my hands onto her shoulders, and she leans back in the rocking chair, still holding Sylvan's hand, as I massage. We have been together in this tiny attic room many times. In delicate whispers, we talk of how we had never met before coming together over this slumbering man, and how close we are now. I finish massaging her shoulders and look over to Sylvan.

As Sylvan's eyes wander, his hands travel randomly over his body. He is sinking into another realm, visiting somewhere else across an invisible divide as Taylor and I chat about our lives and loves. My massage has brought Taylor some relaxation, and she heads off to bed for a little nap as I take her place by Sylvan's side and massage his hands. Like Sylvan, I've slipped into a meditative massage moment, when a jolt of electricity runs through me: Sylvan has stopped breathing. I stroke his forehead gently, talk softly to him about love and letting go. Then his eyes flutter and he inhales deeply. He decides to stay.

I don't move from his side or stop massaging him. His features are still as I run my hands over his proud nose, his broad forehead and large mouth, now slack with effort spent. His lips are shiny with oils and lubricants. He looks handsome in this pose. He seems calmer when I am talking and I find an easy flow of prayerful words. As I stand attending to these moments of Sylvan's ebbing life, I know that he will not live long. But it doesn't occur to me that he is leaving now, that he will die while I am there. His breathing hypnotizes me: the rise and fall of his expansive chest, the sounds of air coming up through water high in his throat, not a death rattle, only soft bubbling.

Then, there is a distinct and intangible shift, and Sylvan's mouth relaxes. He is still breathing, but I can't reach him anymore; he has left, beyond reach.

I call out into the house, down the stairs. I call to Barb. I call to Taylor. I call to announce his passing. I call to break the spell. I call from higher ground.

Barb and Taylor appear at the same time and, finally, Sylvan's body breathes its last breath. The moment suspends itself. I can still feel his warmth and see his peaceful face, at last free of pain, as I watch to see if he is really departed.

Without a dramatic spasm or announcement, he is gone. I have a sense of satisfaction that he died without feeling like he was drowning, that he was gone before his fluids backed up his throat, the flood of his shutting down. He was able to ease out without struggle, slip out without pain, and reach the other side without panic.

---

We stayed with Sylvan for the hours it took for him to cool. By the time he felt dead to the touch, there was a group of five of us gathered around the bed, laughing and telling stories about Sylvan as we continued to anoint him with all his special oils. It was a spontaneous wake. We were hands-on with him in a circle of love and affection, singing songs as we put our star performer to rest.

Sylvan.

# 10

# Grieving in Good Hands

"I do believe that touch and massage are very important for facing and healing from grief."

– Judy Tatelbaum, author of *The Courage to Grieve*

Grieving is part of loving. It comes with the territory. We do not grieve those we do not love. The more we love, the more we grieve. The deeper we love, the deeper we grieve. If we are an active lover of life, then we are an active griever when those we love die.

In times of grief, there is a great deal of satisfaction in knowing that you did everything possible to make a dying person's experience less painful and more peaceful simply by massaging them. At the same time, death brings with it the overwhelming pain of loss. You have lost forever the opportunity to touch your loved one. You had the daily and maybe hourly opportunity to give love and affection through your massages, and now that person has disappeared. You do not have the rhythm and flow of loving and being loved. You are left with a huge tactile emptiness.

For caregivers, widows, and widowers alike, being touched and massaged is deeply settling in this time of transition. Appointments to look after a departed patient's spouses or friends with massages should be part of the aftercare plan. The community of care that surrounded the dying person can now surround those left behind, allowing them to grieve in your hands.

## Grieving Before Death

Grieving doesn't start the day a person dies. It can begin well before the person's last breath. The process of losing someone we love is not easy to handle. It can be hard to let them go. A comforting touch helps to keep a dying person's caregivers thawed out and in touch with their feelings, stopping them from becoming numb.

Massages, like those described in Chapter 9, help keep caregivers talking about their feelings, anxieties, fears, and doubts. The power of touch is therapeutic for caregivers in all the stages of separation while the person they love is dying. Talk and touch relieve the buildup of tension and release tears of relief so the person is not immobilized by their impending grief and loss.

Caregivers often feel helpless as their loved one moves closer to death and there is less "work" to do. They miss the conversations and acknowledgements that they have grown accustomed to hearing. I know I missed my mom's whispers of appreciation as she was dying. I felt the same after my dad died. They always said "thank you" for my massages and commented on how good it felt. I remember noticing how quiet my mom became near the end, and how much it meant to me when my friends would come up behind me and squeeze my shoulders. I could still feel my mom respond to me, but losing her words and not hearing her say my name was very difficult. Those touches from friends helped to keep me feeling well-loved, and they were able to represent my mom's missing endearments.

When my mother was dying, I couldn't take my friends up on their offers of full massages off-site because I didn't like to leave her. But I loved the volunteer massage visitors. I knew that when I went swimming early in the morning, massage volunteers like Miryam would be attending to my mom.

For me, seeing Miryam's hands on my mom was like seeing my own hands on her. She had attended my summer palliative massage course after her dad, Gaston, died the previous May and was paying me back, saying "thank you" by massaging my mom the way I had massaged her dad. I was touched by Miryam's generosity. She gave me the most reassuring time away from my mom.

## Aftercare Plan

Everyone's acute phase of grief is different; loss is an individual experience. Chronic grieving, in which the strong emotions of the heart are not expressed and go looking for trouble, is often where illness and unhealthy coping strategies manifest. The heartache of losing a loved one is often accompanied by symptoms of irritability, loss of appetite, overeating, overdrinking, overspending, and insomnia.

Get volunteers to be hands-on with grieving loved ones of the person who died with the same sense of purpose they showed the palliative patient. Hands-on care for the caregiver can alleviate helpless feelings and express what words of sympathy cannot convey: that caregivers need support in their lives beyond their loved one's death. The power of touch through massage will transport them through their grief and soften the sharp edges of pain, hopefully delivering them to a place of peace.

Massage the grieving person at home. People can be massaged in the same bedrooms and in the same beds where their loved ones died. This can help them reestablish healthy sleep patterns, realign their nervous system, and regain their emotional resilience. The many addictions that face people in bereavement (like alcoholism and compulsive overeating) can be prevented with the laying-on of hands. Widows and widowers can reclaim their sensuality and need for contact, touch, and affection through massage.

Giving these caring massages can also be therapeutic for the person doing the massaging. Once the palliative person has died, physically being in contact with the "out-of-work" care team is the most important aftercare program to implement. The surplus energy of the caregiving lifestyle needs redirection and a new outlet.

### LOSING VALERIE

My stepmom, my brother, and I were hands-on with my dad. We changed him, washed him, massaged him, and kept our hands on him for days until he died. Those massages made a big difference to my ability to deal with my grief. I could still feel him under my fingertips after he died.

The day after my stepmom died, I went back to my 6 a.m. workout class. We did a good workout, although I was feeling a little heavy in the legs and couldn't lift my arms. The workout routine that I knew so well helped to carry me along. I had completed the class and was relaxing deeply in the cool-down part of the session when I started to cry uncontrollably. The music, the endorphins, and the teacher's soft voice all combined to carry me into a tidal wave of emotional release. It started with silent tears, then progressed to weeping, and culminated in intense sobbing.

A friend of my stepmom came over to my mat, knelt down beside me, and put her arms around me. She held me for the rest of the cool down, awkwardly wrapped around me, stroking my hair and telling me that my stepmom loved me and that I would be okay. This reserved Japanese woman was not a cuddly or gushy type of person. But she gave her touch with perfect timing. I was in good hands with her as I grieved.

When my dad died, I found it therapeutic to massage my stepmom because I missed massaging my dad; I missed being in their home and having my designated spot at the side of the bed. The view out the window was the same when I massaged Valerie. The scene had not changed, and I was lifted up by being able to deliver the same care to my stepmom that I had given to my dad.

Taking the key caregivers, including the hospice workers, and maintaining their network with each other through massage is very healing. At the same time, it is respectful to the deceased. The one who passed would be thrilled to have this aftercare alive in their absence. It is a pleasant living tribute; a hands-on memorial.

## When to Offer Massage

The early days after a death may be a good time to offer a massage; however, offering massage after a memorial service may be even better. Relatives and friends often put their feelings on hold until the memorial service. They will undoubtedly be on damage control of some kind, getting the service organized and making all the arrangements, looking at pictures, and sorting through their loved one's belongings. They might be armored with emotional protection or healthy coping behavior. After the service, when "normal" life is supposed to continue, may be when those grieving need more help.

## Emotional Connection

I feel strongly that touch helps people stay emotionally available in the acute stages of grief. It helps the emotions flow as predictably as helping the blood circulate. It is like taking the body for an emotional walk.

We instinctively withdraw into solitude with our grief. We turn inward and lock ourselves up. This is the mask of grief visible for the world to see. The unseeing eyes, the shuffling walk, the weakness of the body, and the heaviness of the heart are all natural symptoms of loss. This tendency to isolate oneself after a death is sometimes accompanied by the urge to self-soothe with bad habits.

When I suffer a loss, I keep close to those who touch me. I need the friends who hold my hand, put their comforting arms around me, massage my shoulders, hold my pain, and hold my soul. They do not try to quiet my tears. It is important that grieving people not have to cope—that they be allowed to fall apart and just feel their feelings.

In 1972, I had a grief paralysis experience—the experience of being literally numb with grief—when my colleague George, who had epilepsy, drowned in a bathtub. When I was talking to a friend the next evening about the experience of being there when George was carried down the stairs on a stretcher, I didn't yet realize that I was numb. As I described how I touched his hair, she quickly came around behind me and put both arms around me. Her touch was intuitively accurate in timing. She held me for a long time. She simply held me tight. The frozen feeling of my body started to melt and I unraveled. I wept, I howled, releasing the pain in tears. Thank god she didn't let me go. Her instincts were accurate, and she had moved quickly on her hunch.

### HEALING REGRETS

I had massaged my mom every day for years in her chronic care facility, and to the last days of her convalescence in my living room. Her death was like giving up my child for adoption—not a natural feeling at all.

The day my mom died, I realized I did not want to stay home that night, so my brother took me home with him. He built an outdoor fire, put my sleeping bed under the stars, and made a huge pot of his best herbal tea. He played the Celtic music of my favorite Canadian performer, Loreena McKennitt, to lull me to sleep. It is one of the most memorable, well-loved experiences of my life.

My brother had been the best person for me to team up with in my mom's dying days. He was strong, brave, and steady in his commitment to help her die comfortably. He took time off work in the North and stayed until we worked through the details in her aftermath.

The day after my mom's death, I was riding my bike along the street about a block from where I lived and where my mom had died. It was the route that I had pushed my mom every night in her wheelchair. I felt such an overwhelming sadness and loneliness. My dog Bert usually filled that place of belonging and longing for contact, but this was different. There was no one to go home to. I felt my phone ring in my pocket, struggled off my bike to answer it, and sat down on the sidewalk. It was my brother, simply wanting to find out how I was doing.

I immediately began weeping uncontrollably. A huge flood of emotion poured out of me. I couldn't talk. I just put my head in my hands and cried because I was really upset—not about my mom's death, exactly, but with myself. I was upset about what I had not done for my mom. I was emphatic in telling him my regrets.

As we talked, he pulled around the corner, climbed out of his truck, and sat down on the sidewalk beside me. With his arm around me, he listened to my tirade. We sat there, two grown adults in their fifties on the sidewalk outside the medical clinic on one of the two main thoroughfares of Nelson, but he acted as though we were alone. He was as thoughtful with me as he had been with my mom. At that moment, his touch was soothing and calming. He told me that I had done everything right, that my mother had died well in our hands.

"You sat with Mummy, you just sat with her, I didn't sit with her," I cried.

I remembered watching my brother sitting with my mom. She was sleeping, and he was reading. Meanwhile, I was doing the laundry. I was cooking, cleaning, doing everything except just sitting with her.

That day on the sidewalk, I was a caregiver tormented by what I had not done and regretting what I had. I was a highly hands-on caregiver, but I was still tormented by the same kinds of regrets that most people experience in the pain of loss.

This memory with my brother is still vividly etched in my memory. I felt cared for on such a basic level that it lifted my pain and replaced it with emotional healing. The feeling of his arm around me and his body up against my left side is a comforting sensation that helped me move through this and other trying times. It helped me get through, and

past, my regrets. I wanted to be proactive. I wanted to take my regret and make it into a positive propeller for change, promising myself in the future to linger longer, to learn to be more like my brother.

We organized a tea for my mom's funeral reception. We prepared some of her best recipes: shortbread; peach, apple, and pumpkin pies; brownies; walnut squares; and her peanut macaroons. My mother was not only there in spirit; she was there in a very tangible way. It was her last tea party.

For the people who couldn't attend her memorial tea, I had three "Margaret dinners" where I cooked her favorite dishes as a way of saying "thank you" to her team of caregivers. Hospice volunteers and friends joined me for different groupings and dinners. I selected copies of my mother's artwork, pieces of her jewelry and clothing, and other items to give each caregiver. These dinners helped me grieve my mom with a gentle letting go.

## Support Groups

When my dad died, I went to a grief support group in Nelson. It was run by two social workers in community care. We met every week for three to four months, talking and sharing our stories of grief and loss. We did an inventory of our own lives, writing about our relationship with the deceased. Simply the act of writing about our feelings helped to release the grip of grief.

Writing groups are good grief groups. If talking is not your easiest outlet for emotional release, then try writing. Writing from the heart is easy when emotions are strong and forceful. Diaries are one of the most common ways people have recorded their survivor pain over the centuries. Writing can also be a way of connecting with a deceased loved one. I still have my parent's diaries to read in their absence. Seeing their handwriting and touching the pages that they touched puts me closer to them, allowing me to be affected by their words. The grief groups I attended after my parents' deaths were very healing for me. It brought me closer to other people and helped me consider my own immortality—the way I will continue to touch and move others after I die—as well.

In one grief group, we designed our own "coping" strategies—and of course, massage was at the top of my coping list. I taught our grief group head, neck, and shoulder massages, and we found opportunities to touch each other weekly after that. Now, I advocate that professionals and laypeople alike encourage safe, consensual, comforting touch in the grief groups they facilitate.

Admittedly, there can be tricky social politics with men asking grieving women if they want a massage when their vulnerability is at such a high ebb. However, a mini-massage, a care for the caregivers shoulder rub, or a hand massage doesn't need to enter into the social politics of male/female touching. Ask for permission and let individuals decide for themselves what they feel comfortable with.

## Memorials and Commemorations

Whether grief is fresh or well-entrenched, it always has some sort of natural and individual time frame; each grief experience follows its own path. Some people do not fully grieve until they fall in love again, often years later. There is something about loving touch that can reactivate the depths of love and loss.

There is, however, a predictable, natural cycle of missing the person. The first anniversary of someone's death, birthdays, and special days are opportunities to grieve again. These are often days we dread; they tend to go better when we share them together, planning special ways commemorate.

My mother's memorial teas and dinners were my way to commemorate but there are many forms a ritual or commemoration of someone's life can take, including a massage memorial. The massages you give or get on anniversaries of deaths can act as a memorial. I usually ask if I can deliver a home-call massage in the place where a person died (if they died at home) to create another positive massage experience. This serves as a proactive eraser of painful and sad memories with a comforting and relaxing new experience. Sometimes, playing favorite music, or music they listened to

while massaging their deceased loved one, is also comforting.

Planning a massage for the anniversaries of my parents' deaths (or even my dog Bert's death) means that I need to ask my friends to help me acknowledge the day. My friends are usually happy to celebrate the life of my deceased loved ones by massaging me and talking about the person I am missing. I have a photo of the person or pet beside the massage table during the delivery of those soothing massages.

Every New Year's Eve for five years, I massaged my friend Dixie. Massaging Dixie from one year to the next was a unique and comforting massage experience. I started her massage at 11:30 in the old year and we ended at 12:30 in the new year. But what I thought would be a unique massage gift for Dixie turned out to be an extraordinary gift to me. We both had reasons to grieve on that day. For me, I grieved the loss of my dad, who died at midnight on New Year's Eve. Dixie felt the grief of losing her son, who was killed on New Year's Eve by a drunk driver, her son's best friend. We put our grief in each other's hands. I felt soothed by the experience of helping someone with a far greater need than mine. We toasted her son and our fathers (who had been friends) and, each year, I felt like the new year got off to the best start possible.

## Courage

Keeping in touch with your massage buddies and with those who may need you after a death often requires courage. You are venturing into territory that is unmapped and emotionally sensitive. You might be hesitant to offer help or to intrude. You might worry you'll be rejected. We naturally don't want to disturb those who are grieving, except to check in with them and provide physical nutrition with food gifting. But remember: when it comes to offering a massage to a grieving person, the worst that can happen is that they refuse your offer. Yet they might reconsider later on—perhaps the next day, or even the next hour. All you need to do is offer. Leave the rest to them.

## CONCLUSION

# Taking It to the Streets

When Grace Chan—the cofounder of the Sutherland-Chan School of Massage Therapy—and I started out, 45 years ago, to change the curriculum standards of therapeutic massage training programs, we wanted to raise the bar high. Both of us believed deeply in the power of touch and the power of massage. We also felt that the program that we had attended and graduated from—a one-year course—was too short, too limited, and neither captured the potential power of massage nor explored all the healing possibilities of touch. We also knew this needed to start with a grassroots movement. If we trained proactive students, they would carry the message forward and make a difference individually, eventually changing the whole profession.

We designed a two-year program to replace the one-year program. We presented our new curriculum to the governing bodies of massage in Ontario and British Columbia. It took some time, but we were ultimately successful—and we did train proactive students, and they did change the profession. The city bylaws in Toronto changed, and the body-rub scene that was using the word *massage* had to use other descriptors for their non-therapeutic use of touch. We saw the standards of public education for massage and massage schools change for the better. The word *massage* gained respectability, and the term *therapeutic massage* was incorporated into healing practice. Today, the public is safe with well-trained massage professionals. Massage therapy became, and continues to be, a serious profession in Canada—and it was an

Grace and me.

enormous compliment when American massage schools began requesting our curriculum.

Our students were trained in community programs and were given experience in all types of facilities, from chronic care facilities filled with seniors to a facility for single mothers and their babies. Our hospice work with Casey House, the only AIDS hospice in Canada at that time, gave our students an opportunity to work with those in palliative care as part of their training program. During their studies, they had many opportunities to give back to the community through the power of touch. All these outreach opportunities awakened in our students the possibilities of massage.

With the latest research at our fingertips, our original goal of creating graduates who would become proactive in building the profession has been fulfilled. Our graduates have started their own schools, and our message to raise the standards of massage has been passed around the world, one therapist at a time.

## The Power of One

One person can make difference by simply massaging one other person. Whether using purely intuitive touch or trained skill, one person touching another makes a difference. In my own times of physical and emotional pain, touch has made a difference. Touch thawed me out, soothed my hurt, and took away my discomfort. Just one person. Just one touch.

The Power of One has been a principle and driving force throughout my life. I was influenced at an early age by a number of special individuals who took an interest in me. The results of their attention and care were practical and powerful. The same is true with my patients: they have individually changed my life.

When Mary Coletti asked me to film her massage team, she wanted to make a difference in the world of ALS sufferers. Joni and Cecil Bund wanted to make a difference for those suffering with cancer. Gaston Huchet wanted to make a difference for families with loved ones dying at home. These patients wanted to be filmed so their stories of palliative massage would be available to the world, so their lives would continue to make a difference after they were gone. They and others asked me to write this book. I would not have done these things without their unique influences.

### The power of the one who is dying

Now let's consider the Power of One from another point of view. If you are the person with the terminal prognosis, you can make a difference by inviting your loved ones to touch and massage you.

It is my wish that every patient feel comfortable asking for hands-on help as soon as they learn their prognosis. This would be the ideal way to start building a team. However, most people are reluctant to ask for help, even when help is desperately needed. They hesitate to ask as soon as they learn of their condition or prognosis. Things don't seem bad enough.

But although you might not be dying right this minute, you may be in need of tender touch. You may indeed have an urgent need for nonemergency care. And speaking to this need, asking loved ones to be involved in your ongoing care will not only ease your pain, stress, and anxiety, but also that of those around you. The Power of One—in this case, the power of one dying patient asking for help—can transform the family's concern into a passionate and natural outlet for their feelings. Loved ones who are invited to reach out and ease someone's pain ease their own pain at the same time. People who feel helpless now feel they have been given a purpose.

It is most important for the dying person to learn to receive love and concern with grace and gratitude, but it is also important to remember that these end-of-life massages are therapeutic for everyone involved, helping them to work through their feelings of sadness, helplessness, and loss. The families that are able to continue massaging each other for better sleep, better emotional availability, and better thinking lead to better grieving, both now and down the road.

## A Tactile Upbringing

Family rituals in death and dying give our children the right upbringing: a tactile upbringing. Children should help care for their grandparents as they age and eventually die. They can begin as young as two years old and continue through their teens into their adult life. When palliative massage is part of a family lifestyle, then the world is going to die in good hands: in the hands of family and friends. Giving massage skills to our youth will ensure a more positive experience for all of us in our dying days.

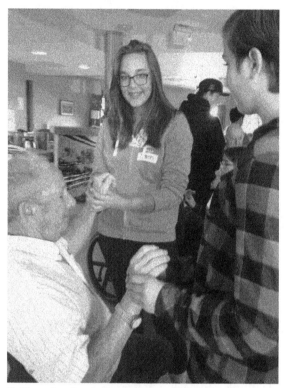

Youth and seniors in Fort St. John, British Columbia. When I teach teens how to massage seniors, I feel like their touch is changing the world. We need our young to be touch crusaders. Through the young, the ancient art of touch can be brought into a contemporary society.

When children see their folks getting massages through the natural cycles of life—through pregnancy, labor, and delivery; in infancy, through baby massage; during special family times, anniversaries, and birthdays; and in times of death and dying, they will know that touch is a natural part of their family life. When I teach kids to massage the pregnant tummy of their mom, I am not only giving them a way to welcome their new brother or sister, but also showing that massage has a place in everyday life. Children need to learn about positive touch. They can cultivate massage in their sports, their home life, and their beauty routines,

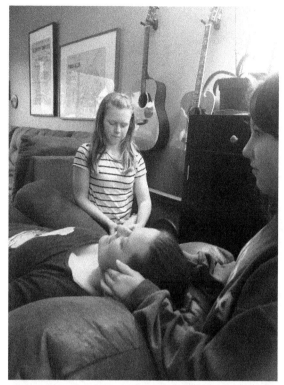

Kids massaging their mom. The dream I had in my twenties of changing the world one massage at a time eventually evolved into a dream of changing the world one massage *workshop* at a time. Now, it has evolved again: I hope to change the children in this world, one massage experience at a time.

and can use massage techniques as practical remedies for drugless relief from headaches, menstrual cramps, and other aches and pains.

### Bridging the gap

When I started to take kids to massage seniors in my hometown of Nelson, I didn't have the Internet to help me spread the message about this community care. Instead, I used the recreational leadership program of the local high school to recruit teenage volunteers.

When I was a teenager, our only outlet for this kind of senior service was volunteering on the library cart at the hospital or visiting seniors to sing Christmas carols. We only had special event opportunities to make contact with chronic care facilities.

Ella gives her mom a massage for Mother's Day.

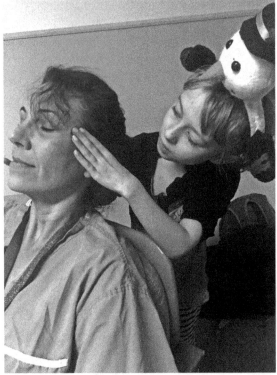

Frosty massages a nurse on a Christmas visit for staff in Fort St. John.

Now, most chronic care facilities have outreach programs with their surrounding neighborhoods. Still, there are not enough young people in these facilities on a daily basis. It is often professionals, not families, who look after the elderly. When I was a child, my grandmother had her own suite in our house. She was independent and came and went as she wished, eating meals with us and going to Friday night movies with me and my brother.

In India, where 85% of families live in multigenerational households, youth and seniors are very often hands-on in caring for one another. In North America, I hope we see more people planning to have their aging parents live with them, or at least—like me—kidnapping their mom and dad to die at home, in their own living rooms. When people can learn the skills to keep their folks at home, they will feel like they have a choice about taking them home to die. They will learn the confidence of a palliative caregiver and take the risk of trying the "die at home" approach. Either way, at home or in chronic care facilities, it is my hope that family care teams will learn palliative massage.

School kids bring parents for family massage class in Guatemala.

## Start Now

Massage for the dying needs to be practiced before the dying happens, in the early stages of disease or simply as people age. If, however, you are on the other side of the world and expect to arrive at the dying person's bedside just before they pass on, then start massaging right where you are. Even during a pandemic, you can look for ways to massage those in your social bubble, whether they are family, friends, or neighbors. There is no time to waste. Do not leave this practice until your parent, spouse, or relative is breathing their last breath.

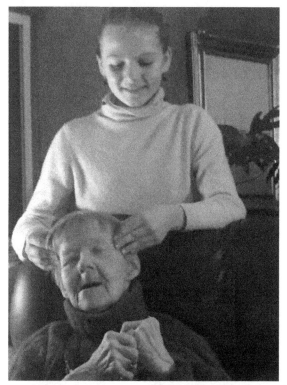

Freya, who lives with Parkinson's, gets massaged by her granddaughter, Alma.

## Pass It on Where and When You Can

After the death of a loved one you've massaged, don't let your massage skills go to waste. If and when COVID restrictions ease, take your knowledge to the streets and pass it on. Volunteer at the local hospice group; show them what you know.

Pass on your skills to those at work, who need their shoulders massaged the same way you massaged the volunteers at your dying parent's bedside. Give your coworkers the benefit of your experience.

### THE BRILLIANCE OF THE TANDEM MASSAGE

Share your massage knowledge with everyone you can. Demonstrating what you know in a tandem massage is the best way to make other people comfortable offering massage on their own. When teaching massage, make your students comfortable about making mistakes and give lots of positive feedback. This will facilitate the learning experience tenfold!

When you arrive to do a massage, invite any friends or relatives who might be available to learn some simple massage techniques. The more people the better! Explain what you are doing as you go along. Have another person join in with you right away. This will lessen their anxiety about trying something new.

Start with the patient's hand. Ask one of your students to take the patient's other hand and follow you. Tell them a bit about the stroke and what it can do, but *keep it simple!* Get feedback from the patient about pressure being used. Since there are two of you working together, your massage time should be cut in half. Be mindful not to overwork an area.

Encouragement will go a long way in opening your students to trying massage, which can also help build a massage team quickly. If there are a lot of people who want to learn, have them practice on each other, or, as the massage tutorial progresses, have them choose a part of the patient's body on which everyone can practice the same stroke. This keeps the learning light and fun.

The four-on-one is a team-tandem with one person on each extremity and taking turns stroking the abdomen and back and face. When everyone knows the routines for each part of the body, all can work simultaneously and a full massage can be done in less than a half hour! The dance of many hands can be very relaxing and satisfying for those doing the massage as well as for the person on the receiving end.

Keep the magic moving through you, easing your grief and bereavement by passing along the gift of touch. Encourage others to learn and massage along with you. All you need is one person to massage, and another to observe or massage along with you, and you, too, can teach massage!

But even with continued restrictions to physical contact, the Internet can help you share your knowledge. With software such as Zoom, I now include students from foreign countries and patients from around the world in the intimacy of the online classroom. I can see into the lives of palliative patients and their families learning to massage them, even at great distances. This epidemic has given teachers like me a boost in bringing what we know to the entire world without leaving home.

## Power to the People

I envision a future with an army of volunteers, retired Zoomers, and high school teens to massage those dying and those in bereavement outreach programs in all Canadian communities. There will be volunteer teams in developing countries working to set up outreach massage projects wherever people are dying with and without palliative drugs. These people will simply be people with experience, not professionals like myself. Ordinary people who are devoted to service above the self. The individual layperson is my ultimate catalyst for change.

Those of us with a gift for teaching will attract students eager to help. Those without a natural talent for engaging a crowd will pass along palliative care techniques by simply allowing others to watch what they do and allowing them to try it themselves. Instructions will be delivered online

High school students learn senior sports massage for the provincial senior games.

Toronto senior citizens get massaged by teenagers and then give their thank you in return.

with films and how-to clips downloaded right to the hospice, hospital, or home. As cars now have phones built into the dashboard, there will be monitors in patients' rooms so the networking of global families can be both virtual and in person.

---

By taking it to the streets, palliative massage can be an extension into that final act of touching and caring that we all anticipate. Practice in the living moments for massaging in the dying moments of life.

Now that you have read this book, combine your intuition with your best massage oil and look for a palliative opportunity to be of service, hands-on. Through the power of touch, we can help each other experience a peaceful and pain-free departure: dying in good hands.

## Online Classroom

Visit brusheducation.ca/dying-in-good-hands to watch these videos:

The power of one
Bridging the gap – Fort St. John
Family learning the skills
Brilliance of the tandem massage
Tandem team massage

# ACKNOWLEDGMENTS

Big thanks for my family, especially my mom and dad and stepmom, Valerie, my auntie Lil, Auntie Ann, and Auntie Flo. You all taught me about the power of palliative touch. Auntie Ann, thanks for taking me to your physiotherapy/massage sessions when I was young to watch the hands-on help that you received. You helped plot the course of my life's work.

Special thanks to my brother, Colin: you helped our parents die in good hands.

To my other five "big brothers"—Charles, Ira, John, Rob, and Peter—like Colin, thank you for your financial literary support to complete this book. To my "big sister"—Anne Stewart—who was the first to finance this project: you paved the way for the In Good Hands series. Thank you.

Thank you Helen Mosby, Marion Hindmarsh, Marion Muth, and Rosemarie Harrop, my team of "big sisters" and financiers for your interest in my work and support in writing this book and filming for the ebook! Thank you Crystal, my daughter, for being a little angel palliative assistant with Jim St James, Brian Carpendale, Joan Renold, and your dying grandparents. You were a great palliative team player from the age of four to 34!

Thanks to Maureen Hyman, who helped me start Bridging the Gap, teaching high school kids to massage seniors over 30 years ago. You helped me get seniors into the hands of youth around the world!

To Lila Taylor, thank you for mentoring with me and bringing your family into my classroom to help them to grieve in good hands. I thrive in your touch!

Thank you to the Harrop clan of Rosemarie, Mark and Joanne and David and family, Leon and Saralynne and the rest of the crew for all the love and support through Rosie's transition west through Parkinson's and beyond. Thank you Leon for sharing your leukemia journey with us all and keeping the love thriving in this special family. Thanks to Donald Grayston, my friend and mentor of 50 years for giving me the most generous gift of living with you at Cottage Hospice for those last months. Special thanks to the hospice staff for making me feel loved and supported and that I belonged. Thank you to Don's kids, Megan, Rebecca, Johnathan, and Ginger, for making me welcome.

Thanks to Brian Carpendale, who told me to follow my dreams and bought all my farm animals (60 chickens, 3 goats, and my horse, Vola) so I could go to massage school.

Thank you Joan, my best friend for all those years, for teaching me the palliative home care dream come true caring for Brian with ALS and coming to teach at Sutherland Chan with Gordon, and Selkirk College with me.

Thank you to my Girls Club of Annie, Colleen, Jill, and Lynn, you kept me going with our long lake swims, paddling the shoreline and massaging each other's feet. I'll be there to rub you the right way right to heaven or welcome you over to the other side. Thanks for all your love over these 27 years of writing *Dying in Good Hands*. Thank you for being there and helping me help my parents to die in good hands.

---

Thank you to all those first students in my first classes at the University of Toronto Advisory

Bureau, when I was a student in training, and then my first professional training programs at the 3HO School of Massage in Toronto, where I met Grace Chan. Your job offer changed the course of my life forever.

To my first business partner, Grace Chan, thank you for all the years of Sutherland Chan and thanks for all your support for my work from the minute we met until today! You and Debra Curties make a perfect team!

Thank you to all the students of Sutherland Chan for teaching me how to teach palliative massage; helping me to *Learn to teach and teach to learn*! Thank you for your feedback and enthusiasm.

Thank you to Rudy Buttignol and Gerry Mosby and all my crew for the first 1984 massage video that we launched!

Thank you to Jim St. James and Casey House in Toronto and the Toronto AIDS community for keeping doors open to massage therapy in the AIDS community globally. You got me started.

Thank you Margo McLean, our palliative nurse extraordinaire, for your professional knowledge and guidance.

Thank you Janice Morrison, our physiotherapist, for teaching me your best lung clearing techniques with Mary Coletti.

To Helen DeWeaver, thank you for teaching my students your wonderful wheelchair transfers.

Thank you to Natalie Berman Biggs for the invitation to volunteer at Camp Kerry. Your bereavement work in this camp is admirable. Thank you Dr. Heather Mohan and Josh Dahling for creating such a needed project for bereaved families. I love working with you all.

Thank you Mona (Ramona Bolton) and your Institute of Traditional Medicine for introducing me to Bridget and her family. Your support in facilitating my workshops over the years in Toronto has been wonderful.

Thank you Dr. Balfour Mount for taking my calls and supporting my work in your field of palliative care. Thank you for all the work you did to create the Canadian Palliative Care Standard, making my work welcomed and respected.

You've made this world a better place for "dying softer."

To the third floor: you are the palliative dream come true. From head nurse, Carla, to the loyal cleaners, you give us the best place to die. Kootenay Lake Hospital third floor has been my highway to heaven over the past 30 years. Thank you for allowing me to teach your families to be hands-on with their dying loved ones. All my students loved their massage experiences with massaging your staff and the family caregivers too. Your CEOs were so progressive in allowing community involvement with your dying patients. Thank you Thalia!!

Thank you to all the local hospices that have supported my work in either sending me their volunteers for training, organizing massage workshops within their hospice volunteer programs, or connecting me with families in need. Thank you especially to Mountain Lakes Seniors Community, Jubilee Manor, and Mount St. Francis for allowing me to teach on site with my students and treat your residents in my outreach program. In Fort St. John, special thank you to Peace Villa for allowing me to teach and film Dr. Kearney High School kids massaging your seniors. Thank you to the Toronto General, Sunnybrook, Mount Sinai, and Toronto Western hospitals for the opportunities to film my palliative patients and tell their stories of the power of touch.

To Jody, Tammy, Dawn, Alexandra, Joanne, Charlene, and Ishi, my first Zoom palliative students, and my team Christine and Romany at Selkirk College, thank you for giving me the laboratory of real life to try out my manuscript before it went to print.

Thank you to the local businesses and families in Nelson that donated memorial scholarships for my summer Zoom classes and textbooks that carried this manuscript into the hands of first-time users before printing and book release.

Thank you to all my families over the years that taught me about the ways to "let Go and let God."

Thank you to all my students that have taught me the most about palliative massage teaching and how to teach the right way. You taught me well!

Thank you to my patients, especially Annie Lalahoff and Jo McBurney, who donated their time to my projects of filming them from ladders, desktops, and tripods. I couldn't have done it without your help and your family's involvement.

To Gaston's family, especially Dominique and Miriam: you gave Gaston a gift of dying in good hands and you gave me a gift of being on your team, thank you. And thank you to all your kids for being so willing to learn.

To Cec's wife, Joni, and family, your trust in my hands was an honor. You showed your love for Cec with your hands-on helpfulness and support till his last breath.

To Brian's daughter, Monica, thank you for helping me put the right finishing touches on Brian's story.

To Carol Wastl, many thanks for the story of Joe, for him dying in good hands, your hands.

To Susan Lucas, thank you for keeping me close with your dying partner and life love, Ted.

To Bob Inwood and daughter Alicia, plus Christine, Sabine, Dorothy, and the clan, thank you for letting me help with Lynnie.

Thank you to the Coletti clan, from Mary's kids, Christine and Mike, to Lou, her husband, and Lorraine, her best friend, and George, Mary's father in law, my current superstar at 99 years old having his first massage for his swollen legs on Zoom for my End of Life Doula grads from Douglas College. Thank you again, Colettis!

Thank you to Melissa Cataford, my student forever. Special thanks for bringing Nik into Mary's massage team.

Thank you to Bridget's Toronto family, Mark, Ruby, Lilly, Michael and Michele and Bridget's many loving hands for the perfect parting. Thank you to Linda Luztono for your song and Darius Bashar for your wonderful film and Jennifer Clibbon for your perfect documentary. You gave me all the story I needed to show how we can take this to the streets.

Thank you to Dawn Richards and her wonderful husband Greg for sharing your palliative perfect wedding on the hospital rooftop and the whole massaging family. Thank you to the Ming-Sun family, especially Warren and his hands-on hockey buddies Joe, Ranji, Joel, Hazel and Tammy! What a massage team!

Special thanks to Marianne Bond for sharing her sister Deb's departure. We set a new standard of divine touch at the hospital with your beautiful battery candlelit massages!

Thanks to Kristie and her daughter for encircling her father, Allan, in a cocoon of love. Thank you Allan for your film footage and photos of respiratory relief, of productive coughing and wonderful rib raking.

Thank you Sydnee for all the "cuddling in" beside your dying mother throughout my massage visits.

Thank you to William's angels, especially Jacklyn and classmates, who gave him his last job of graduating you all, giving you your certificates from his bedside. Thank you to William's partner, Lee Waddell, for sharing her partner's precious palliative time. Thank you to Lee's family for massaging her before her own departure.

Thanks to Nina Beveridge and her extraordinary mother, Margaret, for showing us the way to keep in touch till the end with the practicalities of palliative massage. From our original filming 30 years ago till today, your coaching has kept me moving forward in my filmmaking and hands-on instructing. Thank you for carrying on your mother's professional film legacy.

To Freya, thank you for teaching the world to be hands-on with Parkinson's! Thank you to your loving, hands-on family, especially your husband, Stan, your partner in this disease for over 20 years. You have both taught me about the power of touch—the power of love—with your team of kids, Finn, Alisha, Shona, Catlin, Seamus, Sean, Jay, and the extended family of helpers, Liz and Janet; granddaughter Alma and grandson John; all eagerly learning to give you the best life, the best touch! Thank you for being my first Zoom palliative massage on-site class. My students loved being in your incredible straw bale house via the intimacy of Zoom!

Many thanks to Richard Cima and his kids, Toby and Wren, and grandson River, who massaged him till the end, as well as Jessica Coonen, who gave Richard his last massage on his last day in his garden on the edge of Kootenay Lake. Thank you Jessica, for your literary talent and help in the last days of my manuscript. Thank you Richard, for gracing the front cover of this book forever.

---

Thank you Bev, for showing us your newly renovated tummy and the best stoma-massage illustrations.

Thank you to all the medical artists, especially Frances Keyes, my original illustrator when I was writing the first massage teaching manual for Sutherland Chan. You helped set the bar high with your massage illustrations never before drawn.

Thank you to my current illustrators, Brandon Basharah, Barbara Brown, and Dylan Archibald for all your work through months of photos shoots and sketches, computer mischief, and hospital visits drawing patients and copying images! I had a talented team!

Thank you to my research sources, the queens of research Tiffany Field, Debra Curties, and Tracy Walton, for their wonderful work. Thank you William Collinge for your work with Tracy Walton in oncology massage treatment. It was inspiring to read about your experiments and research.

To Trish Dryden and Linda Novak, thanks for all you did to contribute to Sutherland Chan in your teaching and the work with me in this book. Thank you Dr. Sheldon Wagner, for your medical advice and support and also to Dr. Marc Gabel, for your medical prescription for me to get massage therapy for my back-to-the land "chainsaw overuse strain." That changed my life forever in 1971.

Thank you Beth McAuley and The Editing Company of Toronto: those years of your work on my first manuscript paid off big time, with Brush Education Inc. and Coach House Press as a complement to your talented team!

To my editor at Brush Education, Lauri Seidlitz, thank you for your expertise and brilliant editing, but most of all for your smooth yet acrobatic juggling between my illustrators, photographers, and filmmakers. This one was a challenge! Your steady encouragement helped me over the finish line!

Thank you to all my camera crews: Bongo Kolycius, Dan Caverly, Peter Schramm, Peter McRory, Halley Roback, and Sussi Dorrell. You gave my *Dying in Good Hands* series the best screen shots ever! And the best ebook to come.

Thanks to Camara, Wyatt, and Anthony for your social media support for this book.

Thank you to all my writing team: my longstanding and long-suffering local editor Verna Relkoff; my writing instructors Tom Wayman, Almenda Glenn Miller, Susan Andrews-Grace, Holly Rubinsky, and the Elephant Mountain Literary Festival workshop teachers, Lou Anne Armstrong and Jenna Butler; and lastly Elizabeth Cunningham, writing buddy extraordinaire. For all those years that we wrote weekly together: so many thanks!

To the editors through the past 20 plus years, from Beth in Toronto to Lisa Ross in Kaslo, thank you for your paid persistence to my writing and keeping me on track through those summers and winters of the concentrated past 10 years to get this over the finish line.

Thanks to John Dejesus and Rick Simon at Coach House Press and the talented press crew for helping me get my first edition of *Dying in Good Hands* looking perfect. Thanks to my favourite Cartier font inventor Carl Dair (which was digitally updated by Rod MacDonald) for making that first birth so pretty!

To my literary twins, Nadine Boyd and Leesa Dean, who found me Brush Education Inc.: without you two, I would still be dreaming. Your steady support and intuitive working of my writing helped me find my voice.

To my Ontario literary audio visual partner, Halley Roback, who has burned the midnight oil to give you the best online classroom: I thank you from the bottom of my heart for helping me bring Bridget's story to birth and delivering my work to where it belongs, in the hands of those in need.

Thank you again, Halley Roback and my film editor Jesse McCallum for helping me finish the Bridget story.

To Ben Haab and Eagle Vision Video Productions, thank you for bringing Bridget's story to the screen and to these pages of *Dying in Good Hands*.

Thank you to my faithful manuscript readers, especially the last big read by Wendy, George, Mike, Seneca, Lynn, Crystal, Kristie, Fred and Jay, Amber, Jill, and longest readers, Verna and Bill.

Special thanks to Rick Cepella for helping me in the last read through of Margaret.

Thank you to Terry Lee for the final read. Your soulfulness helped put the icing on the cake!

Special thanks to Cheri Gaynor, my literary labor and delivery assistant. You made that year-long delivery of coding lists a joyful experience. Many, many thanks!

Thank you Dr. Michael Biggs, Dr. Trevor Jantz, and Rev. David Boyd for your quotes and support!

Thank you John McDermott for your song, "One Small Star," my theme song for this work: https://www.youtube.com/watch?v=n5mqYnrAPw0

# NOTES

1. Stewart, H. G. (2013). "The last human freedom." *Queen's Alumni Review, 2013*(2): 26–27.

2. Montagu, A. (1971). *Touching: The human significance of skin.* Harper & Row.

3. Spitz, R. A. (1945). "Hospitalism: An inquiry into the genesis of psychiatric conditions in early childhood." *Psychoanalytic Study of the Child, 1945*(1): 53–74.

4. Harlow, H. (1958). "The nature of love." *American Psychologist, 13*(12): 673–685.

5. Field, T., Diego, M., & Hernandez-Reif, M. (2010). "Preterm infant massage therapy research: A review." *Infant Behavior & Development, 33*(2): 115–124.

6. Cassileth, B. R., & Vickers, A. J. (2004, September). "Massage therapy for symptom control: Outcome study at a major cancer center." *Journal of Pain Symptom Management, 28*(3): 244–249.

7. *Therapeutic massage for pain relief.* (2016, July). Harvard Health Publishing. https://www.health.harvard.edu/alternative-and-complementary-medicine/therapeutic-massage-for-pain-relief

8. Adams, R., White, B., & Beckett, C. (2010). "The effects of massage therapy on pain management in the acute care setting." *International Journal of Therapeutic Massage & Bodywork: Research, Education, & Practice, 3*(1): 4–11. doi.org/10.3822/ijtmb.v3i1.54

9. Trudeau, M. (Moderator). (2010, September 20). Human connections start with a friendly touch [Radio show episode]. On *Morning Edition*. NPR. https://www.npr.org/templates/story/story.php?storyId=128795325

10. Chillot, R. (2013, March 11). "The power of touch." *Psychology Today.* https://www.psychologytoday.com/us/articles/201303/the-power-touch

11. Collinge, W. B., Khan, J., Walton, T., Kozak, L., Bauer-Wu, S., Fletcher, K., Yarnold, P., & Soltysik, R. (2013, May). "Touch, caring, and cancer: Randomized controlled trial of a multimedia caregiver education program." *Supportive Care in Cancer, 21*(5): 1405–1414.

12. Coletti, M. & Sutherland, C. (Directors). (n.d.). *Massaging Mary: Hands On with ALS* [Film]. Sutherland Productions. https://www.youtube.com/watch?v=dq07V0d8ZXU

13. Curties, D. (2000). "Could massage therapy promote cancer metastasis?" *Massage Therapy Journal, 39*: 83–88.

14. Collinge, W. B., MacDonald, G., & Walton, T. (2012, February). "Massage in supportive cancer care." *Seminars in Oncology Nursing, 28*(1): 45–54.

15. *Complementary therapies: Massage therapy.* (2020). Canadian Cancer Society. http://www.cancer.ca/en/cancer-information/diagnosis-and-treatment/complementary-therapies/massage-therapy/?region=ab

16. Coletti, M. & Sutherland, C. (Directors). (n.d.). *Massaging Mary: Hands On with ALS* [Film]. Sutherland Productions. https://www.youtube.com/watch?v=dq07V0d8ZXU

17. Surjshe, A., Vasani, R., & Saple, D. G. (2008). "Aloe vera: A short review." *Indian Journal of Dermatology, 53*(4): 163–166.

18. Hekmatpou, D., Mehrabi, F., Rahzani, K., & Aminiyan, A. (2018, September 29). "The effect of aloe vera gel on prevention of pressure ulcers in patients hospitalized in the orthopedic wards: A randomized triple-blind clinical trial." *BMC Complementary and Alternative Medicine, 18*(1): 264. doi.org/10.1186/s12906-018-2326-2

19. Onigbinde, A. T., Olafimihan, K. F., Ojoawo, A., Adedoyin, R. A., Omiyale, O., & Mothabeng, J. (2010). "The effect of ultraviolet radiation (type B) on decubitus ulcers." *Internet Journal of Allied Health Sciences and Practice, 8*(1): article 7. https://nsuworks.nova.edu/ijahsp/vol8/iss1/7/

20. Even Superman couldn't win battle with pressure ulcers [Blog post]. (2006, August 23). *ScienceDaily.* www.sciencedaily.com/releases/2006/08/060822172344.htm

21. Heat halts pain inside the body [Blog post]. (2006, July 6). *ScienceDaily.* www.sciencedaily.com/releases/2006/07/060705090603.htm

22. Vahedian-Azimi, A., Ebadi, A., Jafarabadi, H. A., Saadat, S., & Ahmadi, F. (2014, August). "Effect of massage therapy on vital signs and GCS scores of ICU patients: Randomized controlled clinical trial." *Trauma Monthly, 19*(3): e17031.

# INDEX

# ABOUT THE AUTHOR

Christine Sutherland is a filmmaker, author, and registered massage therapist. This book and her previous work *Birthing in Good Hands* are massage inspirations to teach both the medical professional and the layperson to alleviate pain and increase comfort during two of life's major transitions: birth and death. She makes Nelson, British Columbia, her home base as she travels the world spreading her message of hands-on healing.

Christine started the Sutherland-Chan School of Massage Therapy with her former student from the 3HO School of Massage, Grace Chan, in 1978. Since then, her career has taken her around the world, touring with musicians all over Europe and North America, working with Olympic and wheelchair athletes, and helping with births (of humans, horses, cows, and other animals) and with deaths.

Teaching massage to others is her passion, and the global classroom—from studying in Germany at the Kneipp School to teaching midwives in a 120-family collective of Guatemalan freedom fighters—is her venue. She has staged massage flash mobs at local hospitals and other events to teach people how to share a healing touch. Her favorite massage activity is "Bridging the Gap," in which she teaches youth in Canada and, using computer technology, as far afield as Africa, Haiti, and Guatemala—to massage seniors. Christine's YouTube channel, which includes films for all stages of maternity and baby massage, wheelchair massage, palliative massage, and pet massage, teaches millions of people 24/7. She has also made a series of documentary films, in collaboration with her patients and massage teams, called *In Good Hands*!

Find Christine at her website, www.christine-sutherland.com.

Facebook: https://www.facebook.com/ChristineLSutherland/

YouTube: https://www.youtube.com/user/SutherlandMassage

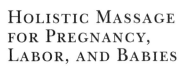

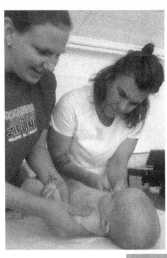
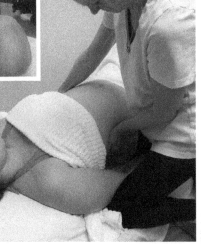